AF717243

Death in Custody

Death in Custody: Inquests, Family Participation and State Accountability

JO EASTON

emerald
PUBLISHING

United Kingdom – North America – Japan – India – Malaysia – China

Emerald Publishing Limited
Howard House, Wagon Lane, Bingley BD16 1WA, UK

First edition 2020

© 2020 Jo Easton.
Published under exclusive licence by Emerald Publishing Limited.

Reprints and permissions service
Contact: permissions@emeraldinsight.com

No part of this book may be reproduced, stored in a retrieval system, transmitted in any form or by any means electronic, mechanical, photocopying, recording or otherwise without either the prior written permission of the publisher or a licence permitting restricted copying issued in the UK by The Copyright Licensing Agency and in the USA by The Copyright Clearance Center. Any opinions expressed in the chapters are those of the authors. Whilst Emerald makes every effort to ensure the quality and accuracy of its content, Emerald makes no representation implied or otherwise, as to the chapters' suitability and application and disclaims any warranties, express or implied, to their use.

British Library Cataloguing in Publication Data
A catalogue record for this book is available from the British Library

ISBN: 978-1-83909-026-4 (Print)
ISBN: 978-1-83909-025-7 (Online)
ISBN: 978-1-83909-027-1 (Epub)

Printed and bound by CPI Group (UK) Ltd, Croydon, CR0 4YY

ISOQAR
REGISTERED
Certificate Number 1985
ISO 14001

ISOQAR certified Management System, awarded to Emerald for adherence to Environmental standard ISO 14001:2004.

INVESTOR IN PEOPLE

I dedicate this book to my Gran, who was always incredibly proud of everything I did; and although she is not here to see me get to the end of this long process, I know she never doubted I would get here.

Table of Contents

Part 3 Participation Benefits for Bereaved Families

Part 4 Bereaved Families Holding the State to Account

Preface

This book considers the participation of bereaved families following a death in custody in the inquest system, which is often the only independent and open process which looks into the causes and wider circumstances of a death. It looks at the legal frameworks in place governing participation, which is set out in the first main part of this book. Relevant theories of justice, participation, procedural fairness and grief theory are all referenced throughout this book. Interviews were carried out with people with personal experience of complex inquests, grouped as coroners, State officials, representatives of the two relevant investigative bodies, bereaved family members and lawyers who represent families. Analysis of the interviews has been used to create a narrative covering three main parts of this book: firstly, how participation benefits families themselves, secondly, how participation of families benefits the wider system and, thirdly, what important aspects are required to achieve effective participation for families. Each part brings together the evidence collected from the interviews and links them to the legal and theoretical frameworks; identifying key benefits of effective family participation and recommendations on how to achieve said benefits.

Family participation can provide families with redress, allows them to represent the deceased as well as being an important part of their grief process. But it is also important in relation to ensuring a fair process, which subsequently impacts positively on accountability and legitimacy. Family participation can improve accountability by maximising the right outcome (via scrutiny) which identifies any failures, they can bring balance and information to the process and they can assist in dissemination of outcomes (preventing future deaths) via media as well as bring Judicial Reviews which reform custodial institutions in terms of preventing deaths in custody and the inquest system itself. Fair and effective participation can impact on perceptions of how transparent, independent and fair the process is – increasing trust, confidence and therefore legitimacy of the system (and sometimes State parties). Fair participation depends upon families being provided with advice and support about the investigation process and their rights, as well as funding for specialist legal representation. Decision-makers who can influence a families' participation should understand the importance of treating families with respect, and openly guaranteeing their rights.

Acknowledgements

The most important people to thank are all of those who I interviewed for this research. I was very fortunate that all interviewees were open with their views and generous with their time. I am especially grateful to the bereaved family members who shared their painful stories. I have treated those stories as respectfully as possible, and hope I have represented their views honestly and fairly.

On a personal level, I am most in debt to Sara and Daragh; who have provided me with endless food and shelter, as well as love and support, over the last few years.

Of course, completing this book would not have been possible without my amazing supervisors. Maurice always seemed to know the right thing to say, especially when I needed a confidence boost. Ellie kindly stepped in to offer words of wisdom when she already had too much to do. And to Lorna, who was there through what felt like an interminable period of time; thank you for somehow seeing the potential through the chaos.

Thanks to the wonderful friends and family who offered to read the thesis when still in draft form. To those of you who struggled with the law, thank you for trying; and to Rachel and Morgane who made it through to the end; you are superstars who obviously had a great teacher! Eternal gratitude to my big brother for proof-reading with an expert eye.

Thank you to Evita and Mark; without whose support I doubt I would have got through the stress of completing a PhD.

Thank you to everyone at INQUEST; especially Debs, Helen and Anna whose expertise was invaluable in giving me the necessary grounding to be able to do this work.

To my colleagues at the Magistrates Association: thank you for indulging my obsession with this piece of work.

Thanks to all my family, friends, work colleagues and random people who I have met along the way who have naively asked about my research topic and been bombarded with hours of detailed discussion about bereavement, deaths in custody and how to achieve accountability. To those who have not abandoned me, I am eternally grateful for your tolerance and I promise to try and find something new to talk about.

To my mum, thank you for everything but especially for reading an early draft and telling me it was perfect, when it was far from it!

Introduction

This book looks at the participation of bereaved families in the investigations following a death in custody. The focus is the inquest system, as this is the primary route by which deaths in custody are investigated, and where there is an established legal right for families to be able to participate. However, in practice, bereaved families are either finding it is very challenging to be able to participate or (where they are able to do so) reporting negative perceptions of whether they found the process fair. This leads to families having little confidence or trust in the process, as well as in State agencies or institutions involved. The author argues that decision-makers are failing to take a process value approach; therefore, they do not sufficiently enable participation by limiting families' access to information, support and respectful treatment. This impacts negatively on the perceived legitimacy of the process, and as the process is the method by which State failings are identified, the legitimacy of the process impacts on the overall legitimacy of the State agencies.

Effective and fair participation for bereaved families can benefit families themselves, as well as improving the accountability of State actions relating to detaining and restraining individuals. Family participation can improve accountability in two ways: firstly by maximising the chance that a fair outcome will be reached, and secondly by increasing the legitimacy of the process. The author believes if decision-makers better understood the wide-ranging benefits provided by family participation, they will be encouraged to take a process value approach, and support families to participate. This book provides evidence showing all the benefits that come from family participation being optimised, and also sets out factors that should be in place to help families participate – including recommendations for different stakeholders. This book is led by the experiences of those interviewed, so focuses on those aspects deemed most relevant or raised most often during the empirical research. The author identifies relevant issues that were not necessarily introduced through the interviews, and uses them to provide context where appropriate. However the aim in this book is to empower those with lived experience, especially those family members who gave their time, and prioritise their voice to influence change.

Human rights are universal and inalienable; they are linked to the inherent dignity of all human beings, regardless of who they are or where they live. And yet we can see that in practice not everyone has equal access to the legal protections

Death in Custody, 1–6
Copyright © 2020 Jo Easton
Published under exclusive licence
doi:10.1108/978-1-83909-025-720201001

that internationally agreed documents set out. You only have to look at countries where political prisoners are held without charge or certain groups are disenfranchised and unable to vote. If they are to be truly universal, people must be able to access human rights. But what if they are not able to access them? This is where one of the most important legal rights comes into play – the right to redress if you suffer a human rights violation. Access to redress not only tries to set right the impact of a violation, or give compensation where this is not possible, but it is also a way to hold State's responsible for violations to account.

Where a violation has resulted in the death of the individual, no system can offer redress to that individual, so it requires looking to the bereaved family and seeing what redress means to them. It can be finding out the truth behind the death, getting compensation or seeing anyone responsible for the death punished. But is that sufficient? If human rights are to be more than merely aspirations, if they are to provide tangible protections, then redress must involve accountability. Not just for an individual violation but to force structural change to prevent ongoing systemic violations. There must be a mechanism for forcing change in State practice to prevent further violations.

Accountability is also key to maintaining public confidence in the visibility and accessibility of human rights. The public must see any State violations identified and addressed in order to be able to trust that their rights are protected. So where a death has occurred as a result of State failings, redress requires a process by which those failings are addressed and future violations prevented. This book looks at the role of the inquest system to provide redress for bereaved families following a death in custody and whether the current law, policy and practice mean access to redress for families is more than just aspirational.

The inquest system is the default process where deaths occurring in State custody are investigated to identify any possible failings. It is vital that a democratic society ensures a system that can hold the State to account for any failings that may have resulted in a death in custody. The inquest system is a very niche area of law in England and Wales that relies on archaic common law processes to devolve Article 2, right to life requirements. Fair participation of victims in a process which is scrutinising possible violations of the right to life goes beyond ensuring the right for the victims to participate but also impacts on the legitimacy of the process. However, numerous case studies, media, enquiries and the organisation INQUEST have all shown that bereaved families are struggling to participate in inquests following deaths in custody. Where there are legal rights, they are not fully implemented; policy decisions undermine participation and there are gaps in both law and policy that mean family participation is restricted. To ensure participation in practice, all decision-makers within a system that leaves large scope for discretion should understand the benefits of family participation, so they can fully support it.

A key part of this book is looking at the legitimacy of the system, which is under siege post Hillsborough. Important lessons for enquiries into tragedies like Grenfell can also be learnt, as the same legal and policy frameworks are used for such enquiries and participation of bereaved families will be similarly restricted. This research also provides insight into the wider concept of access to justice via participation in a process, not just in relation to possible human rights violations but any proceeding where rights are involved. This book is based on empirical research, used to create the author's narrative about why participation for families is so important, and how to achieve it.

The first part includes two chapters describing the overall human rights legal framework as well as the domestic law governing inquests following a death in custody. This part covers the positive legal protections currently in place in relation to families' participating in such inquests, as well as gaps where families cannot rely on the law to ensure participation. Chapter 1 sets out the legal framework governing Article 2 investigations into cases where the State might be held culpable for an individual's death, which covers deaths in custody where the State had control of an individual. It covers the evolution of Article 2, developed through case law, setting out distinct obligations on States to ensure any investigations are compliant. This chapter looks at European as well as domestic (UK) law about what is required for any investigation into a death in custody to be compliant with human rights requirements. Chapter 2 provides a brief summary of the inquest system as a unique process that is now the primary way that Article 2 obligations involving deaths in custody are devolved in England and Wales. The author explains what current legal protections are in place in relation to ensuring families are able to participate in the inquest system, as well as setting out potential gaps in the law where protections are not in place. This chapter looks at the specific domestic legal framework relating to the inquest system, especially for deaths that occur in custody. It also considers relevant legal requirements which relate to the purpose of an inquest, the role of bereaved families and specific rights that exist to allow their effective participation.

The next part introduces the methodology used by the author to carry out the empirical research which forms the basis of this book. Detailed, qualitative interviews were carried out with various people who all had experience of the inquest system following a death in custody. The author followed an Interpretative Phenomenological Analysis approach, which is a relatively new approach for this type of legal research, so the methodology is set out in some detail.

The next part of this book involves three separate chapters which all relate to how the participation of families in an inquest following a death in custody can benefit the families themselves. It includes reference to how participation protects the rights of families' as well as allowing them access to certain forms of redress. Chapter 4 looks at what are considered as the key legitimate interests for families who participate in an inquest. Domestic law allows family participation in order to protect their legitimate interests which are defined as finding out the truth, identification of State culpability and knowing further deaths will be prevented.[1] This chapter looks at theoretical frameworks setting out the overall right for affected individuals to participate in a process investigating potential human rights violations, and what that should look like in practice. The empirical

[1] *R (Joanna Letts) v Lord Chancellor* (2015) EWHC 402 (Admin) (England and Wales High Court (Administrative Court)).

evidence is used to create a narrative setting out how this relates to families' participating in an inquest, including what interviewees considered relevant aspects of the right to participate and redress. Chapter 5 introduces other potential benefits for families' participating in the inquest identified through empirical evidence, focusing on the impact on an individuals' bereavement. The research indicates that participants felt participation could have a positive impact on families' grief process and that families represented the deceased through the process. This chapter introduces complicated grief theory, then uses empirical evidence to show how participating in the inquest process can impact on a families' grief process. Positive aspects of participating include learning the truth about a death, and being able to ensure the voice of the deceased is heard through an inquest. Chapter 6 brings the empirical evidence into the wider context with the author identifying how the existing legal framework allows certain benefits to families to be considered in relation to participation as well as benefits that are not currently considered. It not only underlines how the empirical research reinforced the existing definition of families' legitimate interests but also highlights that additional aspects such as the impact of participating on the grief process are not reflected in the law. It concludes this part by explaining how the legitimate interests as set out in law address some benefits to family participation but coroners and other decision-makers need to better understand other benefits to families if they are able to participate in the inquest.

The next part includes three separate chapters which all relate to how family participation can benefit the wider principles of accountability following deaths in custody by ensuring State agents or agencies are held to account for any actions that might have either caused or not prevented a death where there was an established duty of care on the State. Chapter 7 introduces the instrumental effect that family participation can have on the outcome of an inquest. The author uses the empirical evidence to explain how families' involvement can ensure a fair and accurate outcome. The key themes identified are families' participation could have a positive impact on the likelihood of a fair outcome and disseminating those outcomes; and ensuring the process was procedurally fair. Families can optimise a fair and accurate outcome by scrutinising the evidence, bringing balance to the process and providing information that can be useful in understanding what happened. They also instigate change in a number of ways: examples are given of how families have directly impacted on improving the effectiveness of the inquest process in holding the State to account following deaths in custody. Chapter 8 looks at the importance of the inquest system as a process that holds the State to account being perceived as legitimate and therefore retaining the confidence of the public. Procedural Justice Theory is introduced as it identifies how fair and effective participation impacts on the legitimacy of certain processes. The empirical evidence is used to show that this theory translates to the inquest process. It shows that effective and fair participation can lead to families perceiving the process as fair, independent and transparent which increases their trust and confidence in the outcome; all of which increase perceptions about the legitimacy of the system. Chapter 9 introduces the author's views on how family participation benefits accountability: referencing how the empirical evidence affirms established theories. It sets out how ensuring families' participation can have an instrumental benefit to both the outcome and the wider legitimacy of the system. Accountability through ensuring State agents are not above the law and that their use of powers to restrain or detain individuals are scrutinised is a vital part of our democracy. Increasing the legitimacy of the system that carries out that scrutiny is therefore incredibly important. This chapter also identifies gaps in accountability that are not addressed through family participation, linked to scrutiny of change following inquests and public dissemination of outcomes.

The final part looks at the practical implications of this research, focusing on how the benefits set out in the previous two parts of this book can be achieved. It includes two chapters that set out the challenges that families' face in relation to being able to participate fairly and effectively, relying on the evidence gathered through the interviews, and identify proposed solutions. The final conclusion summarises the findings of the research. Chapter 10 sets out the challenges identified through the empirical evidence in relation to families participating. Some of the main issues include having restricted access to the process in a practical sense, with little information about the process and difficulties physically attending a hearing; limitations on families being able to influence the outcome; examples where families are not given access to the evidence in a timely manner, so they cannot scrutinise it; and lastly the importance of being represented by a lawyer with the necessary specialist knowledge. Chapter 11 brings together all the empirical research to identify all the benefits linked to ensuring the participation of bereaved families in an inquest following a death in custody, as well as setting out recommendations proposing how this can be achieved in practice.

The conclusion summarises the research, and puts it into the context of previous work, while also giving the authors hopes on how lessons can be learnt to improve the fair and effective participation of families following a death in custody, to the benefit of the families themselves, as well as increasing the legitimacy of the system, State actors and helping to hold those actors to account.

It is important to note that interviews were carried out before new legislation was passed in the Coroners and Justice Act 2009: it is clearly stated in the book where this has resulted in a relevant change in law, which might have changed families' experiences.[2] However, although the interviews reflect experiences before this change, most of the issues reflect challenges in accessing rights already set out in law, so this new law alone will not have changed this. The Act did bring in a Chief Coroner, and it is likely that this role has improved the system and provided greater consistency in practice. Similarly, the Independent Police Complaints Commission (IPCC) was replaced by the Independent Office for Police Conduct in 2018, and it is as yet too soon to tell whether problems identified by this research will be resolved by this change.

In this book, the phrase Article 2 inquest is used to describe proceedings following deaths in custody where enhanced procedural duties are engaged. This is a phrase used to distinguish inquests where additional requirements (such as

[2]Coroners and Justice Act 2009.

juries being present) are in place from the majority of more straightforward inquests. The descriptor is used to simplify the text but should not be taken literally to infer specific inquests are Article 2 compliant. This book discusses these enhanced or complex inquests; but it should be remembered that the distinction between 'straightforward' and 'complex' inquests is not always clear. Some inquests that do not engage Article 2 can be very complex in nature and vice versa. And similarly, it is not always clear when Article 2 is engaged, the decision can be complicated and may even change during the process. Enhanced inquests may be held even where Article 2 is not engaged, if the coroner deems it appropriate. Use of this term does not make any judgement on whether any inquests that involve more enhanced requirements are actually compliant with Article 2 for any individual case. The issue of whether any specific inquests are Article 2 compliant is complex, partly as compliance with Article 2 can involve other processes, outside of an inquest, and partly because compliance with Article 2 must be assessed against the individual circumstances of a case. So any judgement about whether a death in custody has been investigated in a manner that is compliant with Article 2 must consider all aspects of investigation and State actions. The author uses a definition of deaths in custody that includes those who have died while being detained by the State (such as in custody, immigration centres or secure mental health institutions) as well as deaths that take place while the individual is in contact with police, whether or not they have been arrested or that happen shortly after that contact.

Part 1
The Law

The first part of this book sets out the relevant law in respect of both the overarching European Court of Human Rights (ECtHR) and domestic legislation for England and Wales. It includes two chapters describing the overall human rights legal framework as well as the domestic law governing inquests following a death in custody. This part sets out the positive legal protections currently in place in relation to families participating in such inquests, as well as gaps where families cannot rely on the law to ensure participation.

Article 2(1) of the European Convention on Human Rights (ECHR) emphasises that a person's right to life *shall be protected by law*. In 1978, the ECtHR found that Article 2 of the ECHR not only prohibits the State from taking life but also places on it a positive duty to protect life.[1] This protective aspect to the right to life has been re-affirmed and expanded upon through numerous decisions of the ECtHR: elucidating on when and what steps must be taken by a State to protect life. In 1995, the ECtHR found in *McCann* that in order to protect life, the State is required to ensure there is a proper investigation into any deaths caused by the use of force by State agents.[2] Any investigation must be 'independent, prompt, contain a sufficient element of public scrutiny, and be capable of leading to a determination of whether State agents are liable'.[3] The investigation must consider not just the actions of agents of the State but also the planning and organisation of the operation governing those actions. European case law has since clarified that situations where a death may have resulted due to a failure on behalf of the State to protect life should also be investigated; this includes deaths in State custody. The ECtHR has also laid out certain minimum requirements which are necessary for an investigation to be seen as compliant with Article 2; including the fact that there must be an opportunity for a bereaved family to participate in the process.

In domestic law, the inquest system is the process which investigates deaths in custody, unless criminal proceedings have fully looked into all relevant factors. Therefore an inquest is the legal process that ensures Article 2 requirements are met. The inquest system is an ancient system; the law which governs the system has evolved over hundreds of years, but in relation to deaths in custody, it is clear

[1] *Association X v United Kingdom* (1978) DR 14 (European Commission (Plenary)).
[2] *McCann v United Kingdom* (1996) 21 EHRR 97 (European Court of Human Rights).
[3] *McCann v United Kingdom* (1996) 21 EHRR 97 (European Court of Human Rights), para 201.

that domestic protections should meet ECtHR standards. It is therefore necessary to set out both ECtHR and domestic law, as well as highlight any diversions between the different jurisdictions that might illustrate potential challenges to ensuring compliance with Article 2 requirements.

Chapter 1 sets out how Article 2 has evolved from protecting life to requiring an investigation in certain situations where there is possible State involvement either in causing a death or failing to take adequate steps to protect life. Chapter 2 then looks at the specific domestic legal framework relating to the inquest system, especially for deaths that occur in custody. It also considers relevant legal requirements which relate to the purpose of an inquest, the role of bereaved families and specific rights that exist to allow their effective participation. But before that, the development of both European and domestic law in relation to Article 2 and the legal requirements around investigations into deaths in custody are discussed in the next chapter.

Chapter 1

Requirement to Investigate Deaths in Custody

1.1 Introduction

This is the first chapter setting out the relevant law relating to deaths in custody. As Article 2 of the European Convention of Human Rights (ECHR) is the primary legal framework governing the requirements in place relating to investigations following a death in custody, this chapter looks at the evolution of Article 2 in European law as well as how domestic law has developed, both in response to European law and as a distinct jurisdiction.

Article 2 of the ECHR protects an individual's right to life. Substantial European case law has established distinct duties on a State under Article 2, described in this book as substantive and procedural duties. Substantive duties on the State are not to take life and take reasonable steps to protect life; the author further distinguishes this latter subset of substantive duties to protect life as administrative and operational duties. Administrative duties are systemic in nature and seek to ensure that appropriate procedures and systems are in place; operational duties relate to protecting an individual or individuals in a specific situation and relate to proactive steps that the State must take in individual situations to protect life. Procedural duties arise from the substantive duties and require a State to ensure causes of death are investigated thoroughly. An investigation must ensure the State has not failed in relation to its substantive duties to not take life and protect life in certain situations. The purpose of any investigation is to also ensure that lessons are learnt to prevent future deaths. Procedural duties are therefore linked to identifying how deaths occur and, in appropriate cases, who should be held liable for the death. So in all cases of sudden and unexpected death, the State must ensure there are systems in place to investigate cause of death – the systems can include criminal and civil justice jurisdictions.

However, in cases where there is possible State liability for a death, case law has established what can be called an enhanced procedural or investigative duty, which sets up additional requirements beyond merely ensuring a criminal or civil justice system is in place to investigate a death. This enhanced procedural duty requires the State to initiate the investigation following a death (so a civil case brought by non-State party would be insufficient), and allow family participation

Death in Custody, 9–22
Copyright © 2020 Jo Easton
Published under exclusive licence
doi:10.1108/978-1-83909-025-720201003

in the investigation. As yet, there is a gap in case law so it is not clearly established which situations should engage this enhanced procedural duty. For example, a natural death in custody does not trigger the enhanced procedural duty unless there is reason to suspect State failures contributed to the death.[1] However, this author sees this as a potential gap in accountability, as even if cause of death is known as natural causes, it can be difficult to judge whether lack of poor medical care might have been a contributory factor.[2] So without an investigation, State failures might not be identified and without evidence of State failures, an enhanced investigation is not required. Although case law is clear that sudden or unexpected deaths in custody will always require an enhanced investigation which is State-initiated with the opportunity for family involvement, it can be difficult to identify whether a death is unexpected without investigation. So there may be cases where there are State failings which are not being identified due to the lack of enhanced investigation.

This chapter will set out the evolution of Article 2 through case law, including the legal protections in relation to family participation in an Article 2 inquest. And as domestic law evolved distinctly from (although taking account of) European jurisprudence, European and England and Wales jurisprudence are considered separately. Under England and Wales law, an inquest is the primary route by which Article 2 enhanced investigative duties are discharged. An inquest is opened within days of a death but then is adjourned to allow other jurisdictions (including criminal, civil and disciplinary proceedings) to take precedence. In relation to deaths that occurred in custody, a coroner must then decide whether other processes have adequately investigated the death; if there remain unanswered questions, the inquest is reopened. It is here that a coroner must ensure Article 2 requirements have been met. An example would be a murder in prison, where a criminal case identified and punished the killer but further questions about possible systemic failings in the prison would need answering.[3]

1.2 Evolution of Article 2 of the European Convention on Human Rights

Article 2(1) of the ECHR states:

> Everyone's right to life shall be protected by law. No one shall be deprived of his life intentionally save in the execution of a sentence of a court following his conviction of a crime for which this penalty is provided by law.[4]

---

[1] *Tyrell v HM Senior Coroner County Durham and Darlington* (2016) EWHC 1892 (Admin) Divisional Court.

[2] Mclean (2017), Harris (2017).

[3] Keith (2006).

[4] Convention for the Protection of Human Rights and Fundamental Freedoms (European Convention on Human Rights, as amended) (ECHR).

Over the last 30 years, the ECtHR has developed extensive jurisprudence on the nature of the rights established by Article 2: specifically, the responsibilities that it imposes on States. Article 2 sets out two substantive requirements for States: first, the duty not to take life except where permitted by law, and, second, the duty to take reasonable steps to protect life. The duty to not take life is sometimes referenced as a negative obligation as it relates to actions the State cannot take or situations when the State cannot use force.[5] The duty to protect life is considered to be a positive obligation as it relates to steps States must actively take to prevent death.[6] This second substantive duty has evolved in ECtHR judgments to create distinct obligations to prevent deaths in certain situations as well as a duty to investigate deaths to ensure anyone responsible for the death is held to account (a procedural obligation).

In general, the substantive duties relate to actions a State should take prior to any death occurring: the State must take steps to ensure force is only used when 'absolutely necessary' and if there is a proven duty of care; the State should take steps to prevent death. The procedural duty relates to actions the State must take following a death: a State must provide a system of investigation allowing any culpability for the death to be established. This obligation was originally considered to only be engaged following a possible substantive breach of Article 2 but is now considered as a stand-alone duty.

In the United Kingdom, the Court of Appeal set out the obligations provided by Article 2 in the *Amin* and *Middleton* cases, 'Article 2 imposes two distinct but complementary obligations on the State'.[7]The domestic courts considered the first substantive duty on States was 'not intentionally to take life' as well as to take any reasonable measures necessary to protect someone whose life was at risk. The second obligation was described as a procedural duty to investigate deaths where there may have been a violation of the first obligation.

1.2.1 Substantive Aspect

1.2.1.1 State Must Not Take Life

European Court of Human Rights Jurisprudence. Article 2(2) states it is lawful for a State to take a life through use of force when 'absolutely necessary' if the State actor needs to defend themselves, someone else, ensure a lawful arrest or stop a riot. In the McCann case, the ECtHR noted that the term 'absolutely necessary' required a stricter test than 'necessary in a democratic society', which is normally used to judge State actions under ECHR provisions.[8,9] However, Article 2 does not just consider when it is permissible to intentionally take life

[5]Milanović (2008).

[6]Mowbray (2005).

[7]*R. (on the application of Amin (Imtiaz)) v Secretary of State for the Home Department* (2003) UKHL 51 (UK House of Lords); *R. (on the application of Middleton) v HM Coroner for Western Somerset* (2004) UKHL 10 (House of Lords).

[8]The first time the ECtHR considered a deliberate action by State officials to take a life.

[9]*McCann v United Kingdom* (1996), *para 1b.*

but also when and how much force is allowed to restrain an individual when such restraint may unintentionally cause death (such as cases involving positional asphyxia).[10,11] A State agent must hold a reasonable belief that it is necessary and proportionate to use force for the reasons given above.[12] If the belief was unreasonable, use of force has been found to violate Article 2.[13] Actions of State agents which may unintentionally result in the death of others (such as dangerous driving) have also been considered by the ECtHR to be possible substantive violations.[14]

If an individual dies while in State custody, and the facts of the deaths are unclear, the State should provide a reasonable explanation for what happened.[15] If the State fails to provide a reasonable explanation, it may be considered a substantive violation of Article 2, even if there is no proof that State actions or inactions were causally linked to the death. In the case of *Salman*, an individual entered into State custody 'in apparent good health' but died of heart failure.[16] The ECtHR did not believe the State's explanation of how the injuries were caused so, even though it was not proven that State actions caused the death, the ECtHR judged the State responsible for the death.[17]

In order to ensure the use of force by State agents is subjected to the 'most careful scrutiny', the ECtHR stated in *McCann* that systemic issues such as the planning of operations, as well as direct actions that resulted in death, should be scrutinised.[18] A further case clarified that the substantive aspect of Article 2 required a State not to just to show any actions of State agents were lawful but that adequate training and planning was part of any operation where agents were permitted to use force.[19,20] This was the first progression of the substantive duty not to take life to incorporate operational obligations to take steps to protect life. This aspect will be discussed in more detail below.

England and Wales Jurisprudence. Prior to the enactment of the Human Rights Act (HRA), use of force by State agents was primarily governed by common law provisions of self-defence.[21] On the issue of self-defence, domestic courts relied on

---

[10]Positional asphyxia was causal to the deaths of Gareth Myatt and Jimmy Mubenga; it will be referenced later in the book in Part 4.

[11]See *McKerr v United Kingdom* (2002) 34 EHRR 20 (European Court of Human Rights); *Bures v The Czech Republic* (2012) ECHR 1819 (European Court of Human Rights).

[12]European Convention on Human Rights, as amended; *Ramsahai v The Netherlands* (2008) 46 EHRR 43 (European Court of Human Rights), paras 376–377.

[13]*Gul v Turkey* (2002) 34 EHRR 28 (European Court Human Rights), para 82.

[14]*McShane v United Kingdom* (2002) 35 EHRR 23 (European Court of Human Rights).

[15]*Aksoy v Turkey* (1997) 23 EHRR 553 (European Court of Human Rights); *Salman v Turkey* (2002) 34 EHRR 17 (European Court of Human Rights).

[16]*Salman v Turkey* (2002), para 102.

[17]*Salman v Turkey* (2002), para 103.

[18]*McCann v United Kingdom* (1996), paras 149–150.

[19]*Andronicou v Cyprus* (1998) 25 EHRR 491 (European Court of Human Rights)

[20]The issue of planning operations is one that must be investigated fully in order to comply with the procedural obligation which will be discussed later.

[21]Association of Chief Police Officers (2003, p. 9).

the reasonableness test to judge whether force was permitted.[22] The test would look at whether the actor reasonably perceived force to be necessary and proportionate.[23] In addition to common law provisions, Section 3(1) of the Criminal Act of 1967 permitted State agents to use force that was reasonable to prevent a crime or make an arrest.[24] This Act provided State agents with legal justification for using force even under an unreasonable belief as long as it was honestly held.[25]

The HRA provides that public authorities must act in a way that is compatible with ECHR rights under Section 6 of the Act.[26] The author considers that domestic law alone sets less stringent requirements relating to the use of force than duties as set out in ECtHR law. State agents merely have to be shown to have been acting in an honestly held belief, which can be unreasonable, but arguably this does not meet the higher test of being absolutely necessary. However, policy and guidance governing the actions of armed police officers indicates their need to adhere to the higher Article 2 standards.[27] In addition, domestic courts have sometimes used the test of absolute necessity when considering force which could be lethal.[28] So the potential diversion in law is hopefully negated in practice through guidance and case law.

1.2.1.2 State Must Protect Life

European Court of Human Rights Jurisprudence. Article 2 sets out a positive obligation on States to protect life, which has been developed through ECtHR case law. In 1978, the European Commission judged that Article 2 goes further than prohibiting the State from taking life and placed on it a positive duty to protect life.[29]

The positive obligation to protect life has now been defined by ECtHR case law as imposing two distinct duties on a State. One is a general duty to ensure effective systems are in place to allow the enjoyment of rights set out in Article 2 – the author will refer to this as an administrative duty.[30] The second is a more specific duty covering situations where States have a duty of care to protect individuals – this will be referred to as an operational duty.

The administrative duty arises in part from the explicit reference in Article 2 to protect life but also reflects ECtHR case law in relation to other rights which do not explicitly impose a positive obligation on States.[31] Generally, many of the

---

[22] *R v Williams* (Gladstone) (1987) 3 ALL ER 411 (Court of Appeal), p 411-9R; *Beckford v R.* (1987) 3 ALL ER 425 (Privy Council), p. 425–433.

[23] Gearty and Kimbell (1995, p. 59).

[24] Criminal Law Act 1967.

[25] Leverick (2002, p. 361).

[26] Human Rights Act.

[27] *Association of Chief Police Officers Manual of Guidance on Police Use of Firearms,* p. 9.

[28] *R (ex parte Beckett) v HM Coroner for Inner South London & Ors* (2006) EWHC 196 (Admin) (England and Wales High Court (Administrative)), para 23; The judge stated that to 'kill when it is not absolutely necessary to do so, is surely to act unreasonably', para 25.

[29] *Association X v United Kingdom* (1978).

[30] *Association X v United Kingdom* (1978).

[31] Alastair Mowbray, *The development of positive obligations under the European Convention on Human Rights by the European Court of Human Rights* (Bloomsbury Publishing 2004).

rights set out in the ECHR only explicitly refer to negative obligations (i.e., what States must refrain from doing rather than actions States must take). The ECtHR has, however, developed implied positive actions States must take to ensure all Convention rights are protected.[32] In relation to Article 2, this involves ensuring systems are designed to deter the taking of life (for instance, an effective criminal justice systems which can identify and punish those taking life) and protect life (for example, health and safety regulations).[33] This can interrelate with the procedural duty to investigate deaths effectively, which will be considered later. Administrative systems must be in place (a proactive and substantive duty on States) as deterrence but the ability to effectively find and hold to account those culpable for a death is part of the separate procedural obligation. A State must ensure effective administrative and legislative systems act to discharge both obligations: the first to prevent deaths (substantive duties) and the second to investigate deaths (procedural duty).

The administrative duty does not require a State to be aware of a specific or known risk but requires measures to be in place to address any inherent or general risks to life. This may include providing information to those at risk so that they may either avoid or mitigate the risk.[34] Various situations have been assessed by the ECtHR to require States to provide systems to safeguard life including the provision of health care services, the disposal of dangerous waste, health and safety on a ship or a building site.[35,36,37,38]

The second substantive duty under the protective element of Article 2 can be described as an operational duty. This relates to specific and proactive steps the State must take in response to specific situations in order to protect life. This obligation covers situations where the State might be considered to have a duty of care to an individual. Violations can include a failure to prevent a murder where specific threats have been made against a named individual, or the suicide of somebody detained by the State.[39]

The ECtHR stated in *Oneryildiz* that the operational duty on a State to take steps to protect life could apply in any situation where an individual's right to life might be at risk.[40] The operational duty is only engaged where 'authorities

[32]Merrills (1993, p. 102–103).
[33]*Oneryildiz v Turkey* (No.2) (2005) 41 EHRR 20 (European Court of Human Rights (Grand Chamber)), paras 69-70; *Osman v United* Kingdom (2000) *29 EHRR 245 (European Court of Human Rights), para 115; Tarariyeva v* Russia (2009) *48 EHRR 26 (European Court of Human Rights),* para 74.
[34]*Koladenko and Others v Russia* (2013) 56 EHRR 2 (European Court of Human Rights).
[35]*Association X v United Kingdom* (1978); *Dodov v Bulgaria* (2008) 47 EHRR 41 (European Court of Human Rights).
[36]*Oneryildiz v Turkey* (No.2) (2005).
[37]*Leray and Others v France* (2001) ECHR 880 (European Court of Human Rights).
[38]*Pereira Henriques v Luxembourg* (2009) ECHR 2244 (European Court of Human Rights).
[39]*Keenan v United Kingdom* (2001) 33 EHRR 38 (European Court of Human Rights); *Renolde v France* (2009) 48 EHRR 42 (European Court of Human Rights).
[40]*Oneryildiz v Turkey* (No.2) (2005), para 71.

knew or ought to have known at the time of the existence of a real and immediate risk to the life of an identified individual or individuals'.[41] States then have a duty of care and a consequent responsibility to take steps to protect the individual or individuals known to be at risk.[42] In such situations, States must show they 'took measures which, judged reasonably, might have been expected to avoid said risk' to discharge their duty.[43] It would violate the operational duty to protect life under Article 2 if States knew or should have known of a real and immediate risk to life and reasonable steps to prevent death were not taken.[44]

The ECtHR has clarified the operational duty but it generally puts a high threshold on expectations of when a State should have taken steps to prevent a death. For example, in relation to murders where previous threats to the victim are known, the ECtHR has acknowledged the importance of States' agencies having operational discretion, and stated Article 2 duties to protect life should not place authorities under an impossible or disproportionate burden.[45]

In terms of deaths that occur in custody, there is an inherent duty of care on the State towards those that they detain, as they control the environment and the individual. The ECtHR has stated 'Persons in custody are in a vulnerable position and the authorities are under a duty to protect them'.[46] This duty requires State agents to take the steps to protect life as well as to only use force when absolutely necessary. As discussed above, under the substantive obligation to not take life, the ECtHR does not necessarily differentiate between the duties on the State to either not take life or to protect life of individuals under their control.

One of the key duties on a State is to take steps to prevent a detained individual taking their own life.[47] *Keenan* involved a suicide in prison where the ECtHR found there was an obligation on the State to take reasonable steps to prevent a suicide in custody, if there was a 'real and immediate' risk of self-inflicted death.[48] In line with other judgments requiring a high threshold before deciding a State should have known about a risk to life, the ECtHR has found there has to be evidence indicating there was an imminent threat of suicide before judging the State 'could have reasonably foreseen' a risk to life.[49] This was affirmed by *Renolde* where a violation of the obligation to protect life was

[41] *Osman v United Kingdom* (2000), para 116; reaffirmed by: *Keenan v United Kingdom* (2001), para 90; *Banel v Lithuania* (2013) ECHR 558 (European Court of Human Rights), para 65.

[42] *Ergi v Turkey* (2001) 32 EHRR 18 (European Court of Human Rights).

[43] *Osman v United Kingdom* (2000), para 116; reaffirmed by: *Keenan v United Kingdom* (2001), para 90; *Banel v Lithuania*, para 65.

[44] *Mahmut Kaya v Turkey* (2000) ECHR 129 (European Court of Human Rights); *Osman v United Kingdom* (2000); *LCB v United Kingdom* (1999) 27 EHRR 212 (European Court of Human Rights).

[45] *Osman v United Kingdom* (2000), para 116.

[46] *Salman v Turkey* (2002), para 99.

[47] *Keenan v United Kingdom* (2001).

[48] *Keenan v United Kingdom* (2001), para 90.

[49] *Trubnikov v Russia* (2005) ECHR 462 (European Court of Human Rights), paras 72–76.

found following a suicide in custody.[50] The ECtHR found there was a real and known risk to life and the State failed in three separate ways to prevent suicide and therefore was in violation of the substantive obligation to protect life.[51]

England and Wales Jurisprudence. UK case law places a specific duty on the State to prevent self-inflicted deaths in custody, partly due to the fact that detention inherently increases vulnerability and therefore results in a heightened risk of suicide.[52] The initial duty related to those diagnosed with a mental illness, but it has now been evolved to cover those without a specific diagnosis.[53,54]

Since the enactment of the HRA, domestic courts have also referred to established ECtHR case law in respect to the duty on States to protect life, with the *Osman* case only being partially affirmed by domestic judgments. In July 2008, a Chief Constable of Police appealed a finding of negligence; and the defensive principle set out in *Hill* was reaffirmed, contrary to the judgment of the ECtHR in *Osman* which found relying on this principle could breach Article 6(1).[55,56] The domestic court did, however, refer to standards set out in *Osman* to find there was no duty of care in this case, stating the standard as to whether the State had a duty to protect life under Article 2 of the ECHR was invariable, not dependant on circumstances. The Osman test was followed more recently in the *Savage* case, which involved the death of a woman who died of suicide shortly after escaping from a hospital where she was being detained under the Mental Health Act.[57,58]

---

[50] *Renolde v France* (2009).

[51] *Renolde v France* (2009), para 110.

[52] *R. (on the application of JL) v Secretary of State for the Home Department* (2008) UKHL 68 (House of Lords); *R. (on the application of Bloggs 61) v Secretary of State for the Home Department* (2003) EWCA Civ 686 (Court of Appeal (Civil Division)).

[53] *Kirkham v Chief Constable of the Greater Manchester Police* (1990) 2 QB 283 (Court of Appeal (Civil Division)).

[54] *Reeves v Commissioner Of Police For Metropolis* (2000) 1 AC 360 (House of Lords); *Orange v West Yorkshire Police* (2001) EWCA Civ 611 (Court of Appeal (Civil Division)); *R. (on the application of DF) v Chief Constable of Norfolk* (2002) EWHC 1738 (Admin) (Queen's Bench Division (Administrative Court)).

[55] This principle states that fear of liability might lead police officers to act very cautiously and therefore prevent them carrying out their duties; *Hill v Chief Constable of West Yorkshire* (1989) AC 53; (1988) 2 WLR 1049 (House of Lords); See also Claire McIvor, 'Getting defensive about police negligence: the Hill principle, the Human Rights Act 1998 and the House of Lords' (2010) 69 Cambridge Law Journal 133.

[56] *Van Colle v Chief Constable of Hertfordshire* (2008) UKHL 50 (House of Lords).

[57] *Savage v South Essex Partnership NHS Foundation Trust* (2010) EWHC 865 (QB) (Queen's Bench Division).

[58] Note: The Policing and Crime Act 2017 amended the Coroners and Justice Act 2009 so that the definition of 'state detention' no longer includes an individual held under 'section 4A(3) or (5) or 4B of the Mental Capacity Act 2005'. It is unclear what, if any, impact this will have on the understanding of State duties under Article 2 for people held under the Mental Capacity Act.

1.2.2 Procedural Aspect

European Court of Human Rights Jurisprudence. The protective aspect of Article 2 imposes a procedural duty on States to provide effective systems to investigate deaths for three reasons: firstly, to provide deterrence to the taking of life, secondly, to ensure those culpable for a death are held accountable and, thirdly, to ensure victims have access to a remedy.[59] This corresponds to the administrative duty discussed previously: frameworks must be in place to protect life through deterring actions that might violate Article 2. The procedural duty relates to the ability of frameworks to determine the cause of a death and hold those responsible for the death to account.[60] The effectiveness of the systems in place to discharge this procedural duty will therefore interrelate to the effectiveness of the system to deter violations of Article 2 and therefore discharge the administrative duty. This wider procedural obligation can be discharged through ensuring an effective, independent judicial system which allows the investigation of the cause of death and identifies any actions that might have resulted in a violation in Article 2. This duty may be discharged through the availability of civil remedies or disciplinary proceedings.[61] In *Banel v Lithuania,* the ECtHR distinguished between deaths caused intentionally and those where negligence was a possible causal factor: stating that in the latter situations, 'a civil or disciplinary remedy may suffice'.[62,63]

The ECtHR has identified certain situations where there is a more onerous procedural duty which requires investigations to be initiated by the State.[64] This duty can be defined as the enhanced procedural or investigative duty, and is linked to the substantive duties on the State to both not take and protect life.[65] This duty has evolved over time to ensure effective investigations are carried out whenever the substantive obligations on the State in relation to Article 2 may be engaged. The key difference between the general procedural duty to ensure systems are in place to investigate deaths and this second 'enhanced' duty is that any investigations must be State-initiated: so a civil system allowing families to bring civil cases would not be adequate to devolve State responsibilities. The distinction between an investigation devolving the general rather than the enhanced

---

[59] *Dodov v Bulgaria* (2008), para 83; *Byrzykowski v Poland* (2008) 46 EHRR 32 (European Court of Human Rights), paras 104–118.

[60] *Vo v France* (2005) 40 EHRR 12 (European Court of Human Rights (Grand Chamber)), paras 90–91.

[61] *Calvelli and Ciglio v Italy* (2002) ECHR 3 (European Court Human Rights), para 51; *Byrzykowski v Poland* (2008), para 105; *Vo v France* (2005), paras 90–1 & 94; *Dodov v Bulgaria* (2008), para 87.

[62] *Banel v Lithuania* (2013).

[63] *Banel v Lithuania* (2013), para 48; See also *Calvelli and Ciglio v Italy* (2002); *Mastromatteo v Italy* (2002) ECHR 694 (European Court of Human Rights).

[64] As referenced in *R. (on the application of Humberstone) v Legal Services Commission* (2010) EWHC 760 (Admin) (Queen's Bench Division (Administrative Court)), para 67.

[65] https://ukhumanrightsblog.com/2012/11/14/no-article-2-inquest-over-14-year-old-overdose-death-despite-failings/

procedural duty is not always clear; for example, in cases involving criminal activity, any State-initiated criminal charges would be in line with general procedural requirements as well as discharging the enhanced duty. It is also not always clear when the enhanced duty is engaged. It is clear that cases where there has been a violation of the State's substantive duty under Article 2 would require an enhanced procedural investigation, but it is not always clear which other cases also engage the enhanced duty. This will be discussed later, and the evolution of the enhanced procedural duty will be summarised below.

The enhanced procedural duty has developed from the initial obligation to investigate deaths caused by State agents. In 1995, the ECtHR found in *McCann* that in order to protect life, a State was required to ensure there was a proper investigation of any deaths which resulted from the use of force by State agents.[66] The judgment stated any investigation must be 'independent, prompt, contain a sufficient element of public scrutiny, and be capable of leading to a determination of whether State agents are liable'.[67] It set out that the investigation must consider not just the actions of State agents but also the planning and organisation of the operation governing those actions. In 2001, four cases from Northern Ireland, all involving situations where death resulted from the use of force by State agents, came before the ECtHR which further developed this duty to include involvement of bereaved families in order 'to protect their interests'.[68] The criteria of an Article 2 compliant investigation devolving the enhanced procedural duty as they relate to the participation of bereaved families and other issues relevant to this book will be discussed in Chapter 2.

A number of key ECtHR judgments reaffirmed and contextualised the procedural duty to come into force whenever there was the possibility of a substantive breach of the operational duty under Article 2.[69] This included situations where a State failed to protect life as well as those in which State agents were directly responsible for causing death. If an unexpected death occurs in custody, the State is taken to have assumed responsibility for the individual so the enhanced procedural duty must be engaged, as the possibility of an infringement of the operational obligation to protect life must be considered. The duty to investigative deaths that occur in custody requires not just the circumstances of the death to be considered but also any potential failings of regulatory systems.[70] A further stated purpose of the enhanced procedural duty, which links to the duty to deter any State actions that might infringe the right to life, is to identify those culpable for a death and ensure they are held to account.[71] This will be considered further in Part 4 of this book.

---

[66]*McCann v United Kingdom* (1996), para 161.

[67]*McCann v United Kingdom* (1996), para 161.

[68]*McKerr v United Kingdom* (2002); *Shanaghan v United Kingdom* (2001) ECHR 330 (European Court of Human Rights); *Kelly and others v United Kingdom* (2001) ECHR 328 (European Court of Human Rights); *Jordan v United Kingdom* (2003) 37 EHRR 2 (European Court of Human Rights).

[69]*Keenan v United Kingdom* (2001); *Tarariyeva v Russia* (2009).

[70]*Trubnikov v Russia* (2005), para 88.

[71]*Oneryildiz v Turkey (No.2)* (2005), para 57.

As mentioned above, the ECtHR has not always clearly distinguished between situations when the general or the enhanced procedural duty might be engaged. There are some cases without substantive failings where the duty appears to have been engaged, and a lack of clarity over those cases with State involvement where it does engage. As the ECtHR evolved the procedural duty over the last decade, it became a distinct obligation on States, not necessarily connected to the possibility of substantive breaches. In 2003, the ECtHR decided that just because there was no State responsibility for the death, it did not preclude the same 'basic procedural requirements apply[ing]'.[72] Three years later in *Slimani*, the ECtHR judged the procedural element of Article 2 was not dependent on a substantive breach.[73] Following this, there were two cases where the State was found to breach Article 2 for not completing effective investigations, even though there was no direct State involvement in the deaths.[74]

So there are situations where the enhanced duty is engaged, even with no State involvement in a death, but there is also some lack of clarity about which cases with State involvement engage an enhanced investigation. For example, there may be deaths where there is a possibility of there being a State substantive violation, but without an enhanced investigation it may not be determined. This includes, as discussed above, a death in custody which is initially judged to be due to natural causes – this might involve substantive obligations around taking reasonable steps to prevent a death but without an investigation this may not be determined. However, unless a death in custody is sudden or unexpected, there is no clearly established requirement that an enhanced investigation is carried out.

So the distinction between the general and the enhanced procedural duty is therefore not as clearly established through European case law as is sometimes argued. It can cover not just those cases where there is State responsibility for a death but where there is a wider responsibility to protect the public. It may not cover all deaths in custody, even where there is an established duty of care on the State. And there is wide discretion as to what the investigatory system looks like – as long as the basic criteria as set out in *Jordan* are complied with, which will be discussed in the next chapter. However, it is clear that in cases where the State may have failed in its duty to protect life (including systemic aspects), an investigation must be able to identify State liability.

The procedural aspect originally set out in *McCann* related to ensuring there were effective investigations in place following deaths that could be attributed to State agents in order to ensure a State was complying with the obligation not to take life unless absolutely necessary. The duty evolved to require an effective investigation process for all deaths where there was a possibility of State culpability, in order to assess whether the State could have prevented the death.

---

[72] *Menson v United Kingdom (Admissibility)* (2003) Inquest LR 146 (European Court of Human Rights).

[73] *Slimani v France* (2006) 43 EHRR 49 (European Court of Human Rights).

[74] *Pereira Henriques v Luxembourg* (2009) ECHR 2244 (European Court of Human Rights); *Angelova and Iliev v Bulgaria* (2008) 47 EHRR 7 (European Court of Human Rights).

The further requirement that the State ensures systems are in place to deter any infringements on the right to life by other parties has led to the procedural duty encompassing any suspicious deaths.[75] The 'suspicious' deaths relate to any death that is not established as natural but as yet there is no clear criteria as to how a State should assess whether deaths can be considered natural or not. It is clear that for all deaths within State custody, there is a chance the State might be culpable (either in terms of causing or failing to prevent the death) so would require an effective investigation. However, what investigation is required to establish whether a death in State detention is natural or not is not clearly defined through European law. This is another potential gap in accountability, as systemic failings may not be investigated for deaths deemed not to be suspicious.

England and Wales Jurisprudence. It was described above that ECtHR case law did not clearly set out criteria for which deaths require an effective investigation beyond the fact that suspicious or unnatural deaths should be investigated, regardless of who might be culpable. Domestic law similarly requires all suspicious or unnatural deaths to be investigated.[76] The domestic courts have clarified two different procedural aspects relating to Article 2: one a general duty to investigate all deaths and the second a duty related to investigations where the State might have substantive obligations. So in cases where there is no possibility of a substantive Article 2 breach by a State, the procedural obligation may be considered to be less onerous. The general duty under Article 2 was set out in domestic law in *Jamieson:* where the court found that Article 2 set out a general investigative or procedural duty to provide a legal system capable of finding accountability for a death.[77] The second duty, sometimes referred to as the enhanced procedural duty, stems directly from the possibility of a substantive breach and therefore relates to deaths in which State agents either caused or failed to prevent the death. Domestic courts relied on ECtHR judgments to define the enhanced procedural duty as requiring States 'to initiate an effective public investigation by an independent official body' following deaths in which State agents may be implicated.[78] The domestic courts reaffirmed this definition in two cases involving the possibility of negligence by NHS staff where it was judged that, although the State had the duty to ensure effective investigations into these cases, they could be considered as distinct from those situations where deaths occurred in State detention.[79]

---

[75] *Nikolova v Bulgaria* (2009) 48 EHRR 40 (European Court of Human Rights), para 57.
[76] The Coroners Act 1988 required 'sudden' deaths to be investigated (s.8(1)(c)) and the Coroners and Justice Act require investigations where the deceased 'died a violent or unnatural death', or 'the cause of death is unknown' (S.1).
[77] *R. v HM Coroner for North Humberside and Scunthorpe Ex p. Jamieson* (1995) QB 1; (1994) 3 WLR 82 (Court of Appeal (Civil Division)).
[78] *R. (on the application of Middleton) v HM Coroner for Western Somerset* (2004), para 3.
[79] *Goodson v HM Coroner for Bedfordshire and Luton* (2004) EWHC 2931 (Admin) (Queen's Bench Division (Administrative Court)); *R. (on the application of Takoushis) v HM Coroner for Inner North London* (2005) EWCA Civ 1440; (2006) 1 WLR 461 (Court of Appeal (Civil Division)).

In respect of deaths that occur in custody, domestic courts have considered the enhanced procedural obligation can be invoked even where there was no evidence the State had breached its substantive duties under Article 2.[80] This was consequential of the enhanced duty of care the State owed to those detained involuntarily by the authorities.[81] It was also acknowledged that when someone died unexpectedly in the custody of the State, the authorities were in a unique position to possess the information concerning the death (including any causal factors), which puts the onus on the State to provide an explanation as to how death occurred.[82]

So, similarly to European law, jurisprudence is not completely clear when an enhanced procedural duty is engaged. Where the State may be deemed liable, the State must initiate an investigation complying with *Jordan* requirements, to be prompt, independent, allow family involvement and adequate public scrutiny. Investigations for all deaths in custody in England and Wales are primarily carried out through the inquest system. However, the same concerns in relation to those deaths in custody that are deemed to be due to natural causes apply as without an investigation it may appear there is no State liability, but conversely, with an investigation, State failings may be identified.

Current domestic law provides a duty for a coroner to investigate following any death in 'custody or otherwise state detention'.[83] Previously, the Coroners Act 1988 had stated all sudden deaths which occurred in either police or prison custody required a coroner to hold an inquest with a jury, unless there were criminal justice proceedings pending.[84] The Coroners and Justice Act now states a jury need not be called for any death in custody that is thought to be natural, even if sudden.[85]

It is recognised that any death in custody occurs effectively 'behind closed doors' and it is therefore likely that the public and next of kin will have questions about the death.[86] The purpose of the inquest to answer such questions and consequently ensure public confidence in the authorities has been affirmed.[87] In 2003, in *Hurst,* the Divisional Court set the precedence that to ensure compliance with Article 2, there must be an effective investigation into possible systemic police failings even where there had been a criminal trial.[88] In 2015, *Letts* found

---

[80] *R. (on the application of JL) v Secretary of State for the Home Department* (2008).

[81] *R. (on the application of Amin (Imtiaz)) v Secretary of State for the Home Department* (2003), para 30.

[82] *R. (on the application of JL) v Secretary of State for the Home Department* (2008).

[83] Coroners and Justice Act 2009, Section 1.

[84] Coroner's Act 1988, Section 8(1)(c).

[85] Coroners and Justice Act 2009, Section 7.

[86] *R. (on the application of Coker) v HM Coroner for Inner South London* (2006) EWHC 614 (Admin) (Queen's Bench Division (Administrative Court)), para 23; *R. (on the application of Amin (Imtiaz)) v Secretary of State for the Home Department* (2003), para 31.

[87] *R. (on the application of Gentle) v Prime Minister* (2008) UKHL 20 (House of Lords), para 195.

[88] *R. (on the application of Hurst) v HM Coroner for Northern District London* (2007) UKHL 13 (House of Lords).

the enhanced procedural or investigative element of Article 2 was triggered whenever there was a possibility State actions might have been complicit in a death but there did not need to be any evidence of a substantive violation.[89] The judgment stated cases which would automatically trigger the enhanced procedural duty include any deaths by suicide in prison and of voluntary psychiatric patients.[90] In *Rabone*, the enhanced procedural obligation arose in cases of 'any death for which the State might bear some degree of responsibility'.[91] However, it is still not clear how it is decided when the State may be liable – for example, natural deaths in custody do not require the same standard of investigation as sudden or unexpected deaths. It is left to the discretion of the coroner to identify whether a case involves possibly substantive breaches, and therefore what investigation is required under Article 2.

1.3 Conclusion

Article 2 case law has evolved to ensure that an individual's right to life is protected not just in relation to governing State actions in using force against an individual but also to require States to take reasonable steps to protect life. This latter duty now includes a distinct duty to investigate deaths, with enhanced duties for those cases where this is State involvement. Any investigation must identify culpability for a death, along with any State failings, with the aim of preventing further deaths. The fundamental requirements under Article 2 should ensure that State liability is established through existing systems, but the lack of clarity around when an enhanced procedural duty is engaged does mean that there is not always a requirement for a State-initiated investigation with family involvement, unless a death in custody is sudden or unexpected. It will become clear throughout the rest of this book that whether Article 2 is engaged or not following a death does have an impact on how an inquest may be governed, as well as affecting other relevant decisions (for example, in dealing with applications for legal aid funding for families) and therefore impact directly on the participation of families.[92] However, the Article 2 requirements are primarily devolved by the inquest system in England and Wales, the domestic law governing inquests is the most relevant law in respect of setting out legal rights for family participation. This will be looked at in the next chapter.

---

[89] *Letts v Lord* Chancellor (2015), *para 74.*

[90] *Letts v Lord Chancellor* (2015), paras 76–77 & 84.

[91] *Rabone v Pennine Care NHS Trust* (2010) EWCA Civ 698 (Court of Appeal (Civil Division)), para 93

[92] Note, in this book, the phrase Article 2 inquest is used to describe proceedings following deaths in custody where enhanced procedural duties are engaged.

Chapter 2

The Inquest System

This is the second chapter looking at the relevant legal framework in relation to investigating deaths in custody. It focuses on the domestic situation in England and Wales, where Article 2 requirements for an investigation described in the previous chapter are usually devolved by the inquest system. The inquest system is an anachronistic part of the legal system that has continued and evolved into the modern day. As described above, Article 2 procedural obligations can be discharged in a number of ways, with some clear margin of appreciation being allowed by the ECtHR. In England and Wales, an inquest is the catch-all process that can discharge procedural obligations if they have not been dealt with in other proceedings.[1] The basic requirements of an inquest are to determine the name of the deceased, where and how death occurred. However, in order to discharge Article 2 requirements, a *Middleton* inquest must take place, which considers wider circumstances related to State substantive duties that might have been causally linked to the death.[2] As all Article 2 requirements must be met for an 'Article 2 inquest', legal rights around the participation of bereaved families are engaged. Although in practice, families still struggle to ensure these rights are fulfilled, without an experienced legal representative supporting them, who can argue on their behalf for the ECtHR requirements to be met.

2.1 Main Reforms of Inquest System

The coronial system has evolved immensely in both its role and its nature over the last 900 years, responding to society as well as to changes within the legal framework (especially the criminal justice system). The responsibility of a coroner to register any sudden deaths within their geographical area of responsibility and establish basic facts such as the name of the deceased and cause of death was mentioned throughout the middle ages.[3] It was understood that in order to investigate the circumstances of a suspicious death, the coroner could call a jury

[1]Home Office (2003), Chapter 10.
[2]As explained in the Introduction, the distinction between different types of inquest is not always clear-cut. This will be discussed later on in this chapter.
[3]Levine and Pyke (1999).

Death in Custody, 23–42
Copyright © 2020 Jo Easton
Published under exclusive licence
doi:10.1108/978-1-83909-025-720201004

to hear the evidence, decide the facts of the case and bring a verdict as to cause of death. Although the manner in which an inquest into a sudden death was carried out did not alter much from the 1500s to the middle of the twentieth century, other duties of the coroner were transferred to alternative bodies or officials.[4]

The coroner has always had a wide discretion as to how their duties are best discharged. Although an inquest has many similarities to a criminal trial, frameworks established to ensure a fair trial in adversarial courts have not necessarily been put in place within the coronial system. For example, evidence given to the Home Affairs Committee (HAC) in 1980 during the investigation into deaths in custody illustrated that coroner's officers had extensive and largely unchecked influence over how an investigation was undertaken.[5]

In 1971, the first modern extensive review of the coronial system resulted in the Brodrick Committee publishing a number of recommendations.[6] This clarified the role of the coroner and inquests within the criminal justice system.

The Coroners Act 1988 set out the legislative framework within which Coroners exercised their powers to investigate controversial deaths.[7] Read together with the 1984 Coroner's Rules, it established the law in relation to the inquest system, stating that for a death in custody, a jury must be present (although other inquests could be held with just a coroner).[8] The importance of public scrutiny was laid out, although restrictions were allowed where there were national security concerns.

In 2001, the Home Office set up a fundamental review of the coronial system, partly in response to cases including the Bowbelle/Marchioness disaster, deaths of children following paediatric surgery in Bristol and the retention of deceased children's organs at Alder Hey hospital. The Luce report was published in April 2003, making a number of recommendations on necessary qualifications and training for coroners; a Council to oversee the coronial system; limiting juries to Article 2 cases and encouraging detailed (narrative) verdicts in those cases.[9] At the same time, an enquiry led by Dame Smith looked at issues which had arisen due to the case of Dr. Shipman, who was convicted of murdering a number of his elderly patients. One area the enquiry considered was the role of the coroner in certification of death as most of the deaths resulting from Dr. Shipman's actions were registered as natural and not referred to the coroner so no inquest occurred. Aspects relating to inquests were published in the third Report from the enquiry in July 2003.[10] It called on the coronial service to be reformed, so every death could be investigated independently, as well as for an overhaul of the way in which death certification occurred. The Government responded with a position

[4]Thomas and others (2014).
[5]Reported in Greer and McLaughlin (2012).
[6]Brodrick Committee (1971).
[7]Coroner's Act 1988.
[8]Coroner's Rules 1984. No 552.
[9]Home Office (2003): http://www.archive2.official-documents.co.uk/document/cm58/5831/5831.pdf.
[10]Home Office (2003): http://www.official-documents.gov.uk/document/cm58/5854/5854.pdf.

paper setting out reforms of the coronial system, including a number of the recommendations from both the Luce and Dame Smith reports, which resulted in the Coroners and Justice Act 2009.[11]

The Coroners and Justice Act collated the existing law relating to inquests into primary legislation with the aim of ensuring greater consistency in practice, as well as amending some aspects of the law.[12] The largest change concerned establishing a Chief Coroner, to take responsibility for ensuring greater consistency through the system via training for coroners as well as collating reports identifying failings of institutions or organisations, so there could be greater national or systemic learning from deaths.[13] Although the Chief Coroner has initiated a number of positive changes to the system, it is important to remember that participants interviewed for this book were discussing inquests before the Coroners and Justice Act 2009 was fully enabled; reference will be made to where positive changes may have changed the situation discussed in the main body of this book. Other important changes to the law were made via secondary legislation, including the Inquest Rules 2013 and the Coroners Investigations Regulations 2013.[14] A policy Charter was also introduced setting out expectations for interested parties involved in an inquest.[15]

2.2 Article 2 Investigations

ECtHR jurisprudence allows discretion as to the appropriate forum for ensuring Article 2 investigations are carried out as long as the relevant criteria for an enhanced investigation are in place. *Jordan* set out the relevant criteria as follows: an investigation must be State-initiated, independent, effective and reasonably prompt; there must be sufficient public scrutiny and appropriate involvement of the next of kin.[16] The enhanced procedural obligation can be discharged through several different but complementary avenues which, when taken together, ensure all criteria have been met. In many situations, criminal proceedings, when associated with subsequent compensation orders, might be sufficient in satisfying a State's procedural obligations.[17] Other proceedings include health and safety

---

[11]Coroners and Justice Act 2009.

[12]For detailed discussion about the changes via the Coroners and Justice Act 2009 see Chief Coroner's Office (2013), Annexes B & C.

[13]https://www.judiciary.gov.uk/related-offices-and-bodies/office-chief-coroner/. Due to the Government introducing proposals to remove the post of Chief Coroner via the Public Bodies Bill in 2010, the post was not fully established until September 2012 and the Coroners and Justice Act not fully implemented until July 2013 via the Coroners (Investigations) Regulations 2013.

[14]The Coroners (Inquests) Rules 2013; No. 1616.

[15]UK Government Ministry of Justice, Guide to Coroner Services (2014).

[16]For a discussion on further relevant case law relating to minimum requirements for an Article 2 compliant investigation see Cross and Garnham (2016), Chapter 7.

[17]Long (2003), See *Mastromatteo v Italy* (2002).

tribunals, institutional or ombudsman investigations, disciplinary hearings, civil cases or enquiries.

An enhanced procedural duty could possibly be devolved by an effective criminal justice system in place which allows the prosecution and punishment of those responsible.[18]An investigation to identify criminal actions must be State-initiated as an effective criminal justice system is necessary to maintain 'public confidence that there is no tolerance of or collusion in unlawful acts'.[19] The ECtHR clarified that in the case of any suspicious death, the enhanced investigative obligation obliged the State to 'act of their own motion' to effectively investigate the death and ensure those responsible were held to account, even where there was no allegation of State culpability.[20] In which case, a criminal court process that identified culpability could satisfy the requirements for an enhanced investigation but often a difficulty arises in that only matters specifically relating to whether an individual is criminally responsible will be addressed in a criminal case. So there are likely to be limitations on what issues are considered as part of a criminal investigation and court case – for example, systemic failings are unlikely to be fully investigated. In addition, there may be limited opportunity for the participation of bereaved families, as necessary to protect their legitimate interests, in a criminal case. Therefore, although there is flexibility within the ECtHR case law as to what an Article 2 investigation looks like, there are at least two reasons why a criminal court case may be insufficient. The ECtHR has judged an inquest as capable of devolving a State's enhanced procedural duty where they are held in public, independently adjudicated, allow family involvement as well as investigating wider aspects related to a death such as planning of operations.[21]

2.2.1 *Inquests as Article 2 Investigations*

In *Amin*, it was noted that the ECtHR does allow a degree of flexibility in how States can carry out investigations that satisfy the procedural obligation of Article 2.[22] As described earlier, the procedural obligation requires a State to ensure there is an investigative process that is capable of ensuring accountability for any death but the ECtHR has judged that if there is a possibility of a substantive breach, the State must ensure that an enhanced, State-initiated investigation occurs.[23] In England and Wales, an inquest is the default process by which Article 2 requirements are devolved, with an inquest usually only going ahead where no

[18] *Oneryildiz v Turkey* (No.2) (2005), para 93, *Angelova and Iliev v Bulgaria* (2008) 47 EHRR 7 (European Court of Human Rights).
[19] *Oneryildiz v Turkey* (No.2) (2005), para 96.
[20] *Rantsev v Cyprus* (2010) 51 EHRR 1 (European Court of Human Rights), paras 232-3.
[21] *Bubbins v United Kingdom* (2005) 41 EHRR 24 (European Court of Human Rights), para 153.
[22] *R. (on the application of Amin (Imtiaz)) v Secretary of State for the Home Department* (2003), para 32.
[23] Hyam (2010, p. 5–6).

other legal proceedings have investigated a death in a manner which satisfies Article 2 requirements.

In *Middleton*, it was noted that in some circumstances, a State's procedural obligation may be discharged through criminal proceedings alone.[24] However, there are other cases where a defendant pleaded guilty (as in *Edwards*[25]) or was not considered mentally fit to stand trial (as in *Amin*[26]), and wider issues related to systemic flaws contributing to a death would still have to be investigated through an inquest.[27] An inquest can be adjourned where there is a public enquiry into the death and resumption in these cases must only occur if the coroner believes there is 'exceptional reason'.[28] But, generally, when there is no ongoing criminal prosecution or public enquiry, 'an inquest is the means by which the State ordinarily discharges that [procedural] obligation'.[29]

In *Takoushis*, the Court of Appeal found that for certain cases (in this instance the death involved medical negligence), the availability of civil proceedings may not be considered adequate to satisfy enhanced procedural obligations but a traditional, non-*Middleton* inquest might ensure States' obligations were met.[30] (A *Middleton* inquest must consider wider aspects which may have contributed to a death and will be discussed in Section 2.2.2). However, a failure of an inquest to fulfil the procedural requirements cannot always be taken as an Article 2 violation as it is only one way the duty can be absolved.[31] An inquest need to only satisfy the procedural duty where the coroner is aware no other investigation (criminal, civil or otherwise) had provided an adequate investigation.[32] Although generally a *Middleton* inquest is relied upon to discharge the enhanced procedural Article 2 duty, any inquest may be considered as discharging the wider procedural duty where other processes have not occurred.

2.2.2 Enhanced Procedural Duty: Considering Wider Aspects Linked to Cause of Death

A coroner has wide discretion to carry out an inquest as they consider is appropriate to each case.[33] However, when an inquest is satisfying a State's

---

[24] *R. (on the application of Middleton) v HM Coroner for Western Somerset* (2004).
[25] *Edwards v United Kingdom* (2002) 35 EHRR 19 (European Court of Human Rights).
[26] *R. (on the application of Amin (Imtiaz)) v Secretary of State for the Home Department* (2003).
[27] *R. (on the application of Middleton) v HM Coroner for Western Somerset* (2004), para 30.
[28] Hyam (2010, p. 4).
[29] *R. (on the application of Amin (Imtiaz)) v Secretary of State for the Home Department* (2003), para 20.
[30] *R. (on the application of Takoushis) v HM Coroner for Inner North London* (2005), para 106.
[31] *Goodson v HM Coroner for Bedfordshire and Luton* (2004).
[32] *R. (on the application of Jones) v Legal Services Commission* (2007) EWHC 2106 (Admin); (Queen's Bench Division (Administrative Court)).
[33] Hyam (2010), *R. (on the application of LePage) v HM Assistant Deputy Coroner for Inner South London* (2012) EWHC 1485 (Admin) (Divisional Court), *McDonnell v HM Assistant Coroner for West London* (2016) EWHC 3078 (Admin).

obligation under Article 2, this discretion is limited in deference to the fundamental nature of the right to life.[34] In 1994, the Court of Appeal in *Jamieson* judged that in reference to the remit of a coroner being limited by Section 11(5)(b)(ii) of the Coroners Act 1998 and rule 36(1)(b) to consider 'how' someone died, this should be interpreted to mean 'by what means' and not 'in what broad circumstances'.[35] However, after the incorporation of the ECHR into domestic law through the HRA, this issue was reconsidered. In 2004, the cases of *Middleton* and *Sacker* involving deaths in prison came before the House of Lords where it was decided the relevant sections of the Coroners Rules 1984 and the Coroners Act 1988 must be interpreted in order to be compliant with Article 2.[36,37] The *Middleton* ruling stated there were instances (for example, where the central issue for the inquest was whether the deceased had died of suicide) where a traditional short form verdict (as described in *Jamieson*) would be adequate for a jury to describe their findings. However, it found that in some cases, this form of verdict would not discharge the enhanced procedural duty fully by limiting the ability of the jury to make conclusions on major issues highlighted during the inquest that did not directly cause death. The judgment referred to *Keenan*, *Edwards* and *Amin* to illustrate that a short form verdict would probably not have met Article 2 enhanced procedural requirements; concluding that in such instances, the coroner had a duty to interpret 'how' to mean not only 'by what means' but more broadly as 'by what means and in what circumstances'.[38] The coroner must still ensure any findings by the jury do not determine any civil or criminal liability on the part of a named person in order to comply with legislation (to be discussed in Section 2.2.3). *Middleton* was clarified in 2009, in *Lewis*, when the High Court took a narrow interpretation of what 'circumstances' might be considered relevant in an Article 2 case and therefore investigated by an inquest.[39] The Court decided that to comply with Article 2 requirements, only issues which either caused or were contributory to the death need be considered. The coroner's discretion to decide whether issues might arguably have been contributory to a death was affirmed in *Speck*, but it was found that once an issue had been judged not to have made any real contribution to the death, the coroner had no discretion to investigate said issue.[40] In 2016, the law was further clarified through *Tainton*, where it was judged that in order to comply with Article 2 requirements, an inquest verdict should

---

[34] Thomas and others (2014).

[35] *R. v HM Coroner for North Humberside and Scunthorpe Ex p. Jamieson* (1995), p 24.

[36] *R. (on the application of Middleton) v HM Coroner for Western Somerset.*

[37] *R. (on the application of Sacker) v HM Coroner for West Yorkshire* (2004) UKHL 11 (House of Lords).

[38] *R. (on the application of Middleton) v HM Coroner for Western Somerset* (2004).

[39] *R. (on the application of Lewis) v HM Coroner for the Mid and North Division of Shropshire* (2009) EWCA Civ 1403 (Court of Appeal (Civil Division)).

[40] *R. (on the application of Speck) v HM Coroner for District of York* (2016) EWHC 6 (Admin) (Queen's Bench Division (Administrative Court)).

reference failures which formed part of the circumstances of a death, even if they were not found to be causative.[41]

In making a clear distinction between *Jamieson* and *Middleton* inquests, UK courts arguably went beyond the ECtHR, where the distinction between the 'normal' and 'enhanced' procedural obligations is not clear-cut. In practice, however, in England and Wales, the distinction is not as clear as case law would suggest; some coroners will treat a case where it is not clear what has contributed to a death as a *Middleton* case (therefore considering wider aspects) until it becomes apparent aspects are not linked to the death, at which point the jury will be directed to not consider those aspects.[42] Other coroners will identify at the start of the inquest aspects which are clearly linked to a death and only allow examination of other issues if new evidence is presented to link them to the death. The Coroners and Justice Act allows coroners discretion to decide what aspects are investigated by an inquest, although it is stated investigations must be widened if necessary to comply with Article 2.[43] The discretion left to coroners, especially when it relates to judging whether Article 2 is engaged, can have an important impact on family participation, as it affects not just what legal rights are engaged to protect a families' right to participate but also whether they will receive legal aid funding. This will be discussed further later on in the book.

2.2.3 Holding the State to Account

Lord Bingham stated that procedural Article 2 obligations should be a high priority for 'a modern democratic State governed by the rule of law'.[44] This is to ensure facts about a death are clearly investigated, including any systemic failings which may have contributed to the death. This is important for two main reasons: firstly, failings should then be addressed, thus preventing further deaths and, secondly, public confidence in the State's compliance with the rule of law by ensuring that State agencies are held to account for any deaths.[45] This means an Article 2 investigation should 'be capable of leading to a determination of whether State agents are liable'.[46] In order to fulfil its Article 2 obligations, a State must ensure accountability of those responsible for a death is possible in practice, not just theoretically.[47] Specifically the ECtHR has recognised the importance of prosecuting any individuals believed culpable for a death. The UK was found to have

[41] *R. (Tainton) v HM Senior Coroner for Preston and West Lancashire* (2016) EWHC 1396 (Admin).
[42] Cross and Garnham (2016), Introduction.
[43] Coroners and Justice Act 2009, Section 5.
[44] *R. (on the application of Middleton) v HM Coroner for Western Somerset* (2004), para 5.
[45] *Enukidze and Girgvliani v Georgia* (2011) ECHR 735 (European Court of Human Rights), para 243, *Da Silva v United Kingdom* (2016) ECHR 314 (30 March 2016) (European Court of Human Rights), para 232.
[46] *McCann v United Kingdom* (1996), para 201.
[47] *Jordan v United Kingdom* (2003), *Dodov v Bulgaria* (2008).

violated the procedural duty in *Jordan* as they 'did not allow any verdict or findings which could play an effective role in securing a prosecution in respect of any criminal offence which may have been disclosed'.[48] The purpose of an Article 2 investigation was clarified in *Menezes*, where the ECtHR stated that an investigation should still be capable of determining whether any force used by State agents was justified.[49]

When an inquest is the primary procedure for discharging the Article 2 obligation to hold the State accountable, it can therefore be in conflict with domestic law which states no civil or criminal liability can be determined in relation to a named person during an inquest.[50] This means an inquest cannot identify anyone responsible for a death, let alone punish them. In *Keenan*, the ECtHR referred to the procedural duty required by Article 2, stating that due to the restricted scope an inquest could not determine liability for a death, which limited the availability of an effective remedy for the next of kin.[51]

However, it is argued that even if an inquest cannot name liability or punish anyone following a death, the State can still respond appropriately – including by taking forward prosecutions where necessary – and therefore Article 2 procedural obligations can still be met. An inquest verdict can be a vital step in ensuring accountability following a death, even though it cannot find liability, as the evidence gathered can be used for prosecutions following a critical verdict. The decision whether to carry out a prosecution following a critical inquest verdict is therefore very important in ensuring accountability. The ECtHR in *Jordan* stated that in cases where there was controversial use of force by State agents, decisions on whether to prosecute should be made by someone independent and reasons should be given in order to satisfy public confidence and ensure the bereaved family can judge whether to challenge the decision.[52] The process followed in the UK was affirmed as Article 2 compliant in *Da Silva*, which found that as long as the use of force was scrutinised and any decision not to prosecute was not taken arbitrarily, it was compliant with Article 2.[53] This narrowed the purpose by clarifying that a lack of prosecution would not necessarily itself be enough to violate Article 2, if the investigation provided sufficient scrutiny of State actions.

The participation of the bereaved family in an Article 2 investigation has been linked to providing the necessary scrutiny required to ensure accountability.[54] This and other reasons as to why family involvement has evolved as a right will be discussed next.

---

[48] *Jordan v United Kingdom* (2003), para 142.
[49] *Da Silva v United Kingdom* (2016), paras 257 & 259.
[50] Coroners and Justice Act 2009, Section 10, Coroner's Rules 1984. No 552, Rule 42; the same language is used in both pieces of legislation.
[51] *Keenan v United Kingdom* (2001), para H20.
[52] *Jordan v United Kingdom* (2003), para 123.
[53] *Da Silva v United Kingdom* (2016), paras 257 & 259.
[54] *Letts v Lord Chancellor* (2015), para 59.

2.2.4 Family Involvement in the Investigation

In 1990, the UN published 'Basic Principles on the Use of Force and Firearms by Law Enforcement Officials', which set out the minimum requirements for an investigation into a controversial death in custody, including the requirement that the family of the deceased should have access to an independent process.[55] The ECtHR enshrined the right of families to be involved in an Article 2 investigation via *Jordan*, where the right of the family to participate in an inquest was stated as necessary to 'ensure the requisite protection of their interests'.[56] The special position of the family has been acknowledged due to their close and personal concern with the death of a loved one. The right for them to participate is therefore held in special regard. For example, although the scrutiny of the public and family is not always distinguished by law, the ECtHR does allow that public scrutiny during an Article 2 investigation may be limited if necessary, whereas family involvement may not be. However, this distinction between public scrutiny and family participation is not always made: in relation to State officials remaining anonymous during inquests, families are often treated the same as the press in not being allowed to see those giving evidence.[57]

UK courts also referred to ECtHR case law in establishing a legal right for bereaved families to be assured of an effective investigation. Lord Slynn in *Amin* indicated the procedural duty was 'partly one owed' to the bereaved family, who, as the representatives of the deceased, had a right under Article 2 to an independent and public investigation following a death in State custody.[58] *Jordan* requirements were followed to find the 'next of kin of the victim must be involved in the procedure to the extent necessary to safeguard' their interests.[59]

Domestically, the rights for families to participate in an inquest were established distinct from Article 2 requirements. The Coroner's Rules 1984 set out rights for bereaved families, including the right to be notified about 'the date, hour and place' of the inquest;[60] to be notified when the post-mortem would take place, if they have given the coroner advance notice to attend or be represented[61] and to examine witnesses.[62] Although the Rules did not explicitly set out what further rights a bereaved family may expect, the importance of respecting their 'best interests' has been referenced in justifying the broad discretionary powers of coroners in a number of well-publicised inquests.[63] These rights were retained

---

[55]United Nations, Basic Principles on the Use of Force and Firearms by Law Enforcement Officials (1990).

[56]*Jordan v United Kingdom* (2003), para 134.

[57]See *R (Hicks) v Inner North London Senior Coroner* (2016) EWHC 1726 (Admin).

[58]*R. (on the application of Amin (Imtiaz)) v Secretary of State for the Home Department* (2003), para 41.

[59]*R. (on the application of Amin (Imtiaz)) v Secretary of State for the Home Department* (2003), para 20.

[60]Coroner's Rules 1984. No 552, Rule 19.

[61]Coroner's Rules 1984. No 552, Rule 7.

[62]Coroner's Rules 1984. No 552, Rule 20.

[63]Including those into Helen Smith's death, the Marchioness disaster and the Hillsborough tragedy, See Beckett (1999).

through the Coroners (Inquests) Rules 2013 and Coroners (Investigations) Regulations 2013 ; the only slight amendment being that families now have the right to be informed when the coroner has opened an investigation[64] and also to be represented at a post-mortem, if they have previously notified the coroner of their wish to be so represented.[65] However, it should be noted that this right rely on the bereaved family being proactive and notifying the coroner that they wish someone to attend on their behalf. The law also allows this right to be restricted if the coroner decides it would be impractical or unreasonably delay the post-mortem to allow a family representative to attend.

It is also important to note that in practice, most of the rights of bereaved families to participate in an inquest are only fully implemented if the inquest is required to comply with Article 2 obligations. In cases that do not involve a death in custody, if there is a failure for the rights set out above relating to families' participation to be respected this does not necessarily require any remedy, such as a new inquest. In an unreported case from 2005, which did not involve State actions, it was found the coroner did not have a duty to adjourn an inquest to ensure the partner of the deceased could attend.[66] Similarly, a more recent case found an administrative error which resulted in an ex-wife not being informed about when an inquest would take place, therefore preventing the deceased's young daughter being represented as an interested party, did not require a new inquest to be called.[67]

Another very important aspect that impacts on family participation is the identification of who actually has the rights set out in law. Some case law (such as *Jordan*) references 'bereaved families', whereas other judgments refer to 'the next of kin'. The ECtHR has stated that an application involving a death does not have to be the next of kin or the closest relative but

> ...if a relative wished to complain about a question as serious as the murder of one of his close relations, that ought to suffice to show that he felt personally concerned by the incident.[68]

In terms of the inquest process, there are distinct rights for those who have been designated the next of kin, and in order to participate, other family members would have to be nominated as an 'interested person'. In situations where deaths occur in custody, the individual themselves will normally have completed a form identifying their next of kin on entering a custodial institution: if this has not happened (for example, when deaths occur soon after interaction with police), the

---

[64]The Coroners (Inquests) Rules 2013, The Coroners (Investigations) Regulations 2013; No. 1629.

[65]The Coroners (Investigations) Regulations 2013; No. 1629, Section 13.

[66]Doyle's Application reported in Thomas and others (2014).

[67]*Chambers v HM Coroner for Preston and West Lancashire & Ors* (2015) EWHC 31 (Admin).

[68]*Yasa v Turkey* (1999) 28 EHRR 408 (European Court of Human Rights), para 63.

coroner's officer will be responsible for identifying the next of kin.[69] The next of kin will be the person notified of the death, the need for an inquest and the time and place of any post-mortem or autopsy that is taking place.[70] The coroner has the discretion to identify anyone as an 'interested person', and under normal circumstances, the next of kin will be so identified; however, other family members may also be given 'interested person' status. Interested parties should be involved in all aspects of the process, although they do not have established rights around being notified about the death, the inquest or the post-mortem.

Although discretion lies fully with the coroner, domestic courts have provided some guidance on who should be given interested party status. In 1993, the sister of a deceased successfully judicially reviewed a coroner's decision not to recognise her as an interested party and it was held that close blood relations who were in contact with the deceased prior to the death should be allowed interested person status.[71] In 2008, the High Court judged that the relevant Rules (the Coroners (Amendment) Rules 2005) should be interpreted broadly to ensure all interested parties were accommodated; in this case, stating the girlfriend of the deceased should not be disqualified from being recognised as an interested person just because they had split up shortly before the death.[72] Although coroners still have the discretion to decide who is named as an interested party, the Coroners and Justice Act provides guidance stating that 'a spouse, civil partner, partner, parent, child, brother, sister, grandparent, grandchild, child of a brother or sister, stepfather, stepmother, half-brother or half-sister' might be an interested party.[73] The importance of being identified as an interested party will be discussed throughout this book, as will the distinct advantages to being named as the next of kin, in enabling effective participation (not least due to the advantage of being more likely to be granted legal aid funding).

2.2.5 Purpose of Family Participation

Jordan clarifies that the next of kin should be involved in an Article 2 investigation to ensure their 'legitimate interests' are safeguarded.[74] 'Legitimate interests' are not clearly defined but the judgment stated part of the procedural duty imposed by Article 2 was to provide the family an opportunity to participate as a remedy beyond a financial or civil judgment.[75] Domestic courts have tried to

[69]The Coroners (Investigations) Regulations 2013; No. 1629.

[70]The Coroners (Investigations) Regulations 2013; No. 1629, The Coroners (Inquests) Rules 2013.

[71]*R. v HM Coroner for Greater London Southern District Ex p. Driscoll* (1995) 159 JP 45; (1994) COD 91 (Divisional Court).

[72]*R. (on the application of Platts) v HM Coroner for South Yorkshire (East District)* (2008) EWHC 2502 (Admin) (Queen's Bench Division (Administrative Court)).

[73]Coroners and Justice Act 2009, Section 47 (2)(a) Coroners and Justice Act 2009; Section 47 (2)(a).

[74]*Jordan v United Kingdom* (2003), para H10.

[75]*Jordan v United Kingdom* (2003), para H43.

establish what legitimate interests a family might have in participating in an inquest. In *Letts*, it was judged that the legitimate interests of a bereaved family included knowing that any State culpability in the death of their loved one was identified, learning the truth and being confident that similar deaths in the future would be prevented.[76]

Although it has been clearly stated that a financial remedy is not the only legitimate interest, it can be an important factor in allowing participation, if State failings are deemed responsible for a death. A consequence of findings of State culpability should be for a family to receive compensation. Participation during the process is key to ensuring families have access to information that might help them decide whether to bring a civil case against either an individual or organisation as well as possible legal challenges to the process itself. The opportunity to challenge the process has been recognised as an important element of an Article 2 compliant investigation by the ECtHR.[77]

The psychological impact an investigation can have on a grieving family is also an important aspect relating to participation.[78] The ECtHR has found the violation of the Article 2 procedural duty did not only merely result in pecuniary damage on the family but also resulted in 'frustration, distress and anxiety'.[79] Australian courts have recognised that an inquest procedure can impact on the grief process of the bereaved, therefore possibly interfering with private life.[80,81] European case law also links interference with grief, as an 'intimate part of an individual's private life', with possible violations of the Article 8 right to a private life of the bereaved.[82] ECtHR judgments have recognised Article 8 rights can impose positive obligations on a State, and State actions that are shown to directly link to a restriction on a person's private life are likely to be considered as a violation of Article 8.[83] In one case, the ECtHR noted lack of legal proceedings which might lead to sanctions intended to remedy an injury might breach the Article 8 rights of the injured.[84]

Families' active participation in the process can go beyond benefitting families or protecting their interests: families can also have a positive benefit on the outcome by effectively scrutinising the evidence. The ECtHR has stated the importance of testing the evidence during an Article 2 investigation through

---

[76] *Letts v Lord Chancellor* (2015).

[77] *Bubbins v United Kingdom* (2005), para 153.

[78] Traumatic bereavement was referenced during the interviews and will discussed in more detail in Chapter 5.

[79] *Jordan v United Kingdom* (2003), para H48.

[80] The Australian coronial system was based on the same framework as the system in England and Wales but has evolved as a distinct system.

[81] Thomas and others (20114, p. 397).

[82] Thomas and others (20114, p. 397).

[83] *Botta v Italy* (1998) 26 EHRR 241 (European Court of Human Rights), Thibaut and others (1973).

[84] *Stubbings and Others v United Kingdom* (1996) 23 EHRR 213 (European Court of Human Rights), Dobson (2012).

examination or cross-examination.[85] It stated evidence or witness accounts must be examined before being assessed as reliable or credible.[86] It further found that untested accounts could be potentially misleading.[87] In the inquest system, families or their representatives are often the ones cross-examining the State's account of a death in custody. Although if the family are not willing or able to perform this role, the inquest system allows the Coroner and the jury to ask pertinent questions of the witnesses; arguably an advantage to bereaved families being responsible for the cross-examination is that they are more predisposed to challenge the State's account.

UK courts have recognised that the purpose of ensuring the involvement of bereaved families in inquests following deaths in custody may go beyond protecting their own interests. In *Main v Minister for Legal Aid*, the court referred to family involvement in an investigation performing a number of duties including assisting the coroner in investigating the death properly, as well as safeguarding the interests of the family and giving them the satisfaction of knowing that lessons would be learnt from the death.[88] Most recently, domestic courts have indicated that family participation can have intrinsic importance and was an 'integral part of the Article 2 duty' linked to the 'need to maintain public confidence in the adherence of the State to the rule of law'.[89]

2.2.6 Aspects of Effective Participation for Families

The ECtHR does not clearly set out what effective participation for families looks like; however, examples of what has been found to constitute a violation of a families' right to participate in an investigation include delays due to lack of legal aid and not being able to attend the inquest for the full hearings.[90] The ECtHR reiterated that the next of kin must be allowed effective access to any investigation into deaths involving State agents in *Aydin v Turkey*.[91]

Although the ECtHR does not set out in detail what effective participation needs to look like, it does distinguish between the outcome and the process in relation to family access to the investigation. The Brodrick Committee was quoted in iterating the necessity of being able to 'judge an issue' through access to the process as opposed to being presented with the verdict once the issues have been judged.[92] This clearly sets out the need for participation to go beyond merely observing the outcome, but ensuring families have the opportunity to scrutinise the evidence for themselves.

---

[85] *Jordan v United Kingdom* (2003), para H14.
[86] *Jordan v United Kingdom* (2003), para 127.
[87] *Jordan v United Kingdom* (2003), para 113.
[88] *R. (on the application of Main) v Minister for Legal Aid* (2007) EWCA Civ 1147 (Court of Appeal (Civil Division)).
[89] *Letts v Lord Chancellor* (2015).
[90] *Jordan v United Kingdom* (2003).
[91] *Aydin v Turkey* (2006) 42 EHRR 44 (European Court of Human Rights).
[92] *Jordan v United Kingdom* (2003), para H70.

In ensuring families are able to effectively participate, there are two important aspects to consider: legal representation and access to documents. These aspects are in some ways complementary – with legal representation being key in not just gaining access to documents but also assisting families to analyse the evidence.

2.2.6.1 Legal Representation

An inquest process is officially an inquisitorial process which does not involve opposing parties.[93] However, there are arguments why legal representation for bereaved families attending an Article 2 inquest might be important. Firstly, the formality of proceedings; for the uninitiated, the process may be indistinguishable from other court proceedings with the coroner sitting as a judge in a courtroom before a jury and witnesses being questioned by legal representatives of interested parties such as the police or prison service. Secondly, the fact that any State agencies involved in an inquest are legally represented; a team of barristers each represents a different facet of the State institutions and State officials. Thirdly, bereaved families have the right to ask questions themselves but the formality of the process, the complexity of the law and their vulnerability through grief (which may well be complicated due to the circumstances of a death in custody), all limit the effective expression of this right. Also, issues that are considered within scope of the inquest are limited by law (they must have a causal or contributory relationship with the cause of death as discussed above); as is the need to ensure the process does not attribute blame to a named person. These legal aspects restrict what questions are permitted, often to the confusion of family members.

As legal representation is an important aspect to ensuring families can effectively participate, the issue of legal aid funding for that legal representation is very relevant. The ECtHR has judged a lack of funding for legal representation for the bereaved family was a contributory factor in finding an Article 2 violation, with the lack of equity of participants also being mentioned.[94]

2.2.6.2 Funding for Representation

One of the key ECtHR judgments relating to a States obligation to fund legal representation for individuals during legal proceedings was *Airey* in 1979.[95] The ECtHR found that in order for rights to be practically accessible, funding should be available if an individual's ability to present their case would be ineffective without legal representation. The judgment stated criteria that should be taken into account in judging whether funding was required included the equity of parties and the complexity of the issues being considered by the process. The challenge on relying on this judgment when it comes to coronial law is the fact that, in principle, inquests are inquisitorial not adversarial, even though in practise this may not be the case, as well be illustrated later in this book.

[93] Home Office (2014, p 1).

[94] *Jordan v United Kingdom* (2003), para H29.

[95] *Airey v Ireland* (A/32) (1979-80) 2 EHRR 305 (European Court of Human Rights).

However, one of the aspects mentioned in *Jordan* as key to ensuring effective participation for bereaved families was funding for legal representation. The lack of funding for legal representation was linked to a lack of equity between families and State parties.

UK courts in *Humberstone* decided that, in certain circumstances, a family should have funding for legal representation in order to ensure they could effectively participate in an inquest.[96] Funding for bereaved families is through the exceptional funding system of legal aid and decided on a case-by-case basis. This remained the case following the enactment of legislation put in place to reform legal aid in 2012.[97] Although criteria governing eligibility became more restrictive, the residence test was successfully challenged in 2016.[98,99] The guidance used in relation to inquests was amended following a judicial review by a bereaved family in 2015: the case will be discussed in more detail in Section 7.2.3.[100]

2.2.6.3 Access to Documents

Without prior access to documents, legal representatives cannot prepare fully for an inquest. Michael Mansfield[101] has been quoted as saying that acting for a family at a complex Article 2 inquest without prior access to documents was like working with one hand tied behind your back.[102] There are two important issues relating to access to documents before an inquest actually occurs. The first is what evidence is provided to the coroner and the second is consequential of that and what evidence is disclosed to the family.

The ECtHR has stated if a death occurs in State custody, the burden is on the State to provide a satisfactory explanation as to the circumstances of the death.[103] It has held that in some situations a State has a duty to disclose all relevant information, as Article 2 cases 'do not in all cases lend themselves for rigorous application of the principle of *affirmanti incumbit probatio* [he who alleges something must prove that allegation]'.[104] In fact if a State fails, without good reason, to disclose all relevant information, this would illustrate a reluctance to fully comply and may also be taken as an indication of the validity of any allegations against the State.[105]

---

[96] *R. (on the application of Humberstone) v Legal Services Commission* (2010).

[97] Legal Aid, Sentencing and Punishment of Offenders Act 2012.

[98] INQUEST (2014), http://www.publiclawproject.org.uk/news/41/press-release-plp-wins-residence-test-case.-proposals-to-introduce-legal-aid-residence-test-are-unla.

[99] *R. (on the application of The Public Law Project) (Appellant) v Lord Chancellor* (Respondent) (2016) UKSC 39.

[100] *Letts v Lord Chancellor* (2015).

[101] Senior barrister in the UK who has represented families in complex inquests such as the de Menezes case.

[102] Scraton and Chadwick (1987, p 85).

[103] *Selmouni v France* (2000) 29 EHRR 403 (European Court of Human Rights), *Salman v Turkey* (2002).

[104] *Timurtas v Turkey* (2001) 33 EHRR 6 (European Court of Human Rights), para 66.

[105] *Timurtas v Turkey* (2001) 33 EHRR 6 (European Court of Human Rights), para 66.

The Coroner's Act 1988 set out the statutory power for coroners to examine witnesses on oath at an inquest but did not compel witnesses to provide a statement prior to the inquest.[106] In 2007, the High Court decided the coroner could request disclosure of certain documents from a witness who was required to appear at an inquest, and if they did not comply, the coroner could apply to the High Court to issue a summon.[107] In fact, a coroner who failed to make such a request for disclosure could be failing to investigate and therefore their decision subject to judicial review.[108] The Coroners and Justice Act 2009 now provides coroners with powers to require disclosure; however, this only allows the coroner to have access to the documents, and predisclosure of the evidence to families is a separate step.[109] This was confirmed in 2013, when the High Court judged that the statutory duty only relates to disclosure to the coroner, but not to other parties, including the public.[110]

The coroner has wide discretion in relation to many aspects of inquest procedure, including what access to documents and evidence interested parties are given before the proceedings commence. In 1979, *Peach* stated that unless an interested party was at risk of facing criminal charges in connection with the subject matter of an inquest, there was no necessity for coroners to guarantee predisclosure of the evidence to them.[111] Following that decision, predisclosure to bereaved families varied considerably depending on the coroner and the case. Some coroners have always ensured families are sent information about what to expect at the inquest, including a list of witnesses likely to be providing evidence.[112] The law now states, if an interested party requests a document held by a coroner, they must either provide them with a copy of the document or make it available to them 'as soon as reasonably practical'.[113] However, the coroner still has wide discretion to redact part of documents or not disclose at all if they decide the request is unreasonable or the document is not relevant.[114] Crucially if consent of the author of any documents 'cannot reasonably be obtained', the coroner can refuse to disclose to other parties.[115] As mentioned above, legal support is sometimes necessary to ensure families not only have access to documents but

---

[106]Coroner's Act 1988, sec. 11(2).

[107]*Assistant Deputy Coroner for Inner West London v Channel 4 Television Corp* (2007) EWHC 2513 (QB); (2008) 1 WLR 945 (Queen's Bench Division).

[108]Thomas and others (2014, p. 149).

[109]Coroners and Justice Act 2009, Schedule 5.

[110]*Worcester County Council and Worcestershire Safeguarding Children Board v HM Coroner for the County of Worcester* (2013) EWHC 1711 (QB).

[111]*R. v HM Coroner for Hammersmith Ex p. Peach* (1980) QB 211 (Court of Appeal (Civil Division)).

[112]Braithwaite (2002, p. 10).

[113]The Coroners (Inquests) Rules 2013, Sections 14 & 15; disclosure may also be refused for legal or statutory reasons.

[114]The Coroners (Inquests) Rules 2013, Section 13.

[115]The Coroners (Inquests) Rules 2013, Section 15.

also are able to analyse them fully.[116] For example, in the *O'Brien* case rare predisclosure led to family's solicitor noticing vital forensic evidence the coroner had missed.[117]

A 2001 High Court decision recognised that common practise had moved on since *Peach* and that effective participation may be restricted if advanced disclosure to interested parties was not guaranteed.[118] The judgment agreed predisclosure to families was not mandatory but that in some cases, fairness decried it should be assured. This was affirmed by *Smith* in 2008, when the High Court judged there should be 'a presumption in favour of as full disclosure as possible';[119] although the Supreme Court reversed this judgment in part 2 years later by deciding this case did not come under Article 2·.[120] A judgment in 2009 acceded disclosure prior to inquest proceedings was generally advisable but that unless it could be shown it altered the outcome of the inquest, a coroner would not be judged to have acted unreasonably to have failed to ensure disclosure to all parties.[121] In 2010, it was reaffirmed that there was no common law duty on a coroner to ensure full disclosure of evidence to bereaved families prior to the inquest unless it was shown that lack of disclosure prevented the ascertaining of cause of death.[122]

This author argues that all interested parties should have access to the same evidence in the interest of natural justice; suggesting families should get predisclosure of documents produced by State parties.[123] In addition to being an issue of fundamental fairness and equity, lack of early disclosure can lead to delays if a family identifies questions they want to ask having scrutinised the evidence at a late stage. In relation to non-Article 2 inquests, the coroner still has wide discretion on whether to disclose evidence to bereaved families prior to an inquest via Sections 14 and 15 of the Coroners (Inquests) Rules 2013; however, following deaths in custody, the bereaved families can rely on ECtHR case law and Government guidelines to argue for full predisclosure.[124]

---

[116]Braithwaite (2002, p. 24).

[117]Ward and Coles (1997, p. 114).

[118]*R. (on the application of Bentley) v HM Coroner for Avon* (2001) EWHC Admin 170 (Queen's Bench Division (Administrative Court)).

[119]*R. (on the application of Smith) v Oxfordshire Assistant Deputy Coroner* (2008) EWHC 694 (Admin) (Queen's Bench Division (Administrative Court)).

[120]*R. (on the application of Smith) v Oxfordshire Assistant Deputy Coroner* (2010) UKSC 29 (Supreme Court).

[121]*R. (on the application of Ahmed) v HM Coroner South East and Cumbria* (2009) EWHC 1653 (Admin) (Queen's Bench Division (Administrative Court)).

[122]*R. (on the application of McLeish) v HM Coroner for the Northern District of Greater London* (2010) EWHC 3624 (Admin) (Queen's Bench Division (Administrative Court)); This case was brought by a bereaved mother whose son had died, and although the post-mortem did not clearly establish a cause of death, since the mother had not received the report (despite repeated requests) she was not in a position to appreciate the importance of asking for a second autopsy or further blood tests before cremation.

[123]*Maksovich v Attorney General 4 NSWLR 318 (Court of Appeal of New South Wales), Braithwaite* (2002).

[124]Thomas and others (2014, p. 148).

The Macpherson report looked into the killing of Stephen Lawrence and the subsequent investigation into his death; one of the recommendations was that evidence and documents to be presented at an inquest should be disclosed in advance to anyone classified as an interested person by a coroner.[125] Following the Macpherson report, the Home Office encouraged pre-inquest disclosure of relevant documents to interested parties in cases of deaths in police custody as a matter of 'normal practise' unless there were 'compelling reasons why certain documents, or parts of documents, may not be disclosed'.[126] It was noted the rationale behind pre-disclosure to the next of kin where possible was to reduce friction in controversial cases and allay suspicions. In 2005, this entitlement to pre-inquest disclosure was extended to other custodial deaths when the PPO developed their policy, referring to the necessity of complying with procedural obligations under Article 2.[127]

Both the police and prison services have now published guidelines suggesting that a policy of predisclosure to families should be followed but this is not a statutory requirement. The Coroners (Investigations) Regulations 2013 empowers a coroner to provide documents to any person they deem appropriate, but does not give coroners the power to force disclosure by other bodies (such as the police or prison service) as their consent is required for documents to be shared with other parties.[128,129] The only domestic legislation that families can rely on to force disclosure would be the HRA, allowing them to introduce ECtHR case law referencing predisclosure. Although in *McCann*, the ECtHR found access of documents for families was not an automatic requirement; in *Jordan*, the ECtHR noted that 'more emphasis of involving the next of kin in procedure and providing them with information' had been made by judgments since *McCann*.[130,131] The importance of the change in policy relating to the disclosure of police witness statements prior to an inquest following the publishing of the Macpherson report was recognised in the judgments. It was affirmed that the next of kin's interests were unlikely to be 'fairly or adequately protected' without predisclosure, especially as it placed them at a disadvantage to effectively question witnesses.[132]

The ECtHR found access to documents for families was important for three reasons. Firstly, as it was a 'positive contribution in the openness and fairness of the inquest'.[133] Secondly, it could benefit the family in preparing for and then participating in the questioning of witnesses.[134] Thirdly, it was important in

[125]Sir Macpherson and Britain (1999).
[126]Home Office (1999).
[127]Prisons and Probation Ombudsman, Disclosing Policy (2009).
[128]The Coroners (Investigations) Regulations 2013; No. 1629, Section 27.
[129]The Coroners (Inquests) Rules 2013, Section 14.
[130]*McCann v United Kingdom* (1996), para 163.
[131]*Jordan v United Kingdom* (2003), para 133.
[132]*Jordan v United Kingdom* (2003), para 134.
[133]*Jordan v United Kingdom* (2003), para 134.
[134]*Jordan v United Kingdom* (2003), para 134.

maintaining equity between all the parties; so if the State had access to documents, then it was important for the next of kin to have similar access.[135] The ECtHR has closely identified the benefit of predisclosure with ensuring the fair participation of families during a process.[136] The ECtHR has judged families do not have an absolute right to access all documents at all stages of the investigation, the requirement being that they had sufficient access to participate effectively.[137]

The lack of legislative protection enshrining the right for families to be given access to evidence in a timely manner leaves them at the discretion of the coroner. In situations where predisclosure is not offered by State agencies involved or ensured by the coroner, families have to rely on legal arguments to access the documents. This can lead to delays in families being given the evidence, in some circumstances only receiving disclosure on the day of the inquest. It is also a concern that all the protections that are in place for families getting disclosure rely on families proactively requesting documents, which presupposes an understanding or knowledge that families may not have without specialist legal support.

2.3 Conclusion

This chapter sets out the legal rights relating to family participation in Article 2 investigations and illustrates that, although bereaved families do have a right to participate in any investigation, there is still considerable discretion left to decision-makers which can impact on participation. This mainly relates to coroners who can determine whether an Article 2 investigation is required, which influences opportunities to participate as well as legal protections in place. State officials including senior police or prison officers and senior individuals in the legal aid office can also influence participation via decisions about disclosure and funding for legal representation. The importance of case law in establishing the legal rights relating to Article 2 investigations has also been shown, and it is worth nothing that these cases can only be brought before both domestic and European courts by interested parties – in this case bereaved families. It is therefore clear that without family participation in all the cases referenced throughout this section, the detailed legal rights would not have been clarified.

ECtHR judgments affirm that in implementing ECHR provisions, an 'outcome-orientated approach' should be taken, so this book will now look at how perceptions influence important aspects for family participation.[138] Within criminal justice procedures, the importance of maintaining the rule of law can be

---

[135]*Jordan v United Kingdom* (2003), para H29.

[136]Although in McCann, the ECtHR stated non-access of documents for families had not hampered their participation in the process, it was noted the families had been represented and their representatives had been able to participate in the proceedings. See *McCann v United Kingdom* (1996), para 162.

[137]*Ramsahai v The Netherlands* (2008), para 199.

[138]Kukavica and Fikfak (2015).

used to argue for procedural fairness in principle, even if it does not alter the outcome. This book will argue this approach can be taken in respect to inquests where the actions of State agents are under scrutiny. This relies heavily on Tyler's work linking procedural fairness within the criminal justice system with the legitimacy of the State agencies.[139] The book will now look at the empirical research which considers the real-life experiences of those with experience of the inquest system. The next part of the book describes the methodology followed by the author to gather those experiences, which are the heart of the book.

[139]Tyler (1990), Tyler and Huo (2002).

Part 2
Empirical Research

The first part of the book has set out the legal framework governing family participation in investigations following a death in custody. The book will now move on to considering the experiences of those who have participated in inquests themselves, in a variety of roles. Gathering the views of those with experience was central to the aim of this book, to understand how the legal framework was working in practice, on a day-to-day basis. Given the relevant rarity of inquests following deaths in custody, the number of people with direct experience is low. So the author took an approach followed primarily in psychological research, which allows the detailed views of a small set of people to be gathered and analysed to create a narrative that represents what is happening in practice.

Chapter 3

Introducing the Empirical Research Approach

The approach taken by the author is relatively new outside of psychological research, so the following chapter describes the approach taken, and why it was the process used by the author. It is important when carrying out research looking at the real world that the research goes beyond the underlying structures governing society and looks at real-life situations to find the context-specific meaning behind any process. In order to reach a deeper understanding of context-specific events, a qualitative research methodology can be used to gather perceptions from individuals who had direct experience of a specific event. Qualitative research is generally concerned with interpreting rather than quantifying data and looks to personal experiences to make sense of the social world.[1] It uses interpretation of experience to understand the world, and provide a fully detailed account of a specific situation. In considering the specific context of the inquest system following a death in custody, the author decided to collect the views of varied stakeholders who have experienced Article 2 inquests. In order to identify what benefits could result from family participation, it was important to hear from people with experience of participating in the inquest system following deaths in custody. Bereaved family members were the primary focus of the interviews but it was also important to hear from State officers and others with the specialised experience. Qualitative data were collected through conducting semi-structured interviews.

Gathering different insights into the inquest system allowed the author to collect a range of views. Commonalities could therefore be interpreted as likely generalities in terms of the specific situation being studied, in this case inquests following deaths in custody in England and Wales. Generalities which in this book are taken from perceptions common to all or most participants interviewed cannot necessarily be translated to the wider population who have not had direct experiences of these inquests, but can be considered as valid for those who have experienced complex inquests.[2] 20 interviews were carried out; five interviewees were bereaved families (FA), six were legal representatives

[1]Smith (2007, p. 2).
[2]Burnham and others (2004, p. 66).

Death in Custody, 45–55
Copyright © 2020 Jo Easton
Published under exclusive licence
doi:10.1108/978-1-83909-025-720201006

specialising in complex or Article 2 inquests (LA), four were coroners (CO), three senior police officers (SP and two recently retired officers who were classified as Ex-Senior Police (ESP)) and two representatives from relevant investigatory bodies (PPO and IPCC).[3]

3.1 Qualitative Research Methodology

Qualitative research through interviewing is a dynamic process with the researcher playing an active part.[4] Interviews collect data that are context-specific; a snap-shot of a particular event or experience. Qualitative interviews are the best way to collect views and opinions which allow the researcher to dig behind statistical data. In gathering opinions and perceptions, this approach must acknowledge that these are likely to change over time. So data gathered by interviews are neither repeatable nor static. For example, all the evidence gathered for this book related to experiences of the inquest system before the Coroners and Justice Act 2009 came into force; it is likely this new legislation will have had repercussions about how the system is experienced. In terms of participants who continue to work in the inquest system (such as coroners and legal representatives), as well as likely changes due to the Act, each case will bring new insight and experience. Although it is to be hoped that bereaved family members and individual State officials (not including representatives of PPO or IPCC) will not experience inquests again, their memory and therefore perception of the experience is likely to continue to change over time. It is also true for some of the bereaved family participants that the process is still ongoing (in terms of appeals, judicial reviews, etc.).

Validity of any research is tested through the honesty and specificity of the data collected.[5] Specific data were collected in this project by gathering personal experiences, not just relying on anecdotal examples. The honesty of the data can be established in a number of ways. Firstly, there was no reason for participants to lie as there was no benefit to be gained. Almost all the participants were self-selecting so there was no requirement or pressure to take part if they did not feel they had any thoughts or experiences to share. This was true apart from representatives from the PPO and IPCC which will be discussed later.

Secondly, the interviews were conversational in approach, which allowed participants to lead the direction taken and therefore the issues covered.[6] Participants only answered questions they were comfortable with, so if they were unsure or had nothing to say in response to a question, they could say so and move on. The interviews collected each participant's perceptions about their experiences and how they had contextualised their involvement in complex

---

[3]Details about how participants were selected will be discussed in Section 3.4.

[4]Smith and Osborn (2003, p. 51).

[5]Marsh and Stoker (1995).

[6]Details setting out the themes and skeleton questions used for the interviews are to be found in ANNEX III.

inquests over time. It must be noted that participants were often referring to their response to a situation in the past but the views they represent during the interviews will actually be their opinion interpreted through a prism of everything that has happened since that situation. So they may say they felt anger at a particular point, but may actually be remembering anger which formed gradually over time rather than being felt at that point. Where participants acknowledged a change of their own opinion over time, this was referenced during the analysis of the interviews.

The data collected in this project rely on the relevance and specificity of the experiences of participants to ensure credible and dependable data. Participants from each group had specialised knowledge; families through their experience; coroners as they all had extensive experience of custody inquests; and the legal representatives interviewed were experts in their field. In terms of qualitative interviews, the objective is to make sense of an individual's experience so the data collected are seen as valid.[7]

3.2 Benefits of Interview-based Research[8]

The purpose of interviewing is to understand 'the lived experience of other people'.[9] One to one interviews allow the exploration of opinions and perceptions in relation to situations or experiences that are either complex or sensitive.[10] Collecting a wide range of views, especially across groups with distinct perspectives, ensures a complete account is given.[11] Although sometimes allowing participants to be self-selecting might be argued to be a limiting factor in research, it is beneficial where lengthy interviews asking for participants to share personal experiences are utilised to gather detailed perceptions. Similarly, for a project where experience is needed of a specific situation or circumstance which is rare, sample size is necessarily small. This is why detailed interviews with a small number of participants were chosen for this particular research, which relies on perceptions of complex inquests following deaths in custody.

3.3 Interpretative Phenomenological Analysis Approach

Qualitative interview research includes many different approaches both in terms of how participants are questioned and how the data are analysed.[12] This book utilised the Interpretative Phenomenological Analysis (IPA) methodology, which is most commonly used in psychological research to interpret first person accounts phenomenologically (using first person experience).[13] IPA is a useful tool to

[7]Seidman (2012, p. 24).
[8]Details of how the interviews were carried out for this research are described in Section 3.4.
[9]Seidman (2012, p. 9).
[10]Hollway and Jefferson (2000).
[11]Burnham and others (2004, pp. 65-66).
[12]Smith (2007).
[13]Larkin (2013).

explore a complex situation in great detail using perceptions of relevant participants.[14] IPA is used to analyse personal accounts of a situation which provide rich, detailed data from a small sample size; so it was an appropriate approach for this project, as only a small number of people have experience of complex inquests into deaths in custody but they can provide detailed information. IPA is most appropriate to answer open and exploratory questions by focuses on the experiences of individuals to identify patterns and themes. IPA is a commonly used methodology in psychological and forensic psychiatric research, but over the last few years it has also been used by researchers working in secure settings such as prisons, as well as being used to gather perceptions about participating in legal systems.[15] IPA was specifically used as the aim of the project was to gather personal experiences from potentially vulnerable individuals. IPA allows the interviewee to 'tell their own stories in ways that were meaningful for them'.[16] IPA also allows the interviewer to engage positively with the interviewee and the issues being raised, which ensures the interview is more focused towards the needs of the interviewee.[17] It was therefore particularly suitable for the research questions answered by this book.

Phenomenology considers how people make sense of their experiences; it describes how individuals perceive the world through interacting with it and what meaning is given to that engagement by each individual.[18] IPA understands personal experiences to reflect an individual's interaction with society through a prism of their own understanding.[19] It allows that an individual will have a unique experience, but goes further in suggesting some aspects can transcend that unique and specific context and provide universal concepts which can be used to explain or describe the experience to others.[20] Shutz describes this as 'reciprocity of perceptions' where a shared framework of meaning allows us to approximate others experiences such as colour.[21] Contentious inquests following deaths in custody involve a relatively small number of people but detailed interviews with people with experience of such inquests can provide insight that can be understood and appreciated by those who have not had a similar experience.

IPA requires the collection of first person accounts through semi-structured interviews in order to gather a rich and detailed record of an individual's perceptions about an experience.[22] The researcher then interprets those experiences in order to gather insights into a particular event or situation. IPA therefore involves two different strands of analysis: the first describing the participants

[14]Smith and Osborn (2003, p. 53).
[15]Gekoski, Adler, and Gray (2013), Kennedy (2014), Back, Gustafsson, and Berterö (2013).
[16]Gekoski et al. (2013).
[17]Campbell (2002).
[18]Smith and Osborn (2003).
[19]Smith and Osborn (2003, p. 52).
[20]Husserl as referenced by Larkin (2013), Ashworth (2003, p. 23).
[21]Schütz (1973, p. 60).
[22]Smith and Osborn (2003, p. 55).

interpretation, the second is the researcher's analysis of that interpretation.[23] Hermeneutics relies on language as the means to shared understanding and conversation can be a form of negotiation to establish that understanding.[24] So allowing for two different analysis strands is known as double hermeneutics. IPA benefits from small sample sizes with purposive recruitment of participants who have specific insight into a situation and homogeneity across the groups in terms of experiencing similar situations. This allows insights into common understandings as well as identification of differences of specific contexts.[25]

This book used data collected by carrying out one to one interviews with people who have personal experience of inquests. Inquests involve different parties who have distinct roles and in order to gather a complete picture of the system, interviews were carried out with individuals from the different groups. The groups identified were coroners, bereaved families, State officials and legal representatives. The aim was to interview four to five individuals from each group, following the IPA approach of small samples sizes for each homogenous group. Each group has a different role to play in the system, so it was important to allow for potential commonalities and differences in perceptions between each group as well as within a group. In that way, descriptive inferences could be used to create generalisations from unique perspectives, using observations to establish agreed themes and issues.[26]

3.4 Participants

3.4.1 Selecting Participants

Interviews allow understanding of context, experiences and meaning so participants should be selected who have particular insight and can provide illustration of an issue, rather than attempting to find participants who are diverse and representative.[27] This research therefore used purposeful selection in identifying sample groups.[28] A combination of gatekeepers and snowballing [29] was followed to select participants. It is important in using gatekeepers that they are seen as legitimate authorities or representatives; so only respected authorities or membership groups were contacted.[30]

(1) A gatekeeper approach was used for contacting coroners through the Coroner's Society.

[23]Smith and Osborn (2003, p. 51).
[24]Larkin (2013).
[25]Larkin (2013).
[26]Burnham and others (2004, p. 172).
[27]Valentine (1997, p. 112).
[28]Seidman (2012, p. 43).
[29]Snowballing is a technique which relies on one participant leading the researcher to another participant with relevant experience; see Bryman (2015, p. 415–416).
[30]Seidman (2012, p. 43).

(2) State officials were contacted in two ways:

   a) Relevant institutions were identified as the two independent investigating bodies whose reports are the basis for inquest proceedings: the Prisons and Probation Ombudsman (PPO) and the Independent Police Complaints Commission (IPPC). These were contacted and in each case, representatives of the organisation agreed to be interviewed. These representatives were chosen by the organisation and these were the only instances where participants were not necessarily self-selecting.
   b) Other participants within this group were individual police officers: one was still an active officer and the others were ex-officers. They were all obtained through the snowballing approach of other participants passing on the researcher's contact details. All freely chose to participate and had specific experience of custody inquests.

(3) Legal representatives were identified through membership of the Inquest Lawyers Group which is open to any lawyer who works in the area of inquest law. All therefore have specialised knowledge and experience but the group is predominantly for those who represent families, so in general this group had less experience representing State parties. Twenty of the most experienced legal representatives were identified, guided by the authors own personal knowledge and expertise in the sector; 10 solicitors and 10 barristers (as they perform different roles in representing families). They were all contacted, and the first six who responded all agreed to participate.

(4) Families were contacted in four different ways:

   a) INQUEST shared the research with families who they had either supported or continued to support via their regular newsletter[31]
   b) Details about the research were shared with a support group via their closed Facebook page (called NO MORE DEATHS IN CUSTODY). This group is open to any family or friend of an individual who has died in custody; membership is only agreed for people known by other members;
   c) One of the lawyers interviewed shared the research with a family member who they thought would want to take part;
   d) One participant was known to the author from their time at INQUEST, and contacted the author directly when they heard about the research.

The author was keen to engage with families who had not necessarily been in the public eye for two reasons, firstly it is likely that such cases have already been analysed in previous work and secondly because where families have either given extensive interviews or evidence (such as in the case of Sean Rigg) or written

[31]It should be noted the newsletter is actually available on INQUEST's website, so families who did not have direct contact with INQUEST but were looking for information about inquests might have found information about the research. No family participants were identified this way.

about their experiences (for example, Audrey Edwards) information about their experiences could be accessed from the public domain.

All initial contact was via email; first contact with participants involved them being sent an information sheet, explaining the purpose of the research and that interviews would be carried out face to face.[32] First contact between the interviewer and participants was very important in establishing a rapport which was vital in ensuring detailed interviews.[33] No one refused to participate having been initially contacted by the author. Interviews took place in locations chosen by each participant and were recorded. All participants were offered anonymity, which involved not just removing all names but other identifying characteristics of cases where participants asked to remain anonymous.

The position of the interviewer in this type of research is an instrument to improve the quality of the data collected; the interaction between the interviewer and the participant is therefore crucial and must be acknowledged as unique to this research project.[34] It was important that the interviewer had expertise and knowledge relevant to the issues under discussion.[35] This ensured the flow of the interview as the interviewer understood the background to much of the answers given as well as references to specific cases or practices and policies specific to custodial institutions. This allowed participants to give more detailed answers without feeling the need to simplify issues or provide detailed explanation to anything said. The role of an interviewer is to create a space within which the participant feels comfortable to share personal experiences and perceptions.[36] One way that this was done was to give each participant control over when and where the interview occurred. Participants were also asked if they would prefer others to be present; FA4 took up this offer and their father (FA4 Father) was included in the interview.

It is also important in conducting semi-structured interviews that rapport between interviewer and participant is established to produce rich data.[37] This was particularly true in relation to the bereaved families who participated in this project. The author had previous experience working with families at INQUEST which was useful to establishing a trusting relationship with participants; allowing them to share very personal and painful experiences. The author's previous role at INQUEST was to provide families with information and support; so they had experience of listening to people's painful stories in a respectful manner.

Understanding for the position of a participant can arguably gain more honest and full answers and the interviewer's previous experience was linked to supporting bereaved family members. It is therefore possible that the views of the families and those that support them through inquests are more strongly

---

[32]Annex I.

[33]Seidman (2012, p. 46).

[34]Seidman (2012, p. 23).

[35]Burnham and others (2004, p. 185).

[36]Smith and Osborn (2003, p. 57).

[37]Smith and Osborn (2003, p. 57).

represented than the voice of State parties in this book. However, direct comparisons were generally not being made between the groups which off-set any disparities in the quality of the interviews achieved with the different groups. It is also true that there is a large diversity in approaches and attitudes among coroners (confirmed by the interviews) but as participants were well aware of the issues covered by this book before agreeing to take part, it is possible coroners with more interest or empathy in relation to families' participation were more likely to offer to be interviewed.[38] In addition, research has indicated if an interviewer is perceived as sympathetic by a participant, they might offer 'additional information on sensitive topics' but not false information.[39] So while the interviews with family members, legal representatives and coroners might have provided fuller and more complex perceptions, this does not make them invalid.

In semi-structured interviews, researchers use an established schedule for all interviews but the process must also be flexible, allowing the interviewer to respond to each participant's specific experience.[40] The researcher followed a semi-structured interview approach, with only a skeleton framework covering a handful of issues which were most relevant to the research questions. Generally, participants were encouraged to talk about whatever they felt was most important; with the interviewer only interjecting to either clarify or examine an issue raised or to guide them towards the skeleton framework where absolutely necessary. This was especially important in relation to introducing sensitive issues and ensuring the interview flowed while discussing complex and sometimes controversial topics.[41] The questions were used as a general guide, with each participant being encouraged to only answer questions if they had relevant personal opinions they were comfortable sharing. This ensured each participant was allowed the space to talk about their own experiences.[42] This did create some disparity between all the interviews as each participant did not necessarily cover exactly the same ground. It did, however, ensure that the data collected were specific and contextual to each individual.

Each interview followed four broad themes:

(1) Participants' perceptions of the inquest process;
(2) What participants considered to be important aspects to involvement of bereaved families;
(3) What participants considered to be the effect of family involvement;
(4) How participants felt the inquest system ensured accountability.

---

[38]It is important to note that interviews were carried out when the Chief Coroner had only been in post for a couple of months, and greater consistency among coroners may well be a consequence of this statutory position.
[39]Burnham and others (2004).
[40]Smith and Osborn (2003, p. 56).
[41]Smith and Osborn (2003, p. 57).
[42]Smith and Osborn (2003, p. 57).

The questions were neutral rather than leading and open rather than closed to encourage detailed responses.[43] The interviewer encouraged more detailed answers by asking for clarification or more details as appropriate, without directing the conversation.[44] Probes were used as minimally as possible to limit how much the interviewer led the conversation while encouraging the participant to continue sharing.[45]

3.4.2 Ethics

The author received ethical approval for research involving human participants from the University of Essex, Law Department's Faculty Ethics Committee before beginning the empirical research. Ethical approval required a detailed plan on how the participants would be contacted, how particular vulnerabilities of proposed participants would be dealt with, how informed consent would be obtained, arrangements for ensuring confidentiality and anonymity if requested, how the data would be securely stored and any possible risks to either participants or the researcher. The most important part of the process was considering the specific vulnerabilities of bereaved families, and how to minimise negative consequences following their involvement in the research. The main risks were addressed by ensuring all participants were very clear on both the process and the aim of the research, and bereaved families did not have any unrealistic expectations about the research affecting their particular case. All bereaved families gave their time and story in the hope of bringing change, not for themselves, but for other families in the future. The author was very grateful for the generosity of all participants and took the responsibility of representing their views very seriously.

Participants shared personal and sensitive information with the author, which puts them in a position of vulnerability.[46] In allowing the author to interpret their experiences, participants were putting themselves in a position where they could be embarrassed or misrepresented. It was therefore vitally important for each participant to give informed consent, not just to be interviewed but for the data to be used. Carefully agreed processes were followed to ensure consent was well-informed, data were stored securely and confidentially. Each participant was given an information sheet, which included a brief synopsis of the research, possible benefits and risks of participating as well as details of how their anonymity and confidentiality would be maintained.[47,48] Any data were only used once the author was confident the participant's personal information could not be identified unless they gave express permission otherwise.

---

[43]Smith and Osborn (2003, pp. 61–62).
[44]Burnham and others, p. 123.
[45]Smith and Osborn (2004, p. 63).
[46]Seidman (2012, p. 61).
[47]See ANNEX I.
[48]As described by Seidman (2012, pp. 61–62).

3.5 Data Collection

General information about the research was provided to each participant so they would have an expectation of what would be discussed during the interview. However, specific questions were not provided as the purpose was to gather insights and perceptions rather than objective knowledge.

Each interview was carried out face to face, which has been shown to the most effective approach for encouraging exploration of opinions and perceptions on very complex and sensitive issues.[49] Each interview was recorded to ensure a better flow of conversation and a more relaxed atmosphere as well as an accurate recording for analysis.[50] A skeleton interview schedule was used to guide the conversation with bullet points to be used as prompts if appropriate.

Each interview was then transcribed verbatim in line with the necessary approach for IPA.[51] Verbatim transcription allows detailed analysis of the data line by line, including the interviewer questions and comments are vital for providing context.[52] Transcription for IPA is done at a semantic level so significant pauses, repetitions and false starts are referenced.[53] Prosodic details such as the tone or emphasis of the conversation are not required for IPA as they are for conversation analysis.[54] This approach also allows for use of quotations so readers can 'see for themselves' and therefore scrutinise the validity of any interpretations made of the data.[55] In order to allow comparability between open interviews, equivalence must be found in meaning, not precise words which requires interpretation on the behalf of the researcher.[56] However is must be clarified that in interpreting the interviews, a double hermeneutic effect is produced as the researcher's own interpretations are added to those carried out by the participants.[57]

3.6 Analysis

Good quality qualitative research must be systematic and transparent so the detailed steps taken during the analysis process are set out below. The qualitative software analysis tool NVivo was used to assist with the coding, comparison and analysis of the transcripts of the interviews. The analysis process included a number of steps carried out over a period of months.

[49]Hollway and Jefferson (2000).
[50]Valentine (1997).
[51]Larkin (2013).
[52]Smith and Osborn (2004, pp. 63–64).
[53]Smith and Osborn (2004, pp. 63–64).
[54]See Drew (2005).
[55]Wolcott (1994).
[56]Denzin and Lincoln (2005).
[57]Larkin (2013).

Step 1: Free coding to reflect researcher perceptions on reading transcriptions.
Step 2: Line by line coding to identify

- Issues that matter to participant;
- Meaning of those issues (experiential);
- Characterise participants' stance in relation to identified issues.

Step 3: Identify patterns (commonalities).
Step 4: Interpretation of patterns to identify themes.
Step 5: Structuring of themes.
Step 6: Development of a narrative using detailed data extracts to take reader through interpretation.

All participants were referred to anonymously, as this was the best way to both ensure anonymity and that the narrative provided by those participants who were happy to be named did not come across more strongly than the anonymous participants. Each participant was identified by group:

FA = Family members
LA = Legal representatives
CO = Coroners
SP/ESP = Police officers/Ex-police officers

The only exception to this coding was to the two representatives of the investigatory bodies which were identified by the acronym of their respective organisation (IPCC and PPO) throughout. This was done for a number of reasons. Firstly, they had both agreed to be named, secondly, they provided perspectives unique to their positions within those bodies and, thirdly, they were selected on a representative basis, whereas all other participants were not taken to be representing their identified group but just an example of that group.

Other than the IPCC and PPO individuals, participants were not taken as representatives of their groups which is why the views were not generally referenced by group (for example, 'families said this') or compared across groups as this would entail endowing participants with a representative function. It also allowed for the fact that with open-ended responses from semi-structured interviews, different issues arose organically and therefore strong inferences should not be made from the fact that a theme came up in one interview but not another.

The rest of this book will now set the experiences gathered by the interviews within the context of different key aspects and use them to consider the different benefits offered by ensuring fair and effective participation for bereaved families in investigations following a death in custody. The next part of this book looks at the benefits that might be directly felt by families themselves.

Part 3
Participation Benefits for Bereaved Families

The previous chapter described how the empirical research for this book was carried out, and the rest of the book will now set out the experiences of those interviewed within the context of different key aspects, with particular focus on the benefits offered by ensuring fair and effective participation for families. This part of the book looks at what benefits might be experienced by bereaved families if they are supported to participate in an inquest following a death in custody.

Chapter 4 considers what are set out in law as the benefits offered to families in relation to participating in an inquest following a death in custody – described as their legitimate interests. It begins with a brief introduction to the theoretical understanding to why a right to participate in a process that affects you is important, and what it needs to constitute in order for people to feel that their participation is effective. This highlights that an opportunity to see the process for yourself (rather than just be presented with an outcome) and influence the process, or at least be confident that your views or input were taken into consideration when a final outcome was being decided, are both key to what constitutes an effective right to participate. This is set within the framework of an inquest following a death in custody, and the author identifies where there are current gaps to how much influence families can have on the process. The rest of this part then looks at how the participation of families in an inquest following a death in custody can benefit the families themselves. The legal framework establishes that families can participate in order to ensure their legitimate interests are protected. Although ECtHR case law does not necessarily go beyond the need for families to access redress – which may be in the form of compensation – domestic law does set out three legitimate interests as identifying State culpability, finding the truth about how and why a death occurred and knowing lessons have been learned. The author carried out interviews with relevant parties with expertise, and these support the understanding that these three factors are important benefits for families who participate in inquests. However, the interviews also identify further factors that families themselves see as benefits of participation – including receiving an apology, seeing those responsible for a death punished or just knowing there is a public record of any failings.

In addition, the author wanted to look at the impact of participation on the grief process of families, which is considered in Chapter 5. It is clear that participation can have a positive impact on grief and reduce the likelihood that a family moves into complicated grief. But this requires families to be provided with timely information about the facts surrounding a death, and being offered the opportunity to ensure the deceased is fairly represented during the inquest, and in press accounts of the death. The author believes that decision-makers (especially coroners) should have a greater understanding on what the right to participate means in practice, to ensure families can effectively influence the process. And they should also be aware of how participation can have benefits to families beyond those established in case law – especially in relation to a healthy grief process. Recommendations relevant to these issues will be set out in Chapter 11.

The next chapter looks at what are described as the legitimate interests, which are the legally defined benefits for families if they participate in an inquest following the death of their loved one.

Chapter 4

Legitimate Interests

This chapter looks at what are considered as the key legitimate interests for families who participate in an inquest. Domestic law allows family participation in order to protect their legitimate interests. As explained in the first part of the book, domestic law aims to protect a families' right to participate as well as the reasoning behind why this right should be protected. Early judgments focused on financial benefits to a family via a civil case or compensation but the recent *Letts* case provided a wider understanding of a family's interests, including finding out the truth, identification of State culpability and knowing further deaths will be prevented.[1] This book is attempting to go beyond the legal protections in place, to provide evidence for a change in not just law, but policy and practice as well. In order to do this, the author is looking for theories that may explain why participation of families is so important. So this chapter begins by looking at how theoretical frameworks relating to the right to participate in a process are relevant to family participation in an inquest. It covers what participation in a process investigating potential human rights violations should look like in practice. The empirical interviews are then used to create a narrative setting out how the author sees participants experience of families' participating in an inquest reflect the theoretical frameworks for the right to participate and redress. Evidence collected through the interviews supported the broad thematic benefits to family participation being that it offers an opportunity to find the truth and ensure failings are identified, which consequentially assists families to receive redress. Redress was described in a number of ways, including families accessing compensation through civil cases, receiving apologies and knowing that future deaths had been prevented.

4.1 Fair and Effective Participation

The theory supporting the right to participation states that for participation to be effective, it must allow an opportunity not just to be heard but also to influence the process.[2] Parties must be confident that their viewpoint is considered and

[1] *Letts v Lord Chancellor* (2015).
[2] FitzGerald and others (2002).

Death in Custody, 59–80
Copyright © 2020 Jo Easton
Published under exclusive licence
doi:10.1108/978-1-83909-025-720201008

incorporated into any final decision.[3] Processes that allow parties the opportunity to be heard before any decision-maker are perceived as fairer, even when the outcome is seen as negative.[4] Initial theories proposed parties perceived a process as more fair if they had the opportunity to be heard as they believed their voice would have an instrumental effect of achieving a better outcome.[5] However, it has now been argued there is an intrinsic value in parties being heard, as it ensures they feel valued regardless of whether their input changes the outcome.[6] An empirical study illustrated there was procedural fairness value in parties being heard, even when the decision had been made but positive impacts are maximised when parties have an opportunity to influence the outcome of decisions.[7] In a process where there are important decisions made at different stages which all have an impact on the outcome, it is very important for parties to have the opportunity to be heard at all those stages.[8]

Thibaut and Walker first put forward the model of procedural justice which argued people were not just concerned about the outcome of a dispute but also equally invested in the process which resolved the dispute.[9] The importance of process was linked to the opportunity to influence the outcome. If people are allowed sufficient input in the process and feel they have had a fair chance to influence the result, they perceive the process as fair. The criteria individuals might see as the most important to assess whether a process is fair are relational and therefore context-driven.[10] So an individual's perception about their standing within society, as well as the fact that people have inherently different points of reference, will alter how they judge whether a process is fair or just. So trust in the authorities, preconceived beliefs relating to status and perceived neutrality of the process influence whether a procedure is seen as fair.[11]

Obviously, any real opportunity to influence the outcome has the potential to have an instrumental benefit of changing the outcome. Professor Adams has asserted that it is the participation offered by an adversarial system, with parties being able to bring evidence before the court, which 'heightens the rationality and acceptability of the result'.[12] So it is sometimes argued that only if participation is seen as effective in changing the outcome, will it be perceived as fair. However, this ignores the benefit that can result from people perceiving a process as fair just by knowing they had an opportunity to affect the outcome.[13] Effective

[3]Allan (1998).
[4]LaTour (1978), Lind and others (1980), Greenberg and Folger (1983), Bies and Shapiro (1988).
[5]Thibaut and Walker (1978), Leventhal (1980).
[6]Lind and Tyler (1988), Lane (1988).
[7]Lind and Tyler (1998), Lind, Kanfer, and Earley (1990).
[8]Price and others (2006).
[9]Thibaut and Walker (1975).
[10]Tyler and others (1998).
[11]Tyler, Degoey, and Smith (1996).
[12]Adams (1973).
[13]FitzGerald and others (2002).

participation in a process does not solely have an instrumental benefit; there can be intrinsic value in allowing the opportunity to influence the outcome, whatever the impact on the final outcome. This can be for a number of reasons, including the fact that participation increases understanding and therefore acceptance of a decision; as well as the fact that allowing an individual to be heard increases the likelihood they feel ownership of the decision and therefore accept it.[14]

The most important factor in ensuring a person will perceive their opportunity to participate as affair is that they must believe that their participation was relevant and taken into account.[15] The opportunity to affect the outcome must be seen as real; so even if the outcome is not altered, an individual must feel their viewpoint was considered. This can be done by acknowledging and recognising the validity of the individuals' input, even if it is then explained why the decision then goes against the individuals' view or input.[16] Giving reasons allows a subject to feel valued and identify with the process, so even if they disagree, they are more likely to accept an adverse decision.[17] It is not clear how far fair participation can counter negative perceptions about an outcome, but as long as people do not feel their input has been ignored, they will have positive perceptions about the process which is beneficial in of itself. However, it is clear the opportunity to participate must be in practice, not just principle and this requires individuals to be heard, and their views considered.

4.2 Right to Participate

4.2.1 Families as Victims

So why should families have a specific right to participate in an inquest following a death? The interviews showed that participants linked this right to families being seen as victims, who have a right to be involved in the process which is determining what happened to their loved ones. All participants agreed families had a right to be heard and participate in the process as those most affected by the death and because the outcome of the inquest was likely to impact significantly on them. Two bereaved family members (FA2 and FA5) felt very let down that the system did not appear to address their role as victims. One family participant (FA5) said there was no space for raising the impact of the death and the process on themselves and the rest of the family. Another (FA2) thought they and their family were unacknowledged as victims. A coroner (CO2) said 'an inquest is not only a judicial system but also a service for the bereaved'. A different coroner participant (CO4) thought it was true that in some ways the inquest was done for the family, so their participation as victims in their own right should be a priority. Therefore, understanding why families have a particular right to participate as victims can ensure their rights are fully respected.

---

[14]Allan (1998, p. 499).
[15]Allan (1998, p. 500).
[16]Brems and Lavrysen (2013, p.181).
[17]Allan (1998, p. 509).

4.2.2 Specific Factors Relevant to Deaths in Custody

Participants identified a number of factors particular to a death in custody that made participation by families in the inquest even more important. Firstly, the fact that families were usually not present when a death occurred was raised as key, as it meant they were unlikely to know what happened through personal experience or even through being able to speak directly to those present. Other sudden deaths may occur when a friend or family member is there and therefore know what happened, but this is unlikely for deaths in custody. Those present at the time of the death are usually State officers, and therefore they hold information that the family cannot get from anywhere or anyone else. Secondly, it was pointed out that families often had little direct contact with the deceased prior to the death and so may find it difficult to understand the context leading up to a death. Lack of regular contact (especially if the person who has died was in prison) prior to a death may leave a family feeling they did not really know what was going on in the day-to-day life of the deceased. Were they particularly stressed or upset about something? Or had they been arguing with someone? Little things we usually know about our family but when there is forcible distance from their loved ones, families are not usually able to be in as close contact as they may wish prior to the death. Thirdly, a lack of knowledge about the situation in custody usually leaves families not appreciating matters directly related to a death. So family members may not know the details of the regime which may either have impacted on the death or just provide contextual understanding about what happened. Fourthly, it was pointed out that deaths in closed institutions meant families usually could not access the location of the death. This has an impact on the grief process, which is discussed in the next chapter as it limits a families' ability to picture what happened.

The fact that deaths in custody meant families were unlikely to be present when death occurred and therefore not have any information about what happened was raised by a number of participants (CO3, FA1, FA2, FA3, FA5, LA1 and LA2). They all noted that participation in an inquest was often the first and only opportunity for the family to see and hear evidence about the circumstances surrounding the death. One legal representative (LA1) said 'the family rely on the process to tell them what happened.' Three family participants (FA2, FA3 and FA5) all said they had to see the evidence for themselves so they could understand what had happened. One (FA3) felt they could not trust summaries or interpretations of the facts produced by others. Another bereaved family member (FA5) found seeing and hearing the evidence made it all feel real.

It was also pointed out that a family might have had limited contact with the deceased prior to the death, especially if death occurred in prison where visits are only possible a certain number of times a month and phone calls are restricted. Another factor that can limit family visits is that prisoners can be held hundreds of miles away from family and friends. A legal representative (LA1) gave examples where the deceased had been in prison, so the family had little involvement in their life for a considerable period of time before the death occurred. In these cases, the family will rely on evidence at the inquest to hear about the life of the deceased leading up to the death, which is particularly important following any deaths by suicide.

Another aspect specific to deaths in custody raised by participants was that families were unlikely to have detailed knowledge about the custodial institutions where the death occurred, especially the policies and practices that govern detention. Both PPO and IPCC noted families did not understand how prisons or police forces worked and therefore could not contextualise decisions and appreciate their appropriateness or necessity. The PPO gave the example of ACCT (Assessment, Care in Custody and Teamwork) documents which are opened when a prisoner is assessed as at risk of self-harm and have to be explained to families so they can appreciate the impact of whether such a document was active at the time of death. They both believed family participation in the inquest system could benefit families by ensuring they understood the context of custody or decisions to restrain an individual. One thing that was apparent in interviewing bereaved families was that they gained a detailed knowledge about many aspects of detention through participating in the inquest process.

Another issue raised was that it could be challenging for families to see for themselves where a death occurred: by definition, access to custodial settings can be difficult to arrange for families. Although PPO said they would expect a family to be given access to the prison cell where somebody died, other participants said this was not usual practice. A coroner (CO3) noted families often struggled to visit the place death occurred. Two family participants (FA1 and FA4) described incredible difficulties associated with visiting the respective cells where their loved ones died.

In conclusion, all participants agreed that one of the reasons families should be able to participate in an inquest is as those most affected by the death. Deaths in custody were shown to inherently mean that without participation in the inquest, families would struggle not just to know what happened, but to contextualise it. The importance of families having a clear narrative about what happened will be discussed further in Chapter 5.

4.3 Right to Influence the Outcome

The right to participate in a process goes beyond either being informed about an outcome or merely witnessing the process but involves a right to be heard and an opportunity to influence the outcome. All participants said they thought this was relevant for family participation in an inquest. One of the coroners interviewed (CO3) said families should feel their involvement was meaningful, not just a 'rubber stamp'. Another coroner (CO2) felt 'very strongly' that families should be 'the focus of the process'. An ex-police officer (ESP2) felt 'families are empowered' by being involved in the process, instead of just witnessing it. A senior police officer interviewed (SP1) agreed, noting that inquests did not always provide clear verdicts (as in criminal cases) or outcomes, so it made being involved in the process even more important.

Participants generally felt that the right to ask questions throughout the process was very important for two reasons. Firstly, the action of asking questions could help families feel involved: with one legal representative (LA6) saying families had 'had enough of being told' and wanted to be able to ask questions. Three other interviewees (LA1, LA2 and PPO) all said the ability to question officers involved in the death of their loved one was very important to families. Family participants (FA1, FA2, FA4 and FA5) explained that the opportunity to question witnesses during their respective inquests made them feel more involved in the process. Two coroner participants (CO1 and CO3) agreed that ensuring families were able to put questions to witnesses helped them feel more engaged with the process.

Secondly, participants thought asking questions allowed families to really understand what had happened: one family member interviewed (FA2) felt that the further along the process, the more questions they had. An ex-police officer (ESP2) said families wanted to scrutinise the evidence and ask questions when one of their loved ones died in custody. One of the legal representatives (LA6) said for families to be satisfied, they had to have the opportunity to clarify inconsistencies or rumours relating to how the death occurred or just about the deceased. This was raised as particularly relevant if the press has reported facts about the deceased which were previously unknown to the family. Some State official participants challenged the idea that families should be able to participate in order to influence the process or outcome as they were concerned about families being given what they called 'too much' influence. IPCC said sometimes families wanted things investigated which were not considered a 'reasonable line of enquiry'. PPO agreed families had to understand what they could and could not influence during an investigation. An ex-police officer (ESP2) said it should be remembered an investigation was not 'just done for the family's benefit'. A senior police officer (SP1) supported this view, querying whether families should be given priority status over other interested parties. Three coroner participants (CO1, CO2 and CO3) felt a balance could be achieved, allowing families to participate but ensuring they did not negatively affect the outcome. One coroner (CO1) believed if the family wanted the inquest to go in a direction which was not helpful in reaching a correct outcome, coroners could be firm in not allowing the inquiry to be 'driven by the attitude of the family'. Another (CO2) agreed as long as it did not unduly influence their decisions, family participation could be assured. A third coroner participant (CO3) said as long as the families' participation were not allowed to negatively impact on the process or influence the jury, it would be unkind not to allow it.

It is worrying that although generally participants agreed a family had a specific right to participate due to their position as victims or the most affected by the death, State officials and coroners still had concerns about family participation being prioritised over other parties. The fact that some participants indicated they felt families could have too much influence over the outcome is concerning, given the theoretical understanding of the importance of having the opportunity to influence the outcome to fair participation. Similarly, the fact that some coroners saw their role as limiting family influence unduly, if their participation is not directly beneficial to the process, is a concern. This suggests family participation is primarily seen as important only in the context of whether it is to have a positive or negative impact on the process and outcome – rather than a legal right. Even if there are legal reasons why family views should not be able to influence the outcome (if they might lead to an unfair outcome or open up inappropriate lines of enquiry), the impact of families perceiving their opportunity to influence the process to be limited needs to be carefully considered.[18] If it is not fully explained to families why their influence must be limited, it could easily be perceived as a way to prevent proper scrutiny of what happened. This links to Chapter 10 which looks at the role of legal representation, which can ensure families participate fully without restricting the validity or efficacy of the process while clearly understanding the limitations to the scope of an inquest process.

And wherever there is no legal reason to limit a families' opportunity to influence the process, this opportunity should not merely be seen within the context of whether it will affect the outcome. It is vital that coroners (in particular) appreciate the wider, intrinsic benefits of families feeling involved, and knowing their input is taken into consideration, even if the final outcome is not changed by their participation. It would therefore be helpful for coroners to understand the theoretical framework which illustrates the intrinsic benefits to families perceiving participation as fair.

The specific factors which were raised as relevant to families' being able to influence the outcome of an inquest will be discussed in the next sections.

4.3.1 Right to Influence the Investigation

Participants pointed out that to ensure families had an opportunity to influence the outcome of an inquest, it was vital they were able to participate in investigations carried out prior to the inquest hearing, as the evidence presented at the hearing was usually decided during the investigation. The evidence presented at an inquest is decided by the coroner but they usually rely on reports produced by investigatory bodes (such as IPCC and PPO) rather than gathering evidence themselves. One of the coroner participants (CO1) said almost all investigations into custodial deaths were carried out by investigatory bodies, not the coroner's staff (including gathering all the witness statements). A legal representative (LA3) noted most coroners 'don't have the time, money or resources' to investigate fully, so had to rely on State investigators. PPO agreed that coroners relied heavily on PPO reports 'to set the scope of the inquest': particularly in terms of the evidence to be presented and which witnesses would be called at the inquest.

[18]For example, there are legal restrictions on what an inquest can investigate or what a verdict may identify – including the fact an individual cannot be named as culpable for a death.

So it is understandable that participants felt families should be able to influence the investigation by asking specific questions for the investigatory bodies to answer, as this subsequently influences the evidence heard by the inquest. Three legal representatives (LA2, LA3 and LA5) all agreed families had to be involved 'before it gets to the inquest stage' (LA5), as all the decisions to do with witnesses and evidence for the inquest were made before the hearing actually started. To have an impact on the inquest, families had to be able to influence which witnesses and what evidence was to be considered. One of the coroners interviewed (CO2) said it was important to make sure families had time to raise concerns to be addressed by investigations. A legal representative (LA3) agreed families had to be involved and supported early enough to suggest issues so they could be looked at by the inquest. One of the bereaved family members (FA4) found there was little opportunity to influence once their inquest had begun as the 'inquest was put in place with all the questions answered'.

Influencing evidence and witnesses to be heard at the inquest was argued to be important not just because families had an opportunity to influence the outcome but also because otherwise the evidence presented at the inquest could be biased by investigatory bodies. Three of the people interviewed (LA2, LA3 and FA3) all noted the investigation could bias the process 'very, very easily by what material you do or don't make available to them [the coroner]' (FA3).[19] A legal representative (LA3) said that too often the IPCC did not investigate 'obvious lines of enquiry'. The example given was the death of Sean Rigg, where IPCC investigators did not watch all of the CCTV and it was only because the family noticed this prior to the inquest that the additional CCTV was presented at the hearing.

Therefore, ensuring families have an opportunity to influence an investigation is one way of ensuring they can bring balance to the process and reduce any bias (to be discussed in Part 4).

A number of participants (LA1, LA4, LA6, FA1 and FA5) raised concerns that the level of involvement offered to families during investigations carried out by bodies like the PPO or IPCC was inconsistent. A legal representative (LA6) said families were not able to participate fully in any investigations carried out by either the PPO or IPCC and were unlikely to get answers to any questions they might have. Other participants distinguished between different investigatory bodies. Two of the lawyers interviewed (LA1 and LA4) said generally the IPCC did not answer families' questions or allow for them to be involved in the investigation but merely provided them with updates. However, one of the lawyers (LA4) noted the PPO usually took the approach of drafting a report then 'asking the family for their views', which they felt was helpful and led to families having more faith in the PPO than the IPPC, who did not take this same approach or take account of feedback from families. One of the family members interviewed (FA5) was able to ask questions of the PPO investigators and make suggestions about the investigation, so they felt their input was valued. However, families are not always involved in PPO investigations with another family

[19]Family participation bringing balance will be discussed in Part 4.

participant (FA1) saying their first contact with the PPO was when they were given the final draft of the report. This can be linked to lack of access to effective legal representation, which can ensure family involvement in an investigation as FA1 did not have early support from specialist legal representatives.

Four of the participants interviewed (CO3, LA6, ESP1 and ESP2) all pointed out that investigatory bodies themselves relied on police and crime scene officers to collect evidence and carry out witness interviews, as they had insufficient resources to do all the necessary work themselves. These participants said police investigations were not set up to allow family involvement, so the only opportunity to influence was through any liaison families had with the investigatory bodies. Although participants generally agreed participation in the investigation prior to the inquest was important for families, in practice, it is clear this is not happening. It was also pointed out by one family participant interviewed (FA3) that investigations into deaths in hospital do not involve the family at all.

Arguably, even where families are being offered an opportunity to comment on an investigation, it is likely to be too late to actually influence the investigation. If all the interviews have been carried out, and evidence collected before families are in contact with the investigatory body, the police are unlikely to be told to re-interview people with new questions or even to carry out new interviews of people suggested by families. Even if this did happen, the longer the time between a death and the gathering of evidence or interviews are done, the more challenging it is to collect valid evidence. Over time, evidence is lost if not collected and stored appropriately, and witnesses' memories may be less robust. Therefore, even if there were an opportunity for families to make representations about any areas where they feel an investigation was lacking, it may be too late for their input to be fully relevant. This obviously has a limiting effect on a families' opportunity to influence the inquest.

4.3.2 Right to Influence the Verdict

The ability to participate by questioning witnesses and scrutinising the evidence during the inquest hearing itself was identified as an important aspect of a family having an opportunity to influence the outcome. This was partly due to the fact that families' participation in investigations could be difficult and partly because the inquest offered opportunities to scrutinise the evidence. All participants were clear that families had to be able to examine evidence and question witnesses in order to be able to influence the outcome of the inquest. This will be dealt with in more detail during Chapter 7, where the opportunity for families to scrutinise and cross-examine the evidence will be shown to impact the outcome.

In addition to influencing the evidence via both the investigation and during the hearing, a few participants also discussed whether families should have the opportunity to directly influence the verdicts. In a general sense, influencing the investigation and questioning the evidence during the hearing allows families to influence what the verdict might be, but there are two practical ways families might be able to directly influence decisions taken by juries. The first relates to the fact that coroners select which verdicts (such as accident, suicide or unlawful killing) are left to the jury for consideration. The second is that it is now usual for complicated inquests (including those following deaths in custody) to produce narrative verdicts in the form of questions put to the jury for them to answer, which consider the wider circumstances around a death.

Generally families do not influence what verdicts are left to the jury, although some coroners will hear the views of interested parties before making a decision. Although one family participant felt it was important their view was heard as to possible verdicts, other participants said family influence had to be limited. One family member (FA2) felt very strongly that misadventure should have been a verdict available to the jury in their case and, with the assistance of their legal representative, convinced the coroner to change the options left open to the jury. Two of the legal representatives interviewed (LA2 and LA3) felt consideration had to be given as to how much influence families should have in terms of possible verdicts as accountability demanded a consistent framework for all inquests, regardless of what the family may want. One legal representative (LA2) pointed out families wanted different things from inquests; with some hating open verdicts but others finding anything other than an open verdict unsatisfactory. Patterns indicating systemic failings involving one or more institutions can only be identified if consistent verdicts are produced. Another legal representative (LA3) supported this, saying families' right to participate in an inquest should not result in inconsistent outcomes, particularly in cases where there might be criticisms of State agents. In order for criticisms to be seen as legitimate, they must be seen to be resulting from an independent and unbiased process, not unduly influenced by a family looking to apportion blame.

There is a strong argument for the need for a consistent approach to be taken in identifying systemic failings – especially if patterns of deaths can indicate a particular problem at a specific institution. However, this author argues that allowing families to put forward verdicts does not necessarily lead to inconsistent or biased outcomes, it just allows juries to have more options open to them. If verdicts are consistent because juries are all limited in their options, it is not an accurate recording of failings. Even if the family has a preferred verdict, it is difficult to see how just allowing the jury to consider it risks the outcome becoming biased. The jury will not just follow what a family wants the verdict to be but should follow the evidence to decide the appropriate verdict. If there is a concern that the views of the family will be given too much weight by a jury, a clear direction can be given by the coroner to follow the evidence. If necessary, the coroner can explain the importance of having transparent and consistent verdicts, to minimise any risk the family views will bias the outcome.

In relation to what questions are put to the jury, it is common practice for all interested parties to be able to suggest questions to the coroner who then selects those (and adds any of their own) which will provide the narrative which best reflects the evidence. One coroner (CO3) explained that they allowed families to put forward questions for the jury to answer, finding it very beneficial as different parties had different angles and therefore provide varied questions. FA5 felt this was one way families could feel 'very involved'. Again, the issue of families wanting to ask questions that might be out of scope should be dealt with sensitively so they do not feel their opportunity to influence is being restricted without good reason.

Participation in both the investigation and the inquest hearing itself was the predominant theme running through all responses in relation to what participants felt ensured families the opportunity to influence the outcome. Two criteria which were identified as beneficial to improving this opportunity were the support of a legal representative and access to documents relating to the death. These will be considered as aspects of effective participation in Chapter 10.

4.4 Legal Right to Protect Legitimate Interests

The right for families to be able to participate should be a framework to allow them the opportunity to participate, if they wish to, but generally families need a reason to want to participate. The fact that there was a legal right to participate was not generally thought by those interviewed by the author to be a reason why families wanted to participate. The law offers an opportunity for families, not an obligation. Families do not participate just because they can – participants were clear that families all had good reasons why they wanted to participate.

Although the fact that participation was a legal right for families was not generally given as an important reason to ensure family participation, some participants (CO4, LA2, LA3 and FA3) did note the importance of the law in framing participation. One coroner interviewed (CO4) referenced the fact that any decisions made by a coroner could be judicially reviewed and that ensuring families were able to participate could make sure a judicial review was 'headed off'. A legal representative (LA3) also referred to the legal framework of the Human Rights Act as being very important in governing participation of families. However, they did note that participation was achievable before the enforcement of the Human Rights Act but only through a lot of hard work by lawyers. The framework allowing families to participate once they had been recognised as interested parties was referenced as vitally important by three of those interviewed (LA2, LA3 and FA3). A legal representative (LA2) said inferring interested party status on family members was the only way of ensuring their participation was possible. One family participant (FA3) thought the legal right to participate was very important, mostly because in their case, the legal right to participate was not as well established following a death in a secure hospital as for deaths in police or prison custody.

The right for bereaved families to participate in inquests following deaths in custody is framed in both European and domestic case law by reference to their 'legitimate interests'.[20] Participants identified a number of varied interests that they thought were relevant and that participation should therefore protect. It was

[20]As described in Part 1.

clear that different families had different legitimate interests that were key to their desire to participate, and, in addition, their individual priorities often changed over time. It is worth nothing that IPCC thought considering family's participation merely as a legal right did not take account of all possible benefits to a family, which was why participation should go beyond access to aspects set out in law. This relates to possible intrinsic values to participation, which will be discussed in Chapter 8.

Most participants acknowledged it could be difficult to assess what a family's legitimate interests were for a number of reasons. Firstly, it was noted that what might be seen as legitimate interests might be unique to each family. Secondly, one participant thought families may not know themselves what their interests were, with other participants saying their interests would change over time. Thirdly, some participants thought specialist lawyers sometimes influenced families, possibly be defining their interests for them rather than representing the family interests.

The uniqueness of families was seen as important by most participants, and something they generally felt was not appreciated by the process or decision-makers. One of the family members interviewed (FA5) was concerned that bereaved families 'all deal with things differently' and yet the State bunched them together by trying to define what 'the families' wanted. One legal representative (LA3) found 'different families want different things' and another (LA5) said families' interest 'just varies from case to case'. A coroner (CO3) agreed, saying each family and each case was unique. PPO thought one of the reasons families' legitimate interests were so variable was because 'people have different grieving processes'. A legal representative interviewed (LA6) said in their experience, families generally fell into two general groups in terms of what they wanted from the inquest process: some wanted the truth and nothing else, others wanted people to be held to account.[21] An additional legal representative (LA1) said it was always difficult to judge what was in the best interests of families as they were all unique. It is also true that different interests are not mutually exclusive; families may have multiple interests in participating, and they may change over time.

The fact that families are grieving, and thrust into an unknown process can mean they do not immediately appreciate what reasons there might be for participating. This also means that as the process goes on, they may change their minds about what they want out of participating. One of the legal representatives interviewed (LA3) thought one of the difficulties in identifying families' legitimate interests was because an inquest was a highly emotional time for them so often they did not know themselves what they wanted. A family participant (FA2) said initially they had wanted to just understand what had happened so they could 'put it to bed', but after going through the whole process they now felt they needed to do something to prevent further deaths happening.

[21]Part 4 will look at how the inquest process holds the State to account; it is important this occurs even if the bereaved family is only interested in hearing the truth.

One concern raised by some participants was that specialist legal representatives (with expertise in similar cases) could sometimes influence families about why it was important for them to participate. IPCC felt legal representatives might have good intentions but did not always take account of the negative impacts for families when they pushed for regular update meetings and every bit of information available on behalf of their clients. A coroner (CO2) also questioned whether legal representatives for families did not sometimes get caught up with achieving a particular outcome and potentially lost sight of what their clients really wanted. One example given was that some legal representatives (particularly those lawyers who took on a lot of similar cases) wanted to use a case to push for change in the system, where families were only focused on the individual death. In the experience of another coroner (CO1), legal teams sometimes 'stoked conspiracy theories in families' minds'. PPO thought this was true, partly due to the fact there were only a small number (6–7) of firms of solicitors who regularly represented families at inquests, which meant that they were sometimes 'operating with their own agendas'.[22] This potential for conflict was acknowledged by two legal representative participants who said they worked hard to counter it. One of the legal representatives interviewed (LA2) said 'the things as a lawyer you home in on and things [that] are the most important legally, are not really always the most important for a family'. This was supported by another lawyer (LA5), who said sometimes families' best interests were very different than getting a particular verdict from the inquest. For example, there may be one specific point families were interested in having clarified; and once that is done, they were not concerned about the final verdict. A good example is following a death by suicide, when a family will often be desperate to know whether the deceased intended to kill themselves or whether it was accidental. It may be that once they hear the evidence of the last person to see the deceased, they will be satisfied, regardless of any verdict.

In the interviews with legal representatives (who were all very experienced with Article 2 inquests), it was clear they were very aware of their responsibility to support families rather than push for a specific agenda. Obviously the expertise they bring from other cases will help inform their work and therefore impact on the support they provide families. But rather than assume lawyers are pushing their interests on families, it could be argued that the reason lawyers push similar arguments again and again is because the same issues arise again and again. And although different families have different reasons for participating, fundamentally, all families want to find the truth. So legal representatives are doing their job if they scrutinise and challenge evidence which helps find the truth.

This section established families might have different interests to protect, but the next section sets out some of the most common interests identified by participants as establishing the truth, achieving redress through verdicts or outcomes and ensuring anyone culpable for a death is held to account.

[22] Difficulties associated with families finding experienced legal representatives will be raised in Part 5.

4.5 Establishing the Truth and Consequential Factors

This section sets out the different interests for families wanting to participate as described by the interviews. As noted above, establishing the truth is often at the core, with consequential interests including families wanting a clear verdict, compensation or just an apology. Ensuring anyone culpable for the death is not just identified but also held to account is also important to families. One important aspect to the right to participate in investigations is to ensure victims of human rights violations receive adequate redress. This can be in the form of finding the truth which can be through a specific outcome and then lead to compensation, an apology or the prevention of future deaths.

4.5.1 Right to the Truth

The primary function of any inquest is to establish the circumstances surrounding a death, and all the families (FA1, FA2, FA3, FA4 and FA5) stated they wanted to participate because they wanted to find out what happened to their loved one. One of the family members interviewed (FA1) said what was important for families was to get 'the complete and whole truth'. Another family member (FA3) said they 'were delighted' to have a coroner who was going to have a proper, detailed inquest as they wanted the truth, whatever it was. A different family participant (FA5) felt satisfied that the inquest gave them 'an understanding of what happened'. This was supported by another family member interviewed (FA2) similarly said that although they had questions that were never answered, they were satisfied that they got the basic facts. The other family participant (FA4) was very clear they participated in the inquest 'for one thing and one thing alone, the truth': they did not care whether it was 'good, bad or indifferent'. One of the family participants (FA4) and their family said the only frustration came from inconsistencies which left them questioning whether they had the truth, with the father of that family participant saying 'if it falls into place, you accept it'.

Other participants agreed it was important for families to hear the truth. One coroner (CO2) saw the primary interest of families to be that they 'want to know what happened'. A legal representative (LA1) felt that not only should the aim of the inquest be to tell the families how someone died; but also 'most families are pretty interested in the detail'. They said this was particularly relevant for deaths that occurred in custody as families were unlikely to have been present when the death occurred and only found out many of the details at the inquest. Another lawyer (LA2) similarly said families rarely knew what had happened before becoming involved in the inquest process and often just hearing the details was the outcome they wanted. One of the other legal representatives interviewed (LA6) agreed that some families just needed to hear the truth to be satisfied with the process, especially if inconsistencies were clarified. One of the ex-police officers (ESP2) thought families mostly just wanted all the answers.

IPCC and PPO both acknowledged families wanted to know exactly what happened but thought as inquests had a narrowly defined scope, families might not always get answers to all their questions. One coroner (CO3) pointed out the scope of the inquest did not have to limit the facts given to the family, as even if an issue could not be part of the verdict, the coroner could acknowledge it during the hearing. A senior police officer (SP1) thought a flaw to the system was that the scope of inquests only allowed the actions of State officers to be scrutinised, when other people may be just as responsible for not preventing a death so sometimes the whole truth was not established. This is not an accurate representation of how the process should work, as the primary purpose of the inquest is to find the truth – regardless of who is responsible, whether they are a State official or not.

All participants agreed families should be informed about the true circumstances around a death; although one of the coroners interviewed (CO4) said there might be situations when they kept facts from the family if they thought it would be painful for a family to hear them. For example, this coroner said they did not necessarily ask a pathologist how quickly or painlessly someone died during the inquest, if they felt the family were not prepared for a negative response. They pointed out, though, that there were disadvantages to this approach, as it could be more painful for families if they learnt these facts later on. This coroner gave an example where the authorities had tried to comfort the family by telling them their child had not suffered (relating to a fatal accident) but the family had then been incredibly traumatised to hear at the inquest that the child had seared lungs, so must have been still breathing during the fire. This links to the importance of families hearing the facts about a death promptly, so they can form a clear narrative about what happened, which benefits the grief process. While decision-makers (including coroners) may mean well, any attempt to keep details about a death from families to 'protect' them is actually keeping the truth from them. It was clear from the interviews that families want the truth, regardless of the consequences. The importance of this within the context of a health grief process is explained in the next chapter.

4.5.2 Verdicts

Getting a clear inquest verdict about what happened was raised as important to families by five participants but there were differing views as to what verdict most families wanted. For example, one coroner (CO2) noted the official and authoritative nature of the inquest meant families listened if the verdict said 'you could not have done more to help'. A legal representative interviewed (LA1) said in some cases families 'were really pleased' with non-critical verdicts and in other cases families wanted failings acknowledged. They gave the example of a family who, during the process, were outraged at the treatment of the deceased in the prison but as these issues were not causative to the death, the verdict was not critical of the prison or its staff. This lawyer thought the family would be disappointed but actually they were pleased and relieved to know nothing could have been done to prevent the death. Two other lawyers (LA2 and LA3) agreed that in their experience, families felt relieved and vindicated if the process gave them a detailed verdict, whatever it may be. This can be linked to knowing people are held to account and lessons are learnt (to be discussed later). Two of the family members interviewed (FA2 and FA3) felt justice for the family and the deceased involved getting a critical verdict which highlighted failings.

Generally it was agreed the more detailed a verdict, the more satisfying it was for families. Three of those interviewed (LA2, LA3 and FA3) all said families preferred detailed narrative verdicts. The legal representative (LA2) said often what was seen as a 'good' verdict by families was one that answered specific questions on issues 'that have formed part of their narrative'. The importance of families having their own narrative about the death is key to a positive grief process (see Chapter 5).

4.5.3 Civil Case

If the truth establishes fault on the half of the State, it can lead to redress in the form of compensation. Achieving compensation via the domestic justice system is through civil cases bought by families against State agencies found culpable for a death. Although only one family participant gave civil action as a priority, other participants thought civil cases were a key reason for why families participated in an inquest because it provides access to compensation.

A coroner interviewed (CO1) said at contentious or high-profile inquests, 'civil litigation is on everybody's mind'. One of the ex-police officers (ESP2) agreed that all parties were aware of the possibility of State agencies getting sued as a result of inquest proceedings. IPCC felt inquests 'usually' led to civil proceedings, with the outcome of an inquest having a big impact on any civil claim. A legal representative (LA5) agreed that inquests where State failings were identified were very likely to lead to a civil case.

However, overall, civil cases were not introduced as important by families, with only one family participant (FA1) saying they were disappointed to be told a civil action would not be successful, after State failings were judged to have contributed to the death of their loved one. Even in this instance, they said they had not initially thought about compensation, but in the end they felt as State agents had failed in their duty of care to protect the deceased, the deceased's child should be due compensation. Both IPCC and ESP1 felt State parties were often more concerned with civil actions than families. One of the ex-police officers interviewed (ESP2) thought it was commonly the legal representatives that were more interested in taking civil cases forward.

A legal representative (LA6) felt even for those families who wanted a civil case, it was more to do with wanting to hold people to account and less about receiving money. Another lawyer (LA5) said in his experience, families were not looking for a civil case to gain financially, but because (unless lawyers were working pro bono) families could only find legal representation if there was a high likelihood of successful civil action to fund the costs.

4.5.4 Apology

In cases where failings have been identified, it was clear that while compensation was not high on the agenda for families, seeking an apology was often key. Some participants (CO1, LA1, IPCC, FA3 and FA5) mentioned the fact that an apology from the State could be a form of redress, as well as being in the best interests of both the families and the process more widely. One of the coroners interviewed (CO1), who answered in respect of their experience as a legal representative for State agencies, thought offering an apology early on in the process was very effective in reducing the adversarial nature of the process. One of the lawyers (LA1) agreed that the State admitting any errors as early as possible was beneficial because when families felt State agencies were not sorry for failures, 'that is what stops people breathing'. Two of the family members who were interviewed (FA3 and FA5) felt frustrated that no one ever admitted any mistakes they might have made, let alone apologised. One of them (FA5) was dismayed that instead of apologising, years later officers were not only saying they acted correctly but even that they would do so again, which was 'another slap really'. The other family member (FA3) felt that, at a minimum, State agents could have said they were sorry the death ever happened 'under their care' without ever admitting liability. IPCC had seen a case where an officer present at the time of the death had apologised (not necessarily for their actions but for the death) and the family had found this incredibly helpful in accepting what had happened.

4.5.5 Identification of Failings

4.5.5.1 Preventing Further Deaths

One purpose of the inquest system relating to custodial deaths is to identify failings which might lead to more deaths. Establishing the truth is key to this and it is clear that for some families, their main purpose for participating in an inquest is so they can know there will be no more deaths because of those failings. Three of the coroners (CO1, CO3 and CO4) all referenced the prevention of further deaths as the most important duty of a coroner. A number of participants (CO2, LA1, LA2, LA5, FA1, FA2 and FA3) believed knowing failures had been identified and further deaths therefore prevented was a legitimate interest for families. One of the coroners (CO2) thought most families were not interested in blaming anyone but in knowing if something had gone wrong, changes were then made as reducing the likelihood of further deaths was a positive result for families. A legal representative (LA1) found families were 'keen to make sure that lessons are learnt'. Another (LA2) agreed that for many families the 'best outcome' was for failings to be identified and changes made. A different lawyer (LA5) thought what most families wanted out of the process was for lessons to be learnt and if that happened, families felt it had been worthwhile participating.

Three of the family members interviewed (FA1, FA2 and FA3) were clear that their primary desire for participating in the inquest process was to know they had made a difference and ensured lessons had been learnt, so no-one else would die for the same failings as their loved ones. One of the family members (FA1) felt strongly that their need to participate was as much about making a difference for 'somebody else's son or daughter or husband', as it was for representing the deceased. Another family member (FA2) felt satisfied when the coroner identified failings and notified relevant agencies but had been devastated when they realised lessons had not been learnt and the same mistakes were still being made across the country. A legal representative (LA2) supported this, saying they found that often the most heart-breaking thing for families was to find the same issues were arising from repeated inquests, with no changes being made.

4.5.5.2 Punishment

For some families, acknowledgement of failings through apology and a promise to change damaging practices is a satisfying outcome. But for others, accountability is only achieved if those responsible for failings are punished. A number of participants linked redress with the punishment of those responsible in some way for the death (FA1, FA2, FA5, LA3, LA5 and LA6). Two of the family members interviewed (FA1 and FA2) thought accountability was far more important to families than other parties. A legal representative (LA3) thought they would only be satisfied by ensuring accountability if someone they loved died because they would want people 'paying for what they had done'. Another (LA5) thought that just because most families wanted lessons to be learnt, it did not stop them also wanting to see people who were at fault to be reprimanded publicly. A third lawyer (LA6) agreed that some families were only satisfied if holding people to account involved some aspect of punishment.

Some participants (FA1, LA3, LA5 and IPCC) noted it could be very frustrating for families that the inquest system did not punish individuals or even lead to other proceedings which meted out punishment. IPCC acknowledged an inquest was only one place where families could get justice but that families were often frustrated when negative verdicts at inquests were not followed or reflected in disciplinary or criminal proceedings. One of the legal representatives (LA5) said it was rare for families to see accountability via criminal cases, which could be very frustrating. Another (LA3) agreed it was very disappointing that there was no will to prosecute police officers for failings identified at inquests. One of the family members interviewed (FA1) said they were devastated when they realised that a critical verdict at an inquest did not automatically lead to charges or disciplinary proceedings, as it was 'not a court of law'.

Another family member (FA5) noted that although inquests did not hold individuals to account, evidence presented during the hearing could establish the need for other proceedings (criminal or disciplinary) which resulted in individuals being punished. However, one concern raised was that even where inquests resulted in disciplinary actions for State agents, such proceedings were not public but carried out behind closed doors, so families rarely knew ultimate outcomes. A lawyer (LA5) said most families preferred any disciplinary outcomes to be publicly available. One of the family participants (FA1) agreed that they were very disappointed to not know the outcome of disciplinary measures; they thought action taken against staff found to be negligent during an inquest should be publicised. Another family member (FA5) felt the inquest had not held anyone to account but thought disciplinary hearings were no better as it became clear to them that 'nothing is ever going to happen to them [the State officers]'. IPCC thought one difficulty was that families did not understand misconduct hearings focused on someone's employment record, nothing else. This meant disciplinary hearings being run along specific rules unrelated to the process of an inquest as well as usually being confidential. This was supported by an ex-police officer (ESP2), who agreed that as disciplinary hearings related to professional standards, they could not be fully publicised for good reason. They also pointed out disciplinary matters could impact on the operationality of the police, which was one reason why they should be confidential.

Holding the State to account was raised as an important issue for families; it will be dealt with later in Part 4 of the book but will be referenced here briefly in terms of how it relates to families' legitimate interests. One of the family members interviewed (FA5) thought accountability meant families witnessing people admitting mistakes and taking responsibility for any actions or inactions that contributed to a death. Another (FA1) said when the jury came back with a critical verdict, they felt 'vindicated' that those at fault had been held to account. A third family member (FA2) felt satisfied that the narrative verdict made clear where faults lay, even though individuals could not be named and there was no public acknowledgement of culpability.

It is clear that even where inquests identify failings and identify evidence that is then used in further processes to identify culpability, families often feel there is insufficient punishment of those responsible for the death of their loved one. Some families may not feel punishment is as important as preventing further deaths, but it is questionable whether accountability can be achieved if there is no punishment. This will be discussed more fully in Part 4 of the book.

4.5.5.3 Public Record

In some instances having a public record of what actually happened was referenced as very important to families, especially when State failings had been identified. The public nature of a record was seen as key for a number of reasons, as an acknowledgement of failings, a sign that lessons would be learnt and a form of reprimand. Two of the lawyers interviewed explained the importance of a public record: one (LA5) said a public record could be a form of redress for families and the other (LA3) thought families were sometimes satisfied by seeing people at fault 'called to account publicly'. They referenced

Truth and Reconciliation processes in South Africa where people responsible for deaths were publicly acknowledged but not punished and stated some families were satisfied when getting similar outcomes from the inquest system. A third legal representative (LA2) believed 'most families [...] want accountability in writing' and the only way this can come from an inquest is a negative verdict given in a public forum. One of the family members interviewed (FA1) agreed that alongside lessons being learnt, it was important that there was a public record reprimanding those responsible following any negative verdict.

The importance of inspectorate reports as the public record was raised as a concern by some, as they do not always reflect inquest verdicts. This can be because they may either be published before the inquest or written before the inquest and not amended before being published. So families were particularly concerned if failings were uncovered through the inquest hearing, but inspectorate reports did not include those failings. Four of those interviewed (FA1, FA4, LA2 and LA4) all mentioned difficulties with the public record being via the PPO reports which were not always amended to take account of new evidence established during the inquest. Two legal representatives (LA2 and LA4) said the PPO reports did not always include key failings identified during inquests: sometimes the inquest verdict 'was the complete opposite' from the investigatory report (LA2). One of the lawyers (LA4) gave an example where a PPO report commended staff for certain actions when it was proved at the inquest failure to carry out these actions were actually causative in the death. One of the family members (FA2) said they were completely supportive of reports being published but only if 'the complete and whole truth' was told. Another family member (FA4) was mortified to find the PPO report was the only public record, as it did not reflect the failings identified during the inquest. One of the lawyers interviewed (LA2) felt an inquest verdict was more important than a PPO or IPCC report as a public record, but family participants disagreed, saying PPO or IPCC reports were easily accessible to all but inquest verdicts were not. This is particularly important following deaths in psychiatric hospitals, as an inquest would be the only public record because investigations into the death by hospitals are kept as internal documents and are not publicly available at all.

In addition to PPO or IPCC reports, other public records of failings can be provided by a Rule 43 report, which coroners produce following a critical inquest verdict.[23] A report is made to agencies, identifying problems and recommending changes that should be made to prevent further deaths. Producing these reports and consequential actions will be discussed further in Chapter 6, but three

[23]Coroners are empowered to produce reports aimed at State agencies identifying any failures contributing to a death and suggested changes to prevent further deaths. The Coroners and Justice Act 2009 changed the name of these reports, so they are now 'Reports on Action to Prevent Future Deaths' (known as PFD reports) but previously they were known as Rule 43 reports; that is how interviewees referred to them, so that is how they are referenced in this book.

coroners interviewed (CO1, CO2 and CO3) all believed families generally saw Rule 43's as a positive outcome, as a public acknowledgement of failures as well as a statement of intent that steps were being taken to prevent further fatalities.

The public nature of inquests was seen as very important but participants did not feel public attendance was usual, and therefore there was little awareness of any findings. Three of the lawyers interviewed (LA1, LA2 and LA5) all pointed out it was very rare to have the public attend an inquest, partly because details about inquests were not publicly listed, so non-interested parties did not know when and where an inquest was happening.

As the public rarely attend inquests themselves, media reporting was introduced as important to informing the public. Two coroners (CO2 and CO3) said press attendance at an inquest could play an important role in informing the public. But others (LA1, LA5 and IPCC) all said that in their experience it was rare to have even local press attending an inquest. IPCC linked press interest to geography, saying contentious deaths outside of London 'never get media attention'. Three of those interviewed (LA1, IPCC and ESP1) all noted that even if there was press interest, they were unlikely to report all the details in a complex case but only certain headlining aspects. Equally, another legal representative (LA5) pointed out it was rare for inquest judgments to be made publicly available if not reported in the media.

Participants said the family do and can take on the role of disseminating the details via the press (to be discussed further in Chapter 6). Three of the legal representatives (LA2, LA3 and LA5) all felt families generally wanted press coverage of the process and a public record of the outcome. Two of the family members interviewed (FA1 and FA2) were concerned that without public dissemination of inquest verdicts, the public would never know what happened. Other participants raised situations where families had concerns about public reporting without family input due to lack of accuracy. Generally participants all agreed that families had a role in feeding into media reporting, which was vital to ensuring accuracy of the public record.

4.6 Conclusion

This chapter has looked specifically at what have been put forward as the legitimate interests for families that are linked to their legal right to participate. ECtHR has not clearly defined what a families' legitimate interests might be that need protecting, although receiving compensation has been named as one key aspect. Domestic law has gone further in stating that legitimate interests include finding the truth, knowing that State failings have been identified and families seeing for themselves that future deaths will be prevented. The interviews carried out by the author reflect this latter interpretation of what families might perceive as their legitimate interests – with hearing the truth about the circumstances surrounding a death being the most common example given. In addition, receiving redress was also seen as important – this could include compensation, an apology or even public acknowledgement of any failings. Ensuring accountability is important to families where failings have been identified – this can be through an admission of failings, but often families want to know that future deaths have been prevented, and in some cases, those held culpable for a death to be punished. However, these are not the only reasons why families may want to participate, and other benefits to families themselves were identified. Specifically, the fact that for families participating in an inquest process directly interacts with their bereavement and how participation can offer a positive impact on the grief process will be discussed in the next chapter.

Chapter 5

Grief Process

5.1 Grief Theory

This chapter looks at how the inquest process, and families' participation in particular, can affect the grief process. We have already introduced the fact that families are specifically vulnerable as those most affected by the death and therefore those that are grieving. The system recognises those that are next of kin as victims who are grieving, and in relation to human rights violations, State responses which impact on grief have to take account of possible interferences in an individual's right to a family life. In respect of an inquest process, one reason for ensuring families are able to participate is to allow them to know the truth about the circumstances of a death. In setting out their reasons for reforming the inquest system in 2004, the Government said they would be 'putting the needs of the bereaved at the centre of the new system.'[1] This recognised the particular vulnerability of people who have been bereaved. However, there is no clear acknowledgement of the impact that participation can have on the grief process, and the specific role an inquest can play in this.

Grief is a natural process following the death of a loved one and, although the process is hugely variable, situations where the response to bereavement is considered to be outside of the norm (either by the length of time grieving or by the extent of the emotional or physical responses) have been defined as complicated grief.[2] The grief process usually includes phases of numbness, distress, despair and acceptance; although it is unusual for people to experience them in logical order.[3] There is no such thing as normal bereavement, everyone has to find acceptance in their own time and in their own way before they can move on. A close bereavement can have negative effects on a person's physical and psychological well-being; including increased medication intake and depression.[4] Academic studies have identified factors which can have a negative impact on the outcome of the grief process.[5] Factors such as the relationship between the deceased and the bereaved;

[1]Home Office (2004).
[2]Stroebe, Schut, and Stroebe (1960, p. 1965).
[3]Love (2007, pp. 75–76).
[4]Stroebe et al. (1960, pp. 1962–1963).
[5]Prigerson and others (1997, p. 616), Neria and Litz (2004, p. 73).

Death in Custody, 81–88
Copyright © 2020 Jo Easton
Published under exclusive licence
doi:10.1108/978-1-83909-025-720201009

the support available to the bereaved; the context prior to the death and the circumstances of the death can all have a significant impact on bereavement.[6]

Research shows that the opportunity to express emotion, communicate concerns or problems and remember the deceased in a supportive environment can encourage a healthy grieving process.[7] Studies also suggest that how the deceased is defined in memory may affect how well the bereaved copes in the future.[8] So where there is a perception of stigma attached to a death, this has a negative impact on bereavement.[9] Perceived stigma can impact negatively on the grief process for a number of reasons; by preventing the bereaved from seeking help, reducing positive communication and memories about the deceased and limiting engagement with rituals that assist the grief process. These factors are likely to be present following a death in custody and can increase the likelihood of complicated grief.[10] Snow and McHugh argue that in cases involving deaths in custody, the bereavement process can therefore be adversely affected.[11] Families may feel shame where a death occurs in custody; particularly if there is negative reporting about the deceased and their lifestyle which leaves families feeling unable to express grief for the death. The bereavement process is then affected by the stigma that is attached to a death in custody that can result in a lack of support from friends, family and society in general.[12] Lack of support or sympathy from a bereaved person's social network is another important factor identified as increasing the likelihood of complicated grief.[13]

Bereavement following sudden or traumatic deaths has been shown to have distinct psychosocial reactions to bereavement following non-traumatic deaths.[14] When someone is bereaved through a traumatic death, there is an increased risk of them developing long-term problems such as post-traumatic stress disorder.[15] It has been suggested that grief is complicated following a traumatic death (including death by murder or suicide) due to the images that will be associated with the death; trying to avoid these painful thoughts can inhibit the healthy expression of grief.[16] Bereavement following death by suicide can be complicated for additional reasons around a family feeling that the death could have been prevented if more support had been available for the deceased; and guilt among family and friends who feel responsible in not having been able to help the deceased.[17,18] Conversely, it has been

---

[6]Love (2007).
[7]Stroebe et al. (1960, p. 1966).
[8]Campbell (1997, p. 329), Dorpat (1972, p. 121), Warren (1972, p. 112).
[9]Hung and Rabin (2009, p. 781).
[10]Love (2007, p. 78).
[11]Snow and McHugh (2000).
[12]Snow and McHugh (2000, p. 137).
[13]Aranda and Milne (2000).
[14]Dyregrov, Nordanger, and Dyregrov (2003, p. 143).
[15]Raphael and Martinek (1997), Prigerson and others (1997), Kaltman and Bonanno (2003, p. 131), Neria and Litz (2004).
[16]Dowdney (2000, p. 823).
[17]Love (2007).
[18]Snow and McHugh (2000, p. 135).

shown that, as suicide may occur not as an isolated event but after a long series of distressing events, some families report feelings of relief following a death by suicide; especially if the person who died was in pain or struggling with life.[19] However, in these cases, families indicated they felt ashamed and guilty because of feeling relief, therefore unable to express their emotions.[20]

It has been shown that interventions are significantly more helpful to the bereaved where they have proactively sought help.[21] However, if there is stigma surrounding the death, then the bereaved are less likely to seek help, even informally.[22] It has also been shown that a healthy grief process requires effective communication so the death can be 'accepted, assimilated and accommodated'.[23] Positive communication about the deceased and the circumstances surrounding their death results in positive outcomes in cases of complicated grief.[24] However, if there is stigma surrounding a death, it can impact negatively on communication in two ways. Firstly, by restricting opportunities for grief to be expressed;[25] and inhibiting communication within the bereaved family.[26] Secondly, stigma can prevent positive memories and result in the creation of negative perceptions about the deceased.[27] Studies suggest that if the deceased is remembered positively, it can be beneficial to a healthy grief process.[28] Research indicates that where children have negative outcomes following bereavement, they were most likely to have had negative perceptions about the deceased.[29] In addition, if a family feels shame about the circumstances of the death, they may isolate themselves and avoid carrying out mourning rituals such as public funerals.[30] Rituals such as funerals or memorial services have been shown to have a positive effect in helping the bereaved come to terms with a death: this can include any hearings or meetings that bring to light the circumstances of a death.[31] However, any such activities must allow the bereaved to remember the deceased in a positive way in order to be beneficial to a healthy grief process.[32] There are a number of factors that can be present following a death in custody, which make complicated grief likely; including stigma, negative perceptions about the deceased, limited

---

[19]Shepherd and Barraclough (p. 272), Snow and McHugh (2000).
[20]Snow and McHugh (2000).
[21]Stroebe et al. (1960, p. 1968).
[22]Hung and Rabin (2009), Moore and Freeman (1995, p. 40), Provini, Everett, and Pfeffer (2000, p. 1).
[23]Love (2007, p. 80).
[24]Nickman, Silverman, and Normand (1998, p. 126).
[25]Demi and Howell (1991, p. 350), Dunne-Maxim, Dunne, and Hauser (1987, p. 234), Mitchell and others (2006, p. 130).
[26]Dowdney (2004).
[27]Hung and Rabin (2009).
[28]Campbell (1997), Dorpat (1972), Warren (1972), Klass, Silverman, and Nickman (1996), Nickman et al. (1998).
[29]Silverman and others (2003, p. 335).
[30]Snow and McHugh (2000, p. 142).
[31]Stroebe et al. (p. 1966).
[32]Nickman et al. (1998).

opportunities for positive remembrance and delays in finding out the truth about how death occurred.

One successful intervention for complicated grief is 'meaning making', which involves the bereaved creating a narrative about what happened to the deceased which is coherent to them.[33] Research has indicated that retelling the narrative of a death can be a beneficial part of treatment for complicated grief.[34] Identifying the facts surrounding a death promptly can help bereaved families to create a true narrative which explains the death to their satisfaction. This can be very difficult for bereaved families if they do not know the circumstances surrounding a death because it occurred in a closed institution. It is also why it is important for bereaved families to be given accurate information about a death straight away, as access to the truth early on in the grief process is vital to ensuring the bereaved do not create a false narrative. Research has shown that changing the narrative about how a death occurred later on is confusing and tends to increase suspicion among bereaved families.[35] Snow and McHugh highlighted that the inquest is an important factor in providing the bereaved with the facts surrounding a death so they can begin to accept it.[36] This does mean, however, that if bereaved families do not know the truth about what happened until the inquest hearing, they will be unable to successfully retell the narrative of the death in a therapeutic environment at an earlier stage. In addition, if the inquest fails to assign culpability for any sudden or unexpected death, it can leave bereaved families feeling frustrated. It has been shown that if the bereaved cannot hold someone responsible for a traumatic death, they find it more difficult to appropriately express anger and resolve their grief.[37] This is exacerbated by normal feelings of anger following any bereavement, which may be expressed towards officials or authority figures.[38]

So theoretically, the inquest process has the potential to be very beneficial to a bereaved family in helping them move through the grief process. But if families cannot participate fully, and therefore do not have the opportunity to identify the true narrative about what happened soon after the death, or are unable to remember the deceased in a positive light, this can exacerbate the bereavement process and lead to a family experiencing complicated grief.

5.2 Bereavement

All participants referenced the role that an inquest plays in the grief process for families. IPCC felt it was important to remember that for families it was all 'part of the grieving process'. Participants all felt the inquest could play a part at different stages of bereavement; some saw the inquest process as just one part of the grieving process, some said the inquest verdict provided closure and others

[33]Neimeyer (2001, p. 171), Park and Folkman (1997, p. 115), Armour (2007, p. 53).
[34]Shear and others (2005, p. 2601), Neimeyer and others (2010, p. 73).
[35]McHugh and Snow (2002, p. 1).
[36]Snow and McHugh (2000, p. 148).
[37]Armour (2007, p. 62).
[38]Snow and McHugh (2000, p. 149).

said the inquest outcome allowed the grieving process to begin. All the coroner participants saw the relevance of the inquest to the grieving process. One (CO1) pointed out families were the ones who were grieving so they needed particular consideration when ensuring their participation due to their 'major emotional connection' to the case.

Participants agreed that for an inquest to have a positive impact on grief, families must be able to participate in the process, not just be given an outcome which they had not had an opportunity to influence. One legal representative (LA2) said it was not enough for families to be told the truth, they needed 'to go through the process' to accept the death. Some family participants felt participating had been beneficial in helping them work through the grieving process. Two family members (FA2 and FA5) said participating in the inquest process had played a positive part of their grieving process. Another family participant (FA3) said the inquest allowed them to work through a lot of grief so they were able to move forward with the bereavement process 'in a more settled, emotional frame'.

Most participants noted that it was only after the outcome of an inquest that families could find closure. Three coroners interviewed (CO4, CO3 and CO2) all thought participation in the inquest process could allow families to come to terms with a death and that it was clear some families 'just cannot move on until after it all [….] as the inquest drags them back' (CO2). One of these coroners (CO2) thought the inquest was undeniably part of the grieving process for families, but their participation had to be managed correctly to ensure the inquest had a constructive impact on bereavement. A lawyer interviewed (LA5) said most families wanted to 'draw a line under it' and move on once they had the inquest outcome. Another (LA6) said families could not 'move on until they've achieved' what they needed from the process. One of the ex-police officers (ESP2) agreed the inquest outcome was often actually 'the start point' of the grieving process for families.

Two participants (LA4 and PPO) said an inquest could help families leave any guilt they felt about a death behind. One of the lawyers (LA4) thought an inquest could help families know they were not at fault over the death. PPO also referenced the unresolved guilt families sometimes felt following deaths by suicide and thought well-managed inquests could help resolve this.

5.2.1 True Narrative as a Part of the Grief Process

A number of participants suggested an inquest process providing families with the truth of what happened could be an important part of a healthy grief process. They (IPCC, LA1, LA2 and LA6) all linked families getting the truth with them finding closure and moving on. One of the lawyers (LA6) thought families who participated in the inquest process needed to hear the truth, so they had a form of closure and then they felt they could 'go home to bed now'.

Most families (FA2, FA3, FA4 and FA5) said constructing a truthful narrative about the circumstances surrounding the death was a fundamental and important part of the grief process. A family member interviewed (FA2) said hearing the truth was very important, as processing all the facts allowed them to settle the narrative in their own mind. Another (FA3) felt knowing the inquest had considered everything properly before coming to a verdict provided closure. A third family member (FA4) felt until they had the truth, 'you are betwixt and between' and cannot assimilate a narrative that makes sense of all the facts. A fourth (FA5) said the inquest gave them a sense of understanding about what happened, which led to greater acceptance about the death.

It was pointed out that potential benefits to the grief process through family participation was often in practice negated by years of delays intrinsic to the system. Some participants (FA1, FA2, FA4 and LA2) made it clear the process only helped the grieving process and provided closure if details about a death were given to families in a timely manner, allowing them to integrate the facts into their narrative about the death. A legal representative (LA2) thought delayed access to information for families after a death could result in an extended grief process. This was reaffirmed by one family member (FA2), who said that while different hearings (disciplinary as well as inquest) were ongoing, it was difficult to process the grief. Another (FA1) similarly thought the length of time and complexity of the inquest effectively stopped them moving on. A different family member (FA4) felt they could not even begin grieving until the inquest process was finished.

A number of participants (LA1, LA2, FA1 and FA2) discussed the fact that if there were delays before families were given information, they were likely to have already formed a narrative to explain the death and it could be difficult for them to readjust the narrative to take into account new facts. One family member interviewed (FA2) opened up about their case, saying some of the information they were given at the time of the death was wrong and not corrected until three or four days later; when they were told the truth it was difficult to process as they felt they had already started 'going down one path' in terms of creating a narrative about the death. In their case, it was particularly heartbreaking as they had initially been told the deceased had killed themselves but later found out the truth was the deceased had actually been calling for help.

With families reporting they were unable to grieve until the process was completed, long delays have huge impacts. But the issue of families being given access to information in a timely manner throughout the process is also relevant; especially if it is years before families get the whole truth. This will be raised in Chapter 11 as a practical solution to ensuring fair and effective participation for families.

5.2.2 Representing the Deceased in a Positive Light

Another aspect of participation that is also relevant for the grieving process is that by participating, families are able to ensure the deceased is represented fairly during the process. Families have a right to participate due to their position as victims (as people directly affected by the process) but are also there to represent the deceased. The opportunity to ensure that the deceased is represented in a positive light is an important part of a healthy grief process. Most participants

(FA1, FA2, FA3, FA4, FA5, CO2, LA2, LA4, CO3 and CO4) believed families saw it as important that they were able to represent the deceased during the process. All the family participants saw themselves as representing the deceased in some way. Three family members (FA1, FA2 and FA3) all reported feeling that the State had already let their family members down so they had to fight on their behalf with one (FA1) saying, 'I needed to do it for [them]'.

In terms of the family representing the deceased, the aspect most commonly raised was that the voice of the deceased should be heard. Two family members interviewed (FA2 and FA3) both felt other parties forgot the process was about someone who had died. One (FA2) gave the example of a birthday cake being bought into the hearing during a break resulting in laughter and joy. Two other family members interviewed (FA1 and FA5) both thought it was very important for them to make sure everybody saw the deceased as a human being who was loved. One of these (FA1) said just because the deceased was in prison, 'it does not matter how you look at it, they are still our children'. The other (FA5) felt it was vital they were allowed to read a statement about 'who [the deceased] really was'.

This was not just important to families, but three coroners (CO2, CO3 and CO4) all noted it was important to allow space for the deceased as a person to be represented. One of these (CO2) felt the family were the only ones who could make sure the inquest heard 'something about the person who died'. Although half of the coroner's who were interviewed felt allowing space for the deceased to be remembered was important, some participants (LA2, LA4, FA3 and FA4) expressed disappointment that this did not always happen at inquests. One of the lawyers (LA2) said in their experience it was all too common for the coroner to not even acknowledge the families' grief, let alone provide space during the process for the deceased to be remembered.

One of the coroner participants (CO2) noted families representing the deceased was particularly important when the details surrounding the death might put the deceased in 'a bad light'. Other participants (FA1, FA4, FA5, LA1 and LA6) agreed: all felt that State agencies tried to blame the deceased in some way, often by referencing their background negatively. One family member (FA5) felt that straight after the death, the initial investigators focused on the background of the deceased rather than the circumstances surrounding the death. Another (FA4) felt State parties were trying to put the blame on the deceased and it was their responsibility to set the record straight; else the process 'can find [the deceased] guilty', with the behaviour of the deceased being blamed for causing the death.[39] This was particularly relevant when individuals had died in prison following a conviction, as their offending behaviour could become central to the process without referencing positive aspects of their lives (including family or hobbies). One legal representative (LA2) referenced inquests where prison authorities tried

[39]See discussion around the Black Lives Matter movement in the United States involving police shootings of black people. For example, Smiley and Fakunle (2016, p. 350), Bonilla and Rosa (2015, p. 4).

to focus on 'some weakness in the deceased'. Another (LA1) pointed out this was not just in relation to deaths in prison but gave the example of the Jean Charles de Menezes shooting where the deceased was blamed and denigrated in the press. A different lawyer (LA6) felt the involvement of the press was a specific reason why families needed an opportunity to represent the deceased so they could challenge negative and unfounded claims made in the media. Family participation ensures a more rounded picture of the deceased is presented and they are not demonised due to an over reliance on one aspect of their lives. Obviously, representing the deceased and ensuring they are presented in a rounded way is an important reason for families to want to participate, but it also has an instrumental benefit as it can ensure a fair outcome. So ensuring the process accurately reflects who the deceased was can guarantee a balanced process. This will be discussed further in Part 4 of the book.

5.3 Conclusion

This chapter has set out how important it is for a bereaved family to be able participate in an inquest process following a death in custody. Specific factors that often relate to a death in custody mean that families may often suffer from complicated grief. The likelihood that deaths in custody are unexpected, and occur in situations which mean families will not know the full circumstances surrounding the death, may mean it will be more difficult for a healthy grief process. In addition, the fact that there may be stigma attached to any interaction the deceased had with the criminal justice system makes it more difficult for families to access processes which can assist them coming to terms with the death (such as public statements of grief). The inquest process itself offers families the opportunity to find out the true details surrounding a death, which is important in allowing them to construct a narrative explaining the death. It can also offer the chance for them to represent the deceased in a positive light and counter any stigmatising narratives that may have portrayed the deceased negatively. This all means that if families are allowed to participate fully, including being given access to information about the death early on in the process, then this can benefit their grief process.

The next chapter sets out the empirical research analysed in Chapters 4 and 5 in the wider context of existing structures and the understanding offered by relevant theoretical frameworks.

Chapter 6

Participation Provides Benefits to Families

This chapter brings the empirical evidence gathered through the interviews into the wider context. The author identifies how the existing legal framework allows certain benefits to families to be considered in relation to participation as well as noting that some benefits are not currently considered. Participants understood the importance of the legal framework setting out the rights families had in relation to participation but it was felt that ensuring participation for families was still very much left to the discretion of the coroner. Although the main themes of learning the truth, identifying culpability and preventing other deaths are established in law as legitimate interests that families may have, participants felt that the interests of families were not effectively represented for two reasons. Firstly, how the inquest process relates to a family's grief process is not recognised; for example, delays to a family learning the truth negatively impacts on how that family process their grief. Secondly, the fact families represent the deceased through the process is not acknowledged – especially in cases where the deceased is often 'othered' as a prisoner or criminal. These two aspects need to be taken into account for the effective protection of families' interests. So the conclusion to this section is that the legitimate interests as set out in law address some benefits to family participation but coroners and other decision-makers need to better understand other benefits to families if they are able to ensure their right to participate in the inquest is adequately protected.

6.1 Legitimate Interests of Families

Participants generally felt families should be able to participate as those most affected by the death as victims in their own right; rather than solely as representatives of the deceased, who are the direct victims of any Article 2 violation. Where families were participating in an inquest as victims, participants suggested their legitimate interests might include the right to the truth, financial compensation or receiving an apology. All of these could come under the broad definition of families receiving redress for any violation. Participants generally thought it was difficult to clearly define what might constitute the legitimate interests of a family partly because families are all unique and partly because they thought legitimate interests could be very context specific. Participants who were legal

Death in Custody, 89–96
Copyright © 2020 Jo Easton
Published under exclusive licence
doi:10.1108/978-1-83909-025-720201010

representatives said there was difficulty in defining what a family's legitimate interests might be because, firstly they might not know themselves, and secondly their interests could change during the lengthy process. It was acknowledged that a family's interests may divert from what their own lawyers might see as important, let alone what decision-makers may see as families' legitimate interests. Case law establishes assessing State culpability, learning the truth and knowing future deaths are prevented as possible legitimate interests for families.[1] It was important for the author to analyse what participants saw as legitimate interests for families, to assess whether the law fully covers all interests.

Participants said they thought families all had different reasons for being involved in an inquest; although understanding what happened to their loved one was often fundamental. Deaths in custody usually occur in a closed environment; even deaths following interaction with the police usually occur when the individual is already in police custody. This means it is unlikely for family members to be present immediately prior to any death and therefore they rely on the police or prison staff who were present to tell them what happened. The importance of participation in a process looking at a death which occurred in a closed environment was raised as key by participants. The likelihood that families would have no other way of finding out about the circumstance surrounding a death was central to why participants said participation in the inquest process was vital, so families could understand for themselves what happened. It was also pointed out (particularly in reference to deaths that occurred in prison) that families may have had limited contact with the deceased prior to their death; with the inquest being the only opportunity for families to hear about the circumstances prior to any death (not just the circumstances causative to any death).

Participants agreed that for many families, their main aims in participating were to ensure mistakes or failings were identified and State agents were held to account for any actions which were causally linked to a death. Accountability will be considered later in Part 4 but identifying issues that were causally linked to a death was thought to be important to families for two reasons. Firstly, any finding of negligence could be linked to a family receiving compensation through civil action. Secondly, participants felt it was very important for families to hear acknowledgement of any mistakes and be assured that lessons had been learnt so future deaths could be prevented.

One legitimate interest referenced by both families and their legal representatives was being able to access the civil system to be awarded compensation if an inquest verdict found that failings or negligence contributed to a death. Civil cases were referred to as important by participants, primarily as compensation could assist families with the costs of participating in the inquest process. Families were clear that participating in a complex inquest could be very expensive for a number of reasons and in particular because of the cost of specialist legal representation. The expense of specialist legal representation will be discussed in Part 5 of the book but it is worth noting here that some legal representatives said civil cases

---

[1] *Letts v Lord Chancellor* (2015).

were the only way families and their lawyers managed to recoup some of their costs. Participants made it clear civil compensation did not always cover all the costs, especially when additional expenses included the need to take time off work, travel costs and funding child care for multiple meetings and hearings over a period of years, during a lengthy and drawn-out inquest process.

Participants also thought that receiving compensation represented an acknowledgement on behalf of the State authorities that they had failed in their duty of care to the deceased. Family participants referred to the importance of some sort of apology from the State, which could take different forms, including simply stating regret for the death, acknowledging mistakes or failings, making firm commitments that lessons had been learnt and actually apologising for any culpability in the death. All of these have distinct nuances, as State officials can regret the death occurred without acknowledging responsibility for it but it is clear that for some families, even the former can provide comfort. For some families, the most important thing to result from the State apologising for a death is an assurance that future deaths would be prevented. This form of redress for families is linked to holding the State to account but relies on the truth being established. Accountability can mean many different things, but the small part an inquest may play relates to ensuring the facts of a death are established and any State failings identified.

Participants understood the importance of the legal framework protecting the right of families to participate in the process. European case law only gives families a right to participate in order to 'protect their legitimate interests', which leaves broad discretion to decision-makers on how to ensure compliance with this aspect of Article 2. Domestic case law defines legitimate interests as including being able to assess State culpability, learn the truth and be confident future deaths will be prevented.[2] Participants pointed out that domestic law provided more specific guidance to coroners as certain rights are established in statute (such as the right to be present or to send a representative to witness the post-mortem) which give families, lawyers and coroners a reference point.[3] Such clarity is beneficial to coroners if they are interpreting Article 2 protections, as participants felt that often families and their legal representatives had to remind decision-makers of the rights established in law to ensure families managed to access the process. The lack of protections if Article 2 is not engaged was referenced as a problem, specifically in relation to deaths that occur in secure hospitals.

It is also important for the right to participate in a process that affects you to be fully respected. This requires an interested party not just to observe a process, but have an opportunity to influence it. In relation to families participating in an inquest, in order to be able to influence the outcome, they must be able to participate in the investigatory part of the process, before an inquest hearing is actually held. It is clear that this is not fully understood by those working in the system, and, in fact, some decision-makers raised concerns about families being

[2] *Letts v Lord Chancellor* (2015), para 70.

[3] The Coroners (Inquests), Rules 2013; The Coroners (Investigations) Regulations 2013, No 1629.

able to influence a process unduly. Family participation should not be limited unless required by law, and ensuring a family is supported by a specialist legal representative can be one way of making sure they understand why and when their influence has to be restricted. Conversely, it is important that decision-makers (especially coroners) understand that a right to participate includes a right to influence the process, and they must therefore ensure families are offered relevant opportunities to do this.

6.2 Participation Impacts on Grief Process of Bereaved Families

Learning the truth is set out as a legitimate interest for families in UK case law, but participants also linked learning the truth with assisting families to come to terms with their grief; with the facts established at an inquest playing a key part in families getting closure following a death.[4] This can be linked to grief theory, as described above, following sudden deaths which suggests that knowing the truth about what happened can be important for a bereaved family member to be able to process their grief following a death. Family participants said how important it was to know the truth; and for what they were told to make sense. One family member (FA4 Father) said 'If it falls into place, you accept it. Fine, if it is done properly'. It is therefore very important that families have confidence in the facts as presented either by State agencies or the outcome of the inquest; so they can trust the narrative and are able to then move on through the grief process.

Participants were also clear that any delays before they were given the truth had a negative impact on their grief. Access to information as soon as possible is therefore very important in helping families create an understanding of what happened. It was also clear that mis-information at an early stage could be damaging for two reasons; firstly it could be painful for families, and secondly because it allows families to create an inaccurate narrative. Mis-information also means that if families were initially given information that was wrong, it makes it harder for them to trust what they are told by the State later on. This impacts on bereavement, as families can then only trust evidence they have seen and tested for themselves. This in turn makes the opportunity to participate even more important.

Effective participation can therefore benefit the grief process, if families can be confident of the facts about a death presented to them in a timely manner and therefore incorporate the facts into a narrative to help them understand the death. However, lack of effective participation, which leaves families without access to, or trust in, what they are told about the circumstances around a death can decrease opportunities for families to go through a healthy grief process following a death.

Any death in custody that results in a complex inquest is likely to take years before the investigation process is completed, with some families waiting 10 years

[4] *Letts v Lord Chancellor* (2015).

before an inquest hearing is held. If learning the truth is an important step in bereavement and the truth is only settled at an inquest hearing, this has obvious implications on families suffering complicated grief. Even for those families who process a death and manage to move on in some positive ways, attendance at an inquest hearing years later can open up old wounds. Also, there is the likelihood that additional details about how the death occurred only come to light during the hearing, which means families may have constructed a narrative to help them understand how the death happened; and years later, that narrative could be shown to be wrong or based on inaccurate facts. This leaves families having to re-create a new narrative to fit new facts. Consequently, the inquest process itself may prolong the grief process, if family participation does not ensure they are informed of all the facts at an early stage.[5] Participants felt participation in the inquest process could benefit a families' grief process, but only if participation was fair and effective. Where families' participation involves accessing adequate support and information about the process and the death itself, it can reduce the likelihood of complicated grief and help families come to terms with their bereavement.

6.3 Representing the Deceased

An additional legitimate interest for families was identified by participants as the opportunity to represent the deceased throughout the inquest process. This was also linked to a healthy grief process, as being offered the opportunity to remember the deceased in a positive light, and reducing any stigma around the deceased both help families process their grief. Families and coroner participants were clear that it was important for the deceased to be remembered and referenced respectfully during the inquest. Families welcomed any space during the process which allowed all parties to remember the deceased. Families and legal representatives felt very strongly that the voice of the deceased could be lost during the process; this was thought to be particularly important where the actions of the deceased were called into question or in some way argued to be causative in their death. If people die in either police or prison custody, there is sometimes a presumption that they are in some way at fault, with the inquest often being the only place this presumption can be questioned. Even if the deceased was shown to be involved in illegal activities; as one family member (FA1) said '[the deceased] went to prison to lose [their] liberty, not [their] life'.

Coroner participants gave examples of how they ensured the voice of the deceased was heard; including allowing families the opportunity to read out a statement about the deceased. This was important as it allowed families to counter any negative descriptions about the deceased. Families felt it was also very important to ensure other aspects or dimensions of the deceased to be referenced during the process, so their life beyond any interaction with the criminal justice system was recognised. Families felt very strongly that part of

---

[5]Snow and McHugh (2000, p. 144).

their role in participating was to ensure an alternative and fuller account of the deceased was reflected during the process.

The more media interest there is in a case, the more important it is for families to ensure different sides of the deceased are represented. This can be for two reasons: firstly, that families want an opportunity to correct misapprehensions about the deceased which have already been publically disseminated and secondly, if there has not been any media reporting before the inquest but there are press present during the hearing, the bereaved family want to ensure there is a fair and representative record of the deceased. Mis-representations or inaccuracies in the press can either involve skewed and unfair views of the deceased or a false and misleading reporting of the facts surrounding the death. The first situation is often inevitable in relation to a death in prison where, by definition, the deceased is perceived by the public as an offender convicted of a serious crime which posed such risk that it was necessary to imprison them. Academics agree that there is a stigma to being identified as a prisoner as they are generally demonised by the public.[6] Specifically, prisoners are often seen as having 'achieved stigma' due to their own behaviour, so the public are less likely to be sympathetic towards them.[7] This ignores issues relating to whether the deceased was on remand at the time of death (and therefore not convicted of any offence)[8] or a failure of understanding that imprisonment does not automatically mean the offender was violent.[9] Of course, regardless of what offence may have been committed, a prisoner is still a human being with inherent dignity and ensuring they are seen for more than their crime is an important point relating to families wanting the deceased to be fairly represented during an inquest. Although deaths following interactions with police involve people who have not been convicted but are merely suspected of a crime, public opinion can still be very negative about someone who the police arrest, as it has been shown that just being accused of a crime by authorities can result in stigmatisation.[10] Deaths resulting from police use of force often lead to media reports of the victim's behaviour being responsible for the police actions: including phrases like 'resisting arrest' and 'hostile manner'.[11] Of course, a large

---

[6]Gaubatz (1995), Young (1999), Harding (2003), LeBel (2008), Hirschfield and Piquero (2010), Goffman (1963).

[7]Falk (2001).

[8]11–13% of prison population in England and Wales from January to June 2016 were on remand: 68–71% of those on remand in the same timeframe were untried. See Table 1.1, Prison Population Statistics at https://www.gov.uk/Government/uploads/system/uploads/attachment_data/file/541229/population-q1-2016.xlsx.

[9]The proportion of individuals in prison sentenced to an immediate custody sentence for a non-violent offence was on average 47% from January to June 2016. See Table 1.2b, Prison Population Statistics at https://www.gov.uk/Government/uploads/system/uploads/attachment_data/file/541229/population-q1-2016.xlsx. Violent offences are defined by the Ministry of Justice as violence against the person, sexual offences and robbery: all other offences are defined as non-violent. See response to FOI here: https://www.whatdotheyknow.com/request/non_violent_crime.

[10]Schwartz and Skolnick (1962).

[11]Lawrence (2000).

number of police interactions are with the most vulnerable people, not necessarily those suspected of serious crime but where the behaviour of people suffering from an acute mental health condition is arguably being seen as combative by police.[12]

It is also true that families generally do not have pre-existing links to the media when a death occurs, so any initial narratives about the deceased will be presented by State agencies. Snow and McHugh found the public nature of the inquest (with the possibility of media presence) can make families feel powerless.[13] For example, Mark Duggan was portrayed in the media as an incredibly dangerous criminal, although he only had a criminal record for two minor offences.[14] In this case, the family found it challenging to persuade the media to present an alternative view.

The second situation where misleading details about the circumstances surrounding a death might be presented in the media also links to the fact that initial details about a death (whether in prison or in police custody) will be released by the State agencies. As families would be unlikely to know the facts immediately after a death, if there are any inaccuracies, they cannot correct them at this stage. Many people will remember press reports about Jean Charles de Menezes jumping over a barrier and running from police before he was shot on the tube, but will not realise this report was inaccurately based on a witness statement given to the media. In fact the witness was referring to one of the police officers, not Mr de Menezes, who actually calmly went through the barrier and walked down to the tube.[15] It is particularly important that families are able to counter distorted views like this as they can become embedded in the consciousness of the public. Where families are well supported by experienced legal representatives, they may be able to present alternative views about the deceased or the death itself but if not, it is only where the press report inquest hearings that families can have the opportunity to ensure there is a fair and accurate representation of the deceased in the media. The interviews showed that a key benefit to fair and effective participation for families is so they are able to ensure the deceased is fairly represented both during the inquest hearing and consequently in media reporting.

6.4 Conclusion

It is therefore clear that the current legal references to what may constitute the legitimate interests of families, and therefore key benefits to the families themselves of being able to participate, do not fully cover all important aspects. This research has supported the relevance of families being able to participate so they can see for themselves any State culpability for a death, understand the true circumstances of a death and be confident that any failings have been addressed

[12]Constabulary HMsIo (2015).

[13]Snow and McHugh (2000, p. 144).

[14]http://www.independent.co.uk/news/uk/crime/mark-duggan-among-europes-most-feared-and-violent-criminals-before-his-death-sparked-the-2011-riots-8835363.html.

[15]http://news.bbc.co.uk/1/hi/uk/4177082.stm; Independent Police Complaints Commission (2007).

so future deaths are prevented. However, it is clear that there are further benefits to families participating, connected with a healthy grief process which requires understanding the true narrative of a death early on, and also being able to remember the deceased in a positive light. The impact that participation can have on these two key aspects of grief is not currently acknowledged, which means that when ensuring a families' right to participate is enabled in order to protect their interests, the impact on a healthy grief process is not reflected. In addition, the interviews highlight the current process does not always allow families to influence the process (either through the investigation, or via influencing verdicts), and some decision-makers raised concerns about allowing families undue influence to the process. This illustrates a lack of understanding about what a right to participate must constitute, and suggests families' right is not being fully respected. All of these factors only focus on what the benefits of participation might be to a family themselves. Part 4 will go beyond this narrow focus, and look at what wider benefits might result from families being able to participate in an inquest.

Part 4
Bereaved Families Holding the State to Account

This part of the book includes three separate chapters which all relate to how family participation can ensure there is accountability following deaths in custody by providing scrutiny of State actions that might have either caused or not prevented a death where there was an established duty of care on the State. It is vital for a democratic society that empowers State agents or agencies to restrain or detain individuals for the overall benefit of society to make sure they have a robust system which will scrutinise any State actions, identify failings and hold people to account. As has been shown, the inquest system is the primary process for investigating deaths in custody, so how it provides accountability is vitally important. As accountability relates to public confidence in the actions of the State, the transparency of any system holding the State to account can impact not just on the legitimacy of the system itself but also the legitimacy of State actions. Therefore the ability of the inquest system to hold State agents or agencies to account is intrinsically important, as are any factors that affect the perceived legitimacy of the system.

Ensuring effective and fair participation of bereaved families is linked to making sure the inquest process is fair; and a fair process can have both an instrumental and intrinsic impact. An instrumental impact focuses on whether factors directly influence the outcome. So a fair process would only be important if it had the effect of producing a fair outcome. Allan argued the fairness of procedures were important primarily in justifying the accuracy and therefore validity of outcomes.[1] However, just focusing on the instrumental impact ignores the intrinsic value of a fair process beyond whether it directly ensures a fair outcome. A fair process can have intrinsic value in two ways. Firstly, public perceptions that a fair process will lead to a fair outcome will increase their confidence in a process that is seen as fair. Secondly, ensuring a fair process has value in of itself, regardless of whether it impacts on the outcome, as it is morally important for the State to act in a fair way.

The first intrinsic benefit is linked to an understanding that a fair process makes a fair outcome more likely, even if it cannot actually guarantee it. Fair procedures can minimise the dangers of coming to incorrect decisions, therefore

[1] Allan (1998, p. 497).

maximising the opportunity of the outcome being correct.[2] This is distinct from the instrumental benefit as argued by Allan for a number of reasons. Firstly, a fair process cannot guarantee a fair outcome. Secondly, whether an outcome is fair or not can be disputed. There can be a difficulty in objectively judging the fairness or correctness of the outcome as perceptions of fairness of outcome may differ among participants. So it is therefore important that regardless of the actual impact on outcome, participating in a fair process increases the perception that a fair outcome will be achieved.[3] Fuller has pointed out that if 'the function of law is to create an orderly interaction among citizens' then the perception of how a fair outcome is best achieved will be fundamentally important.[4] So as fair procedures offer the highest opportunity for a fair outcome, perceptions of fairness will then have a positive impact on the belief in the fairness in the system.

There is a second intrinsic benefit of a fair process regardless of whether it increases the likelihood of a fair or accurate outcome. This follows Kant's belief that to act in a moral way has value regardless of the outcome.[5] In respect to justice, Lerner argued that there was such an intrinsic value to justice.[6] This is particularly relevant if the actions of State authorities are being scrutinised. Kessler described due process as important not just because procedural rules have the benefit of providing a mechanism for ensuring the truth but because compliance with certain principles also ensures the State does not use its power arbitrarily.[7] So the State complying with basic principles of fairness is of benefit to ensure the legitimacy of the State as a democratic authority.

In summary, incorporating both the distributive and procedural theories of justice, a fair process can have instrumental and intrinsic value. The instrumental value of a fair process relates to the effect on the outcome; so factors like the quality of decision-making and the parties having the opportunity to influence the process affect whether a fair outcome is achieved. A fair process can also have intrinsic value, distinct from the impact on the outcome but often linked to the morality of fair treatment for all. So this part of the book will consider both instrumental and intrinsic impacts of a fair inquest system allowing effective and fair participation for bereaved families. The instrumental effect of bereaved families participating in an inquest is considered in Chapter 7: it looks at how families can have a direct impact on the outcome of an inquest, as well as instigating change in the law or policy by campaigning or bringing legal challenges. The intrinsic value offered by families participating in the inquest process focuses on increasing the legitimacy of the process, and this is described in Chapter 8.

Bereaved families can benefit the likelihood the inquest system holds State agents to account in different ways. The first is an instrumental effect, as by increasing the likelihood that an inquest will reach a fair outcome, families can

---

[2]Newman (1985, p. 1648).
[3]Greenberg and Folger (1983).
[4]Fuller (1969, p. 229).
[5]Kant and Gregor (1996).
[6]Lerner (1982).
[7]Kessler (2004, pp. 1213–1214).

ensure any failings by the State are identified. The second way relates to the role some families take on to disseminate and publicise outcomes, which increases the transparency of the process. The third way families benefit accountability is by improving the intrinsic value of the system by increasing the perceived legitimacy of the system itself. The author relied on procedural justice theory to link fair participation of participants in a process to increased legitimacy, and this research proves this theory is relevant for inquest processes. Chapter 9 considers how families' participation can ensure the State is held to account in relation to any failings relating to a death in custody.

Chapter 7

Instrumental Effect of Family Participation

This is the first chapter that looks at the wider benefits that can arise where families are able to participate fairly and effectively. It introduces the instrumental effect that family participation can have on the outcome of an inquest. The author uses the empirical evidence to explain how families' involvement in the process can ensure a fair and accurate outcome, as well as taking a lead role in disseminating those outcomes. The interviews linked the role of a bereaved family participating in an inquest to ensuring State accountability in a number of ways. Firstly, participants suggested families have an instrumental effect by optimising the likelihood an inquest would reach a fair and accurate outcome. This happens in two main ways; by providing or uncovering evidence to be presented at the inquest and by scrutinising the evidence. Although some coroners could carry out this scrutinising role, difficulties with lack of time or resources as well as the need to be seen as being unbiased meant it was thought families were better placed to take on this role. Effective participation therefore increases the likelihood that the final outcome will be fair and accurate. Secondly, families were argued to play a key role in disseminating the inquest outcomes, which is particularly relevant where media interest is either non-existent or inconsistent. Dissemination of inquest outcomes can ensure any lessons to be learnt reach beyond the specific institutions involved in a death, but it is also important that the outcomes of any processes holding the State to account are publicised. Thirdly, families were argued to drive through positive change; both in calling for any necessary reforms to prevent deaths and improving the inquest system itself. Obviously all the case law references earlier in the book, all relied on families bringing cases to push for change, but three very specific examples are given here of how families have directly impacted on improving the effectiveness of the inquest process in holding the State to account following deaths in custody.

Death in Custody, 101–118
Copyright © 2020 Jo Easton
Published under exclusive licence
doi:10.1108/978-1-83909-025-720201012

7.1 Instrumental Impact: Ensuring Inquests Hold the State to Account

7.1.1 Purpose of an Inquest

The primary purpose of an inquest is to ascertain who the deceased was, how, when and where they died.[1] However, the Coroner's and Justice Act 2009 states an inquest must also ensure HRA rights are not breached by ascertaining how the death occurred.[2] Where the inquest system in England and Wales is the primary way Article 2 requirements are met, this should include ensuring any State agents culpable for a death are identified.[3] All participants linked the purpose of the inquest system with the aim of ensuring State agents were held to account for their actions. Although participants interviewed understood there were limitations as to what accountability could be achieved by the inquest process, as punishment is not a possible outcome; it was felt that ensuring failings were identified and publicised was still an important purpose of the process. Both PPO and IPCC were clear the purpose of their investigations were to identify failings by State bodies which might have contributed to a death, with inquests playing an important role in ensuring accountability. One legal representative (LA6) said there was recognition that the inquest system was 'one of the few ways in which you can begin to bring about a modicum of accountability for a system'.

All participants thought accountability via the inquest system went beyond identifying failures or culpability but ensuring lessons were learnt to prevent further deaths. Two coroners interviewed (CO1 and CO3) agreed it was 'terribly important' (CO3) to make sure any failures were identified and therefore not repeated so the likelihood of future deaths was reduced; with one (CO1) saying 'the only useful thing [they could do] was to stop other people dying'. Another coroner (CO4) thought there were two aspects to accountability: the first being identifying culpability for a death (which the inquest was not able to do) but the second was ensuring that lessons were learnt and future deaths prevented, which is where the inquest system had a fundamental part to play. A legal representative (LA2) said the law was very clear that an inquest verdict should record failings related to a death and Rule 43 should be used to identify changes needed to prevent future deaths.[4] Two family members (FA1 and FA2) both thought inquests should identify such changes; with one (FA2) saying it was 'ridiculous' for lessons not to be learnt considering the cost involved with a complex inquest.

A number of issues were raised by participants relating to whether the inquest system worked effectively to identify culpability. Two problems with the inquest system itself were identified; firstly, that the scope of inquests were limited so that failures which were either not directly linked to a death or by agencies not party to the inquest were often not considered. Secondly, the fact an inquest cannot name

---

[1]Coroner's Rules 1984. No 552, Rule 36; Coroners and Justice Act 2009, Section 5.

[2]Coroners and Justice Act 2009, Section 5.

[3]See Section 2.3.4.

[4]See Chapter 5; *n*6.

any individuals who the jury might consider to be liable for a death was mentioned as restricting the opportunity for establishing culpability.

In relation to ensuring all systemic failures were identified, one lawyer (LA6) said inquests were meant to do this. However, one of the family members interviewed (FA2) felt there was no opportunity for systemic issues to be identified and resolved (as you would if you held a corporation to account for any deaths). Another lawyer (LA4) thought all systemic failings were rarely identified due to limitations related to the scope of verdicts, so failings could only be mentioned if they contributed to the death. So a failure in procedure could be identified that did not actually contribute to the death being investigated but could be a risk for the future; for example a failure to carry our regular checks on someone who was at risk of harming themselves. A senior police officer (SP1) identified another problem as the remit of an inquest only focusing on the immediate circumstances relating to a death, not what may have been organisational failings that ultimately led to a death. So, for example, if a person killed themselves in police custody, the people involved in arresting and detaining the person were investigated but not the wider health service that might have failed the person previously.

Some participants (IPCC, PPO, CO4, LA1, LA6 and FA2) mentioned the fact that inquests were not allowed to identify who might be culpable for a death as a challenge to ensuring accountability. Both IPCC and PPO said neither the investigation nor inquest could apportion blame and had to identify what happened without naming any individual who might be responsible for the death. One coroner (CO4) said while this allowed inquests to focus on making sure lessons were learnt from a death, it also meant no individual was held to account. A legal representative (LA6) said inquests were meant to assess accountability but were not able to judge liability even though European jurisprudence indicated these were 'almost synonymous'. Legally inquests are not allowed to apportion blame but two participants pointed out that it was often clear which individuals were to blame, even though they could not be named in a verdict. One of the family members (FA2) felt the narrative verdict made it quite clear who the jury thought was to blame; 'it was obvious who they meant' even though they could not name names. A lawyer (LA1) agreed that although an unlawful killing verdict could not name someone, often the truth was everyone who participated in the inquest knew who was culpable.

Although participants raised concerns about the limitations which prevented the inquest system effectively holding the State to account, generally participants felt the biggest problems related to the lack of State response following negative inquest verdicts. The 1984 Coroners Rules set out the power for coroners to write a 'Rule 43' report to any agencies identifying failures that contributed to the death, as well as making suggestions for necessary changes which should happen to prevent further deaths.[5] The Coroners and Justice Act 2009 made changes to the provisions of these reports, including making it a statutory duty (instead of being discretionary) for coroners to order 'Reports on Action to Prevent Future

---

[5]Coroner's Rules 1984. No 552, Rule 43.

Deaths' (known as PFD reports).[6] However, the reports will be referred to as Rule 43 reports in this book.[7] One coroner (CO1) said Rule 43's were very important 'to protect other people from dying'. Two others (CO2 and CO4) believed their power to ensure lessons were learnt came from the fact that State agencies had to respond to Rule 43's and explain what steps had been taken to address identified failings. However, an ex-police officer (ESP1) pointed out a Rule 43 only required a response; there was usually no follow-up. One family member interviewed (FA2) agreed, saying agencies only reported back what steps had been taken to address failings but no one ever checked up to ensure these changes were sufficient or complete. A legal representative (LA2) suggested that there should be a team following up on Rule 43's to make sure necessary changes were made. The Chief Coroner now collates PFDs and they are published on the Internet, but there is still no process to check whether specific changes have been carried out.

Some participants (LA2, LA3, LA4 and SP1) said even if there was no follow-up on Rule 43 reports, they could still be important in achieving change by providing a public record of identified systemic failings. Three legal representatives (LA2, LA3 and LA4) all thought public Rule 43's could be used to push agencies to make necessary changes. A senior police officer (SP1) agreed, saying publication of Rule 43's was one way to ensure a State agency responded to the report. Although one coroner (CO4) agreed it was important Rule 43's were made public, they acknowledged that conversely this made agencies fight hard to prevent them being given and the fact Rule 43's were public inhibited some coroners from making them. This was illustrated by the views of two participants (CO1 and SP1) who questioned whether Rule 43 reports were the most effective way to bring about change; both believed if coroners had private constructive dialogue with State agencies, there was sometimes no need for a public document. One lawyer (LA2) thought the most effective coroners were those who produced Rule 43's and also engaged with relevant institutions to find out what changes had occurred. Two participants (SP1 and LA4) agreed the most important thing (regardless of whether a Rule 43 was public or not) was whether State agencies provided evidence when necessary changes had been made. It is inimical that critical Rule 43's are seen as important to instigate change as they require resources to be directed towards correcting failings but because of this, State agencies fight harder to prevent them being ordered.

One of the concerns raised by participants related to the fact that coroners took very different approaches as to ordering Rule 43's. Some participants interviewed (LA1, LA2, LA5 and SP1) said coroners ordered Rule 43's in different circumstances; with some coroners producing a lot of reports and others none at all. The main differences in approach related to whether the necessary changes had already been made by State agencies. Due to delays in the system, participants said years often passed between a death and the inquest hearing, which meant agencies often informed coroners that changes had been made in the interim period. Two lawyers (LA1 and LA4) said in such cases, some coroners

[6]Coroners and Justice Act 2009, Schedule 5

[7]Partly because participants were referencing the old-style reports.

would agree not to order a Rule 43 report, whereas others would still produce a report so there was a public record of the identified failings. One coroner (CO3) said the only reason for ordering a Rule 43 was to prevent deaths, so if the necessary changes had been made, there would be no need to order a report. Some participants (LA1, LA4 and LA5) identified a problem with only ordering a Rule 43 report if changes had not been made, as this did not allow for any national learning to occur. So one prison might have made the necessary changes to prevent a death but if a Rule 43 was not made, other institutions might not be aware of the potential problem. A coroner interviewed (CO4) said before making a Rule 43, they considered not just whether the necessary changes had already been made by the institution in question but also whether similar failings might be a problem elsewhere. Another (CO2) agreed Rule 43's could be useful in sharing concerns so others could learn lessons from a death.

Another concern raised by participants relating to inadequate State responses to inquest verdicts was where neglect or unlawfulness was identified during an inquest but no prosecutions followed. One family member interviewed (FA2) felt the lack of criminal proceedings in cases where neglect was identified limited accountability and made them feel the process was just 'a huge exercise to clear the [State]'. Two lawyers (LA1 and LA3) said lack of prosecutions following negative inquest verdicts limited accountability as 'the desire or the will to prosecute police officers has been poor' (LA3). Another (LA5) agreed, saying it was very frustrating for families when there was no way of 'getting accountability through the criminal law'. One legal representative (LA3) thought prosecutions were only due to public pressure after campaigns led by bereaved families.

So the interviews established a number of fundamental problems that limit the capacity of the inquest system to hold the State to account fully. Some of these are structural (such as the restriction on an inquest naming an individual deemed to be culpable for a death), and others related to the discretion offered to the coroner. Some of this discretion has been reduced slightly by the Coroners and Justice Act change from Rule 43s to PFDs, but the wider discretion left to the coroner as to managing the inquest can still limit what failings are identified. And although there is more public dissemination of PFDs (therefore allowing wider institutional learning), the lack of State follow-up – either to check changes have been made to prevent further deaths or to punish individuals responsible – is still a problem. The next section will look at this and other roles families play in enhancing accountability via the inquest system.

7.1.2 Impact of Bereaved Families Participating on Optimising a Fair Outcome

This section considers whether participants felt family participation had a positive impact on achieving a fair outcome of an inquest. One coroner interviewed (CO1) was clear an inquest was not specifically for the family so their participation should only be allowed if it helped achieve a fair outcome. A number of ways this could happen were identified, including the fact the family play a role in scrutinising the evidence, can ensure the process is equitable and sometimes even provide additional information relating to a death.

7.1.2.1 Family Provide Scrutiny

Participants felt the most important impact on an outcome from family participation was through scrutinising the evidence. All participants felt that for inquests following a death in custody, cross-examination and scrutiny of the evidence was vital in ensuring a fair outcome. One lawyer (LA1) said whenever it was possible the State might be responsible for a death, scrutiny had to be stringent. Another (LA2) agreed, saying without cross-examination of witnesses during the inquest, you would not get 'the proper verdict'. A third legal representative (LA6) said good cross-examination could be 'very effective, teasing out what really happened'. A senior police officer (SP1) agreed the 'British method is that evidence is subject to scrutiny'. An ex-police officer (ESP2) thought somebody had 'to be in a position to probe and test' the evidence, otherwise there could be no confidence that the system would reach the correct outcome.

A legal representative (LA5) pointed out the need for families to scrutinise the evidence depended on the quality of the investigation itself. Another (LA3) felt the two State investigators (PPO and IPCC) were 'hopeless' and that it was therefore families and their legal teams who had to examine the evidence to find the truth. Two other lawyers (LA2 and LA4) had experienced inquests where the verdict had been the complete opposite to the PPO report due to the scrutiny of the evidence during the inquest process. One of these lawyers (LA4) said 'in a PPO report [it] is regarded as a positive, and by the time we get to the inquest it's turned into a negative'. They gave an example where (even though an ACCT document had been open) very few of the consequential actions requirements had been put in place but the PPO had commended staff in their report. The failings were identified during the inquest and the PPO acknowledged they should never have commended people who had actually failed to do their job. Two participants (LA4 and ESP2) agreed that however thorough an investigation was, the full story could only be identified through probing the evidence and witnesses.

Two coroners (CO1 and CO3) pointed out that they examined all the evidence as it was gathered, so they thought the process was not as reliant on families where the coroner was effectively investigating the case. However, two legal representatives interviewed (LA3 and LA5) thought coroners rarely had the time or resources to 'sit down and think critically' (LA3) or scrutinise the evidence thoroughly, so it was very important that families took on this role. One coroner (CO2) was clear that when family members were actively involved in an inquest, it usually ensured negligence was identified. A lawyer (LA2) said often the only scrutiny came from legal representatives acting for the family and a coroner (CO1) admitted there were examples of coroners who 'abdicate the questioning to the representatives'. Two lawyers (LA5 and LA6) thought, even though some coroners were very good at asking questions, there was always the danger this could affect perceptions about their independence and open them up to charges of bias. One of them (LA5) thought it was therefore inappropriate in the most contentious cases for coroners to cross-examine the evidence. An ex-police officer (ESP2) agreed somebody needed to take 'the adversarial position' to scrutinise the evidence but coroners could not do this as they had to remain independent.

Participants agreed that where coroners did not scrutinise the evidence or cross-examine witnesses, families had to take on this role to ensure a fair outcome. But even where coroners were actively involved in questioning, participants still thought it was important for families to be able to question parties. Two coroners (CO1 and CO3) felt the most contentious inquests should allow all parties to scrutinise and cross-examine the evidence. One lawyer (LA2) said any restriction of questioning by the family limited the likelihood of reaching a fair outcome. Another (LA5) said families provided greater scrutiny by 'pushing boundaries, trying to find things out'. A third lawyer (LA4) agreed, saying families were always going to 'press ahead [.........] trying to find things out', which made sure everything was questioned closely.

Some family participants felt they had to take on the responsibility of scrutinising the evidence. One (FA3) thought the family were 'there as the prosecutors', and it was very positive to have the family (with good legal support) to take the lead in scrutinising evidence, which was why inaccuracies and mistakes not identified by the investigation were brought to light during the inquest. Another (FA2) agreed families had to be persistent to get the truth from State agencies. And a third family member (FA4) felt 'like I am an investigator half the time' as they had to 'do the job' the investigators failed to do.

Some examples of family scrutiny identifying new evidence relating to a death were given during the interviews. One lawyer (LA3) talked about the Sean Rigg case where it was the family, not the IPCC, that identified the police were lying about analysing CCTV evidence. Similarly, a family member (FA2) said through scrutinising the evidence and questioning witnesses, they identified inconsistencies: 'a lot more came out from the witnesses than [had been] in the statements' through cross-examination. Another family member (FA5) said as a result of their legal representative questioning witnesses, stories were changed and evidence of perjury was established. A different family member (FA4) said it was through questioning that it became clear mistakes had been made in the investigation. For example, in their case, the time of death had been wrongly noted down, the ligature found in the cell had been lost and not all possible causes of death had been considered by the medical examiner.

Some participants (LA2, LA3, IPCC, FA1, FA3 and FA4) thought one reason families could be so effective in scrutinising the evidence was because they wanted to know all the details. One lawyer (LA2) said families generally 'live those cases' so were in the best position to scrutinise the evidence. IPCC agreed families sometimes knew the case in exhaustive detail. Three family members (FA1, FA3 and FA4) all knew the files in great detail and scrutinised every bit of information; identifying gaps or errors. The Rigg case mentioned above by one lawyer (LA3) illustrated how families sometimes know the case better than anyone else. They said that it was the family (with the assistance of their lawyer) who went through all the videos; and such detailed scrutiny could not be provided by the coroner 'who would not have had time to look at hundreds of hours of CCTV'.

Families taking on this role in specific cases were identified as a potential problem in relation to how accountability was achieved, if the system relied on families to scrutinise the evidence. It was pointed out that this meant scrutiny may not happen if families could not or did not want to take on the role. One lawyer (LA2) said they felt families were expected to analyse all the evidence and then examine witnesses. Two family members (FA2 and FA3) acknowledged not all families would be happy to go through everything in as much detail as they did or to challenge State parties. One of them (FA2) said the process required them to be 'like a dog with a bone'and they thought 'a lot of families would have just gone along with it'. In their case, they challenged the verdicts to be left to the inquest jury and managed to ensure all possible verdicts were considered. The role of a legal representative was raised as vital in assisting families scrutinising the evidence, and will be discussed later.

One coroner (CO2) said ably represented families could provide scrutiny but coroners needed to be aware that when family members were not actively involved, they had a 'bigger burden' to scrutinise the actions of State parties themselves. One of the legal representatives interviewed (LA1) agreed a 'progressive coroner' should take into account whether the family either were not involved in the inquest or not represented and ask the questions necessary to scrutinise the State in either of these situations.

One family member (FA3) thought some juries might help scrutinise the evidence via questioning. However, other participants (PPO, LA1 and LA3) said this was rare, with PPO saying juries had a few questions in about 50% of cases but were 'not massively engaged in the process' the rest of the time. Two participants (ESP2 and LA6) both thought an independent (of all parties) advocate examining all the evidence during an inquest was a better approach than leaving it to families.[8] The financial burden has to be met by the coroner for any such legal advocates. Although some participants agreed that scrutiny could be carried out by the coroner, jury or an independent lawyer appointed by the coroner, families are often considered the ones best placed (with the support of their legal representatives) to challenge and question the evidence.

7.1.2.2 Family Bring Balance to the Process

As well as scrutinising evidence, families also bring balance to the process which is necessary where State parties are not actively seeking the truth. (Providing balance and equity to the process can also be linked to the perceived fairness and legitimacy of the process to be discussed in the next chapter). Some participants (CO1, LA1, LA2, LA3, LA4, LA5, LA6, FA3 and FA5) felt the system was set up so State parties were either not actively seeking the truth, or fighting during the process to ensure all the facts were not brought to light in order to avoid possible civil cases or Rule 43 reports. One coroner (CO1) said instructions to lawyers representing State parties would often be 'to avoid a Rule 43 report by any way you can'. A family member interviewed (FA3) agreed, saying they thought State institutions would always be on the defensive as they had to 'protect their image

[8]A coroner can appoint an independent advocate as 'Counsel to the Inquest' for certain high-profile cases including the 7/7 bombings: see http://webarchive.nationalarchives.gov.uk/20120216072438/http://7julyinquests.independent.gov.uk/int_persons.htm

[...........] to avoid at all costs to be publically criticised'. One legal representative (LA1) found that in their experience, State parties had 'a bottomless pit of resources' aimed towards avoiding a critical verdict and any evidence they presented was 'entirely self-serving'. They thought this was partly as a result of the Manning case which created a requirement for the DPP to review any case following a critical inquest verdict, which had left State agencies even more concerned about receiving a negative or critical outcome. This case will be referenced in more detail later in this chapter. Four other lawyers interviewed (LA2, LA3, LA4 and LA6) all thought State bodies were primarily focused on limiting any criticism of themselves: with one (LA6) saying that following a death in custody, any State agency involved 'does not want to admit anything if they can avoid it'. The other lawyer interviewed (LA5) agreed State agencies were sometimes more interested in 'muddying the waters' than finding the truth.

Two participants (FA5 and LA5) felt that even when the State was not actively working against finding the truth, all non-family parties provided a cohesive front, with the only balance provided by family participation. One family member (FA5) experienced every other interested party sticking together during the inquest; with the doctors covering for the police and vice versa: 'it was like a little club really'. In fact they felt some individuals involved probably did feel remorse for what happened but could not express it as they had to stick together with the other officers. During the inquest hearing, they (FA5) witnessed interactions between all officers that led them to believe that the one officer whose statement had originally disputed the others had been ostracised; this made them question their confidence in the State agencies. A lawyer (LA5) supported this view, saying usually different State authorities 'sweep up' any inconsistencies for each other.

The participation of families was linked by a number of participants to ensuring a fair and balanced process that is not dominated by State parties. Two coroners interviewed (CO1 and CO3) thought because custodial inquests always had the potential to be contentious, it was important for legal representatives for all parties to be involved to provide balance. Two legal representatives (LA2 and LA3) thought in order for coroners to run an independent and balanced enquiry, they had to hear the families' perspective. One family member (FA2) agreed, saying if coroners were only hearing from State parties 'then inevitably that's the side they are going to come down on'.

Participants thought an important benefit to families' participation was that they provided a different viewpoint from other parties, who tended to be experts on issues arising after deaths in custody. One legal representative interviewed (LA3) said the family could usually identify new questions to be answered.[9] Another (LA4) thought families provided different perspectives than other parties, so their participation brought 'a new slant'. One coroner (CO3) agreed

[9]Again the role of legal representatives assisting families with this was pointed out, which will be discussed in Chapter 10.

that families asked questions 'from the heart or about things that trouble them', so it could be very constructive to have them feeding into the process.[10] A family member (FA2) said they sometimes thought of angles or questions that even their legal representative had not. IPCC and PPO agreed families were often the most likely to have interesting and 'very relevant' (PPO) questions, which usually benefited the process greatly.

The participation of families can therefore ensure that the process is not dominated by State parties, who have good reason to limit scrutiny and critical outcomes. Families, as those most affected by a death, provide a unique viewpoint and perspective that cannot be provided by any other parties. This can ensure the process is more balanced, and the opportunity for a fair outcome maximised.

7.1.2.3 Family Provide Information About Deceased

Families can also assist an inquest by providing important evidence about the background of the deceased and, in some cases, even details relevant to the circumstances around a death. Process wise, one coroner (CO3) said 'sometimes there are things they [the family] need to say' about the deceased. Although IPCC pointed out whether families could provide relevant information to assist the process was heavily reliant on 'what kind of contact the family had had with the person before they died'. In terms of police deaths, two lawyers (LA3 and LA4) said the family may have vital information about circumstances before an individual came into contact with the police. For example, cases where the family call the police to assist them when they have concerns about the behaviour of someone. Two participants interviewed (LA3 and FA1) said even when the deceased had been detained and therefore separated from the family, families still might have insight about their state of mind or other things linked to a death. For example, if an individual is worried about an upcoming criminal hearing or having problems in prison that might lead them to take their own life.

Participants also gave examples of families gathering evidence where investigatory bodies were not effective. One family member (FA4) felt they were acting as investigators in gathering, assessing and scrutinising evidence because they 'had to do the ground work'. Their father (FA4 Father) pointed out a photo was not taken of one key piece of evidence (the ligature), so investigators asked him to do it; 'that is the only way we got a photograph'. These photographs were essential evidence, as the pathologist had to change his mind about some aspects in their report when showed the photographs at the inquest. Another family member (FA3) gathered evidence to support their case, with the help of their legal representative. One legal representative (LA6) said they knew of cases where the family 'dug up some fresh material', necessitating a new inquest. Similarly,

---

[10] CO3 did note, though, that legal representation was very useful in helping families frame the questions appropriately: as referenced in Chapter 10.

another lawyer (LA3) had seen cases like this, including when Sean Rigg's family were responsible for identifying the fact CCTV evidence was missing.[11]

So families can affect the accuracy of the outcome by scrutinising and questioning the evidence, bringing balance as well as introducing relevant facts to the process.

7.2 Families Instigating Change

As well as taking a proactive role during the process, families can also instigate positive changes once the inquest has concluded. This includes pushing for State responses following critical inquest verdicts (as discussed previously) either to achieve accountability or to ensure further deaths are prevented. One lawyer (LA3) said often decisions to prosecute officers depended on families and their lawyers 'pushing for prosecutions'. A family member interviewed (FA1) said they had written countless letters, trying to ensure lessons were being learnt from the inquest. IPCC agreed that families were often key in getting wider learning following identification of failings as they often pushed for inquest outcomes to be publicised and shared.

In some cases, families go beyond pushing for change in relation to substantive failings linked to a death, and instigate change to rules for detention State institutions as well as changes to the investigatory system itself. In respect of the inquest as an investigation holding the State to account, reforms have been interlinked with the evolution of Article 2 via ECtHR case law. The ECtHR identified the ECHR as a living instrument, illustrated by the manner in which Article 2 obligations have broadened since the inception of the ECHR.[12] Fundamentally, changes have been in response to societal evolution and to ensure Article 2 is interpreted in a way that ensures the protections are effective.[13] Cases are brought before the courts by those affected by a State's actions; so in relation to Article 2, cases are brought by bereaved families.[14] One legal representative (LA6) was clear that 'families are very active [.............] they are the ones who bring about the changes'.

Bereaved families, with support from organisations like INQUEST or JUSTICE, also play a vital role in judicially reviewing decisions relating to the inquest system, thus changing the law, police and practice governing the system. Two legal representatives (LA4 and LA6) both said families were key to important legal changes increasing accountability via the inquest system. One example provided was that before the *Middleton* case, juries were limited to one-word verdicts so it was difficult for failings that might have contributed to a death to be raised. Achieving 'the betterment of the system' was a key aim for one family member (FA3), who challenged the investigative system for deaths in a mental health setting. The following section describes three areas where families

---

[11]This is in addition to the family then scrutinising the CCTV evidence as mentioned previously.

[12]Mowbray (2005, p. 60–71).

[13]*R. (on the application of Amin (Imtiaz)) v Secretary of State for the Home Department* (2003).

[14]Often with the support of campaigning organisations.

instigated change in the inquest system related to achieving accountability and family participation via case law; the importance of what verdicts are left for the jury to consider, how the State must respond to certain verdicts and when legal aid must be available for families.

7.2.1 Inquest Verdicts

An important part of the inquest process is the final verdict produced by the jury. The verdict of unlawful killing is by far the most critical verdict, and the one that is most likely to have repercussions. As discussed previously, an inquest cannot name an individual as the person culpable for any death, but the jury can state that they believe the death was due to unlawful behaviour, without naming who is responsible. A verdict of unlawful killing therefore indicates that it is likely an 'unnamed individual' is culpable for the death. So it is a vitally important outcome from any inquest. A series of challenges by families to existing practice have clarified the law around when the verdict of unlawful killing should be left for the jury to consider. Juries are only allowed to choose a verdict if it is an option left to them, so what verdicts should be left open to them is vitally important. This is especially important in relation to a verdict of unlawful killing following a death in custody, as this can be an indication that there is State culpability for a death. Due to the importance of such a verdict, at an inquest, the criminal standard of proof is required for a jury to bring a verdict of unlawful killing; so they must consider it proved beyond a reasonable doubt.[15]

A number of cases initiated by bereaved families or in response to campaigns on their behalf have clarified the law around this issue of when an unlawful killing verdict should be left for the jury to consider. In 1999, Roger Sylvester died after being restrained by police, and an inquest jury gave a verdict of unlawful killing but the police judicially reviewed the decision, which was subsequently quashed.[16] The High Court found police actions could not be proved to have caused the death, so no jury would have been likely to find the officers guilty of manslaughter in a criminal case, and therefore unlawful killing should not have been left to the inquest jury.[17] In 2005, the police involved in the shooting of Harry Stanley successfully judicially reviewed the decision of the coroner to leave the verdict of unlawful killing to the inquest jury.[18] The judgment found a jury could not have concluded beyond a reasonable doubt that the shooting did not occur under an honest belief of self-defence and therefore an unlawful killing verdict should not

[15]Note that normally, the standard of proof at an inquest is on the balance of probabilities as in civil courts; *R. (on the application of Cash) v HM Coroner for Northamptonshire* (2007) EWHC 1354 (Admin) (Queen's Bench Division (Administrative Court)).

[16]*R. (on the application of Anderson) v HM Coroner for Inner North Greater London* (2004) EWHC 2729 (Admin) (Queen's Bench Division (Administrative Court)).

[17]It was proved the restraint may have contributed to hypoxia but a causal link to the death was not proved.

[18]*R. (on the application of Sharman) v HM Coroner for Inner North London* (2005) EWHC 857 (Admin) (Queen's Bench Division (Administrative Court)).

have been left to them. This was even though Mr Stanley was unarmed and walking away from the officers at the time of the shooting and the forensic evidence did not support the police description of what happened. The law restricting a coroner to only leave unlawful killing to an inquest jury when the evidence would support a criminal conviction was affirmed in the *Bennett* case; where the application by the bereaved family to judicially review the coroner's decision was refused, as the *Galbraith* test had been correctly applied in deciding which verdicts to leave to the inquest jury.[19,20]

The importance of allowing a jury to return an unlawful killing verdict if appropriate has since been recognised. In 2007, a bereaved family took a case to the High Court, which found the coroner was wrong to not leave unlawful killing as a possible verdict at the inquest into the death of Darren Cash (who died after being restrained by police).[21] The judgment said if there was evidence on which an inquest jury might decide a verdict of unlawful killing to a criminal standard; this option should be left open to them. This was reflected in *Tainton*, where it was judged that issues which could not safely be left to the jury as possibly causative to a death (as it would be unsafe for the jury to make such a decision) should still be referenced in a narrative verdict if judged as a wider circumstance linked to the death.[22]

Generally, any coroner's decisions on what verdicts are to be left open to a jury can only be challenged on Wednesbury grounds (the action or decision must be established legally as fully unreasonable or irrational).[23,24] It has been clarified that coroners have greater discretion than a judge would have in a criminal jurisdiction to decide what options can be left to a jury. In 2008, in refusing a family the right to judicially review a coroner's decision, the Court stated that the coroner had a duty to ensure the jury was not allowed the opportunity to choose any verdicts that might risk determining liability which would be illegal as set out in the Coroners Rules 1984.[25] Previous judgments decided coroners were able to consider the interests of justice in deciding what verdicts to leave to an inquest jury.[26] It was clarified in *Menezes* that this distinguished coroners from criminal judges, as they were unable to 'act as a filter for unmeritorious cases'.[27] Although

---

[19] *R. v Galbraith (George Charles)* (1981) 1 WLR 1039; (1981) 2 All ER 1060; (Court of Appeal (Criminal Division)).

[20] *R. (on the application of Bennett) v HM Coroner for Inner South London* (2007) EWCA Civ 617 (Court of Appeal (Civil Division)), para 4.

[21] *R. (on the application of Cash) v HM Coroner for Northamptonshire* (2007).

[22] *R. (Tainton) v HM Senior Coroner for Preston and West Lancashire* (2016).

[23] *Associated Provincial Picture Houses Ltd v Wednesbury Corp* (1948) 1 KB 223; (1947) 2 All ER 680 (Court of Appeal).

[24] *R. (on the application of D) v Inner South London Assistant Deputy Coroner* (2008) EWHC 3356 (Admin) (Queen's Bench Division (Administrative Court)), para 25.

[25] *Da Silva v United Kingdom* (2016), paras 122–123.

[26] *R v HM Coroner for Exeter and East Devon ex parte Palmer* (2000) Inquest LR 78 (Court of Appeal); *R. v HM Coroner for Inner London South District Ex p. Douglas-Williams* (1999) 1 All ER 344 (Court of Appeal (Civil Division)); *R. (on the application of Bennett) v HM Coroner for Inner South London* (2007).

[27] *Da Silva v United Kingdom* (2016), para 219.

wide discretion is still with coroners as to which verdicts should be left to juries, the detailed case law resulting from families challenging decisions has helped clarify the law, and therefore improve consistency.

7.2.2 State Response to an Inquest Verdict

One aspect of achieving accountability is for the State to respond to any issues identified during an inquest. In relation to cases where liability for a death was established, this would include seeking criminal conviction of those culpable. As inquests only proceed once any criminal proceedings are completed, if an inquest hearing is being held it is likely either a prosecution failed or the decision was taken not to prosecute the case. As explained above, an inquest cannot name an individual liable for a death, but can indicate that the inquest jury decided the death was due to an unlawful killing. If the evidence from an inquest can be used to identify the individual, then where an inquest results in an unlawful killing verdict, it might be expected prosecutions would follow, given the fact unlawful killing can only be found using the criminal standard of proof. This leads to questions as to why unlawful killing verdicts do not automatically lead to prosecutions; let alone convictions.[28] In relation to State actions, the lack of prosecutions can be seen as a limitation to achieving accountability but bereaved families have been key instigators in even requiring the State to respond at all in these cases.

Although there are still questions as to how effectively the process is working, families challenging decisions were key in requiring the State to officially respond to unlawful killing verdicts. In 1997, the decision by the Director of Public Prosecutions (DPP) not to prosecute police officers involved in the deaths of Shiji Lapite and Richard O'Brien (after both inquests concluded with unlawful killing verdicts) was judicially reviewed by the bereaved families.[29] During the judicial review, the DPP conceded the decisions not to prosecute in these cases were flawed.[30] A Government enquiry was initiated following these cases; the subsequent report influenced the changes in guidance explained below.[31]

In 1998, the inquest into the death of Alton Manning in HMP Blakenhurst returned a verdict of unlawful killing.[32] The CPS decided not to prosecute anyone

---

[28]There have been 11 unlawful killing verdicts at inquests where State actions resulted in a death but only three unsuccessful prosecutions: see INQUEST, *Learning from Death in Custody Inquests: A New Framework for Action and Accountability* (2012).

[29]In conjunction with the case of Derek Treadaway, who was found to have been tortured in police custody; *R. v DPP Ex p. Treadaway* Times, October 31, 1997 (Divisional Court).

[30]In relation to the second death, it transpired the decision not to prosecute the officers had relied on their evidence alone and had not taken into account statements by other witnesses.

[31]In response to these cases, the Government set up the Butler Inquiry to look into the Crown Prosecution Service (CPS) decision-making process relating to deaths in custody and other serious cases; Gerald Butler, *Inquiry into Crown Prosecution Service decision-making in relation to deaths in custody and related matters (Butler Report)* (1999).

[32]Mr Manning had died in 1995 after prison officers had used a neck hold to restrain him.

in relation to his death but in 2000 his family judicially reviewed this decision.[33] The Court concluded that when there was a death in custody and the inquest returned a verdict of unlawful killing, the family was entitled (unless compelling reasons existed) to hear the reasons behind CPS decisions not to prosecute any officers identified as failing in their duty of care through the evidence from the inquest.

In 2001, the ECtHR in *Jordan v UK* commented on the need for the State to reassess any decisions regarding prosecutions if inquest verdicts indicated it was necessary.[34] The ECtHR also referenced the importance of the DPP giving families reasons explaining any decision not to prosecute following a controversial death, so they could 'challenge the decision legally if they should wish'.[35]

Subsequent to these judgments, in 2001, the Attorney General announced a review of the role and practices of the CPS in cases of a death in custody. The report published in April 2003 recommended 'A new package of measures to increase the transparency of the decision-making process and to involve families more'.[36] Current guidelines for the CPS now state that on completion of an inquest, all the evidence will be considered (including any new evidence exposed through the inquest process) before a decision on whether to prosecute is taken.[37] If there will still be no prosecution, families will be informed and given reasons for the decision.[38] The CPS also offers to meet with families so the 'decision can be explained to you in more detail'.[39] Domestic courts affirmed this process is necessary for an inquest to satisfy Article 2 procedural obligations following a death in which State agents may be implicated.[40] Similarly, the ECtHR has stated that the fact any verdict of 'unlawful death' now meant the DPP must reconsider any decision not to prosecute was a key aspect of the inquest system's compliance with Article 2.[41] The High Court decided in 2006 that the review process as set out in *Manning* was compatible with Article 2 obligations as described in *Oneryildiz*.[42] Families have played an important part in ensuring that the State must respond to any unlawful killing verdict; and now, if a prosecution is not taken forward, reasons must be given to families to explain this decision.

---

[33] *R. v DPP Ex p. Manning* (2001) QB 330 (Queen's Bench Division (Administrative Court)).

[34] *Jordan v United Kingdom* (2003), para 142.

[35] *Jordan v United Kingdom* (2003), para 123.

[36] The Rt Hon The Lord Goldsmith (2003, para 6.8).

[37] Crown Prosecution Service *Prosecution Policy and Guidance: Deaths in Custody* (2004).

[38] Crown Prosecution Service, *Prosecution Policy and Guidance: Deaths in Custody* (2004); Retrieved from http://www.cps.gov.uk/publications/prosecution/death_custody.html#a10

[39] Crown Prosecution Service, *Prosecution Policy and Guidance: Deaths in Custody* (2004).

[40] *R. (on the application of Middleton) v HM Coroner for Western Somerset* (2004), para 16.

[41] *Bubbins v United Kingdom* (2005), para 153.

[42] *R. (on the application of Da Silva) v DPP* (2006) EWHC 3204 (Admin) (Divisional Court), para 43.

7.2.3 Legal Aid for Families Participating in an Inquest

Families have also been key in instigating change that makes the process fairer by improving the opportunity for bereaved families to effectively participate, which can then increase accountability (as discussed above). A recent example of a bereaved family driving change within the inquest system itself related to the guidance for Legal Aid Agency (LAA) officers deciding whether to provide families with legal aid funding to pay for legal representation during an inquest process via the exceptional fund system. In 2013, Christopher Letts died of suicide, shortly after being released from a mental health clinic; his sister, Joanna Letts, applied to the LAA for legal aid funding for a lawyer to represent her during the inquest process. Initially she was refused legal aid; although after she started to judicially review the decision, the LAA reversed its decision. Mrs Letts continued with the judicial review, however, to ask whether the criteria used by the LAA on granting legal aid for inquests were fair and legal.

Under Section 4 of LASPO 2012, the Lord Chancellor was empowered to produce guidance for the LAA, governing how applications for legal aid should be dealt with; including applications for funding for legal representation during an inquest.[43] The guidance gave two criteria which had to be met before granting legal aid; firstly the case should come under the remit of Article 2 and secondly legal representation must be deemed necessary for a family member to be able to participate in the inquest.[44] It was the first criterion that was questioned by Joanna Letts, as the guidance suggested that in deciding whether a case was within the remit of Article 2, the LAA should judge whether the State had arguably breached substantive Article 2 obligations. Joanna Letts argued that in some cases, the procedural or investigative duty under Article 2 was automatically engaged, regardless of whether the State could be shown to have been responsible for the death. The Lord Chancellor acknowledged there were some deaths where Article 2 was automatically engaged but disagreed as to which cases came within this category. The Court found the procedural duty went beyond cases where there was State culpability for a death; and stated the guidance did not allow for the fact families should be involved for the purposes listed in cases where there was no State culpability.[45,46,47] The Court therefore judged the existing guidance contained an 'error of law' that was likely to lead to wrongful decisions.[48]

Following the *Letts* judgments, the Lord Chancellor published updated guidance which gave new criteria for the LAA dealing with an application for

---

[43] Legal Aid, Sentencing and Punishment of Offenders Act 2012.

[44] Lord Chancellor's Exceptional Funding Guidance (Inquests), 2013.

[45] *Letts v Lord* Chancellor (2015).

[46] To discover the truth, to be comforted by the fact the state was shown not to be at fault or to know lessons would be learnt to prevent future death (*Letts v Lord Chancellor* (2015), para 64.

[47] *Letts v Lord Chancellor* (2015).

[48] *Letts v Lord Chancellor* (2015), paras 100–101.

exceptional legal aid funding for an inquest process.[49] The first criterion now states that cases should engage the procedural obligation of Article 2; the second criterion remaining the same.[50] Clear guidelines are provided as to when the procedural obligation would be engaged, including the fact that it can be triggered automatically in such cases as 'intentional killings by State agents, violent deaths and suicides in police or prison custody or during the course of arrest or search, and all violent deaths and suicides of persons detained in mental hospitals'.[51] The guidance still includes reference to cases where the procedural obligation might not be automatically triggered but where there is evidence showing the State might have arguably breached either of the substantive Article 2 obligations.[52]

Without the Letts family bringing the challenge, and without them continuing with it once they had been awarded legal aid themselves, the first criterion would have remained as non-compliant with legal understandings of Article 2 procedural obligations.[53] The second criterion is still in place, requiring the LAA to judge whether legal aid would be required to ensure family involvement in order to protect their legitimate interests. The guidance suggests considerations which might indicate legal aid funding was required would be 'the nature and seriousness of any allegations' likely to be made against any State agencies; any particular vulnerability of the next of kin; and whether the family had already played 'an active role' in an investigation into the death.[54] So the test to receive exceptional legal aid funding is still a high one for families to reach, which is likely to continue to make it difficult to get the legal support they need (as referenced in the Chapter 10).

7.3 Conclusion

This chapter has explained how the effective and fair participation of bereaved families in an inquest following a death in custody can have a positive instrumental impact on the process. Accountability of State agents is linked to identification of any failings, linked to deaths in custody and steps being taken to change processes so that these failings do not continue. Family participation can benefit this both by optimising the chance of any failings being identified, and by pushing for positive change to prevent future deaths. Family participation can

---

[49]Lord Chancellor, *Lord Chancellor's Exceptional Funding Guidance (Inquests)* (2015).

[50]Lord Chancellor, *Lord Chancellor's Exceptional Funding Guidance (Inquests)* (2015), para 7.

[51]Lord Chancellor, *Lord Chancellor's Exceptional Funding Guidance (Inquests)* (2015), para 11.

[52]Lord Chancellor, *Lord Chancellor's Exceptional Funding Guidance (Inquests)* (2015), para 14.

[53]It should be noted this change was only possible because Joanna Letts was legally represented by a specialist solicitor and two barristers as well as being supported by INQUEST.

[54]Lord Chancellor, *Lord Chancellor's Exceptional Funding Guidance (Inquests), paras 21-23.*

ensure there is a greater likelihood that the inquest will reach a fair and accurate outcome in a number of ways. The main way in which this happens is through the family influencing what evidence is presented at the inquest, and scrutinising the evidence provided on behalf of State bodies, and investigatory bodies. As those most likely to want to find out the truth about how and why a death occurred, bereaved families are best placed to push for all the relevant evidence to be presented, and question the evidence presented by others. It is generally agreed in our justice system, that cross-examination of the evidence and witnesses is the most effective way of ensuring its validity, and families will often take on this role at an inquest. It is agreed that one of the main purposes of an inquest process is to identify failings, and ensure where there are any lessons to be learnt, these are disseminated so that future deaths can be avoided. Families often take a lead in not just ensuring failings are identified (through scrutiny) but also in pushing for lessons to be learnt, especially by encouraging dissemination of outcomes. This chapter also provided examples of how bereaved families have been the key drivers beyond reform in relation to the inquest process, improving accountability.

The next chapter will look at the intrinsic impact of families being able to participate fairly and effectively, which primarily relates to increasing the legitimacy of the process as well as the wider system.

Chapter 8

Legitimacy Provided by Family Participation

This chapter looks at the intrinsic value of a fair process: in particular, the correlation between families being able to participate fairly and the perceived legitimacy of the process. Legitimacy is especially important in relation to the inquest system as a process that holds the State to account for possible human rights violations. The theoretical framework set out in this chapter relies on procedural justice theory, as it illustrates how fair and effective participation impacts on the legitimacy of certain processes. This theory has been identified as relevant in relation to interactions that individuals have with different strands of the justice system; particularly the police and prison service. The empirical evidence is used to show that this theory is equally relevant to the inquest process. It shows that effective and fair participation can lead to families perceiving the process as fair, independent and transparent which increases their trust and confidence in the outcome; all of which increase perceptions about the legitimacy of the system.

8.1 Fairness of a Process

Dworkin argues that achieving a fair outcome should be the priority of any process; if a biased process leads to a fair outcome, it does not injure anyone; so the law should be interpreted to maximise a moral and fair outcome.[1] Dworkin himself acknowledges, however, that it is impossible for a process to always come to the right decision.[2] Even though authorities cannot guarantee that a justice system provides just outcomes, they do have a moral duty to ensure fair processes and rely on them to produce a just outcome.[3] This moral duty is linked to the fact that there is societal harm if a process leads to unjust decisions. Authorities with limited resources can minimise this moral harm by ensuring a fair procedure.[4] So in constructing normative values of justice, it is important to focus on maximising

[1]Dworkin (1986, p. 165).
[2]Dworkin (1963, p. 624).
[3]Allan (1998, p. 513–514).
[4]Allan (1998, p. 515).

Death in Custody, 119–138
Copyright © 2020 Jo Easton
Published under exclusive licence
doi:10.1108/978-1-83909-025-720201013

the opportunity of a just outcome rather than expecting a just outcome to always be achievable.

Fairness in procedures is important, even if it does not change the outcome, as it allows for the potential of fair distribution of resources, which can reduce oppression or disadvantage. The same argument can be made in terms of shared values such as justice: fair processes which govern how concepts are translated into real-life situations will allow for the concepts to be applied to all fairly. Procedural justice theory as set out by Tyler argues that people do not necessarily consider the outcome when perceiving fairness but evaluate the process.[5] Therefore, the perceived fairness of a process can be linked to an understanding of whether the system is fair and concepts are being applied equally. This is particularly relevant in relation to marginalised groups, who may feel the justice system does not treat them fairly.

Transparent and accessible fair processes can be used to counter perceptions of unfairness which can exist in marginalised or disadvantaged groups.[6] It is particularly important that fair processes are in place in relation to the criminal justice system as perceptions of injustice are present especially in disadvantaged and minority groups in terms of interactions with law officials.[7] For example, reports like the Lammy Review highlight the disproportionate negative outcomes from criminal justice interventions amongst those from Black, Asian and Minority Ethnic background.[8]

Aspects of both outcome and process have been argued to interact to influence perceptions of fairness.[9] Perceptions of how fair the outcome is will influence how fair people consider the process to have been and conversely, perceptions about how fair the process was will influence how fair people consider the outcome.[10] So the impact of a fair process is vital in relation to affecting a fair outcome (as set out in the previous chapter) as well as being of intrinsic value.

The person who receives the most favourable outcome may perceive the outcome as fair, whereas the reverse may be true for the person who receives an unfavourable outcome. In terms of resolving a dispute, the perception of whether the outcome is fair or not may correlate closely to whether participants receive a favourable or expected result.[11] However, belief that the process was fair can lead to a belief that the outcome was fair even if not favourable (see below). What is perceived as fair is a subjective concept that can depend on many factors.

Cropanzano and Ambrose argue that both perceptions of how fair the outcome and the process are can be influenced by pre-existing expectations.[12] If expectation is an important aspect in perceived fairness, pre-existing

[5]Tyler (2003, p. 283).
[6]Buckler and others (2011, p. 370).
[7]Buckler and others (2011, p. 370).
[8]https://www.gov.uk/government/organisations/lammy-review
[9]Brockner and Wiesenfeld (1996, p. 189).
[10]Lind and Lissak (1985, p. 19), Van den Bos, Vermunt, and Wilke (1997, p. 95).
[11]Crosby (1976, p. 85).
[12]Cropanzano and Ambrose (2001, p. 120).

understanding about a process will be used to evaluate that process when someone experiences the process. So if individuals go into a process with certain expectations of what should be happening, especially in relation to what opportunities they should have in relation to participation, this might impact on whether they perceive the process of fair or not. This is an important point in relation to inquests as the process is not widely understood outside of those who have personal experience of the system. It is therefore likely that general understanding about the way courts and the justice system works impacts on the expectation of how an inquest should proceed.[13]

So achieving justice can relate more to the process than the end result. Fairness requires doing everything possible to ensure a just outcome is achieved and a fair process is the best way of maximising the likelihood of achieving a fair outcome. The fairness of a process must be evaluated against a normative definition of justice, which means looking to standard, accepted norms to guide what 'fairness' should look like. Society, over time, creates these norms by establishing what might be considered fundamental aspects to a fair process. These norms may be set out as legal standards such as the principle that no one is above the law or that justice is applied impartially and predictably.[14] There may also be moral values that are deemed central to a society such as treating everyone fairly and with respect, which would need to be reflected as norms or standards that must be complied with in any process used to settle disputes or conflicts.

Objective criteria used to assess fairness were first proposed by Levanthal who suggested that the most important aspects were consistency, accuracy and freedom from bias, opportunity to correct unfair decisions, compliance with moral or ethical norms and the representativeness offered to all participants.[15] These were summarised as intrinsic (as opposed to instrumental) aspects broadly established under three areas: trustworthiness of the decision-maker, neutrality of the decision-maker and how the perceptions about the process affect beliefs about participants standing.[16] Although these aspects rely on perceptions by those experiencing the system, Leventhal also stated the importance of objective criteria to judge the quality and fairness of the decision-making.[17]

Tyler and Blader put forward a more detailed four-component model which explained how people evaluate the fairness of a process; addressing the importance of aspects which are believed to influence the outcome and those that counter different initial viewpoints.[18] Firstly, the perceived quality of the decision is decided by the neutrality of the decision-maker, how transparent the process is in coming to the decision and the potential for participation by the subject.[19]

[13]This will be raised later in this book in relation to families being provided with sufficient information about the process.

[14]Principe (1999, p. 357).

[15]Leventhal (1980).

[16]Heuer and others (2002, p. 1469).

[17]Leventhal (1980).

[18]Blader and Tyler (2003, p. 747), Tyler and Blader (2000).

[19]Tyler and Blader (2000).

Secondly, the subject's perception of the treatment they receive will also affect their perception of how fair the process is.[20] Criteria such as whether an individual is treated with respect and dignity through the process would be relevant to this.

Tyler and Blader further separated each component into the general and the specific: with the general represented by the rules governing a process (the formal) and the specific represented by the specific process the individual is party to (the informal).[21] The four components are therefore described as the rules governing how decisions are made through the process, the rules governing how parties are treated, how the decision was made in a specific instance and how the parties were treated in that instance.[22] This model is useful for two reasons, firstly it combines the theories which argue the predominant reasons behind procedural justice are either that perceptions of fair processes influence perceptions of outcome (such as argued by Thibault and Walker) or to counter relational issues such as perceptions about standing.[23] The importance of this was argued by Heuer et al., when they suggested the two theories were not mutually exclusive but that people used aspects such as trust and neutrality of the process to evaluate not just relational concerns but also the fairness of outcomes.[24]

Secondly, the four-component theory recognises two criteria which other literature does not: namely the aspect of formal rules dictating quality of treatment and the influence of informal aspects (such as how individual officials translate rules in practice) on decision-making.[25] This four-component theory consistently covers how people evaluate fair processes and therefore perceptions of procedural justice.[26] This allows for Fuller's assertion that in applying laws or rules to govern interactions or behaviour, the systematic structure must be respected and the social context appreciated.[27] This understanding of how people perceive the system highlights the importance of the laws or rules governing a process, and whether people perceive them as ensuring fairness, as well as the relevance of how people are treated in an individual situation. In relation to the inquest system, this means that the rules governing decision-making, and opportunities for families to participate (such as whether the rules ensure access to documents) as well as the individual perceptions of families in relation to whether decisions were made fairly, and whether they were treated fairly, will all impact on perceptions about the legitimacy of the inquest process.

---

[20]Tyler and Blader (2000).
[21]Blader and Tyler (2003).
[22]Blader and Tyler (2003).
[23]Blader and Tyler (2003, p. 756).
[24]Heuer and others (2002, p. 1470).
[25]Blader and Tyler (2003, p. 756).
[26]Blader and Tyler (2003, p. 756).
[27]Fuller (1969, p. 229).

8.2 Legitimacy of State Actions

The intrinsic value of fair processes relates to theories including social contract theory, natural justice and maintenance of the inherent dignity of individuals.[28] The importance of fair processes when State authorities are making decisions impacting on individuals correlates to the perceived legitimacy of the State. Societies require a mechanism of social control by the State to prevent and punish those who do not comply with social norms set out in law. Legitimacy can be defined as the perception by people that 'an authority is entitled to be deferred to and obeyed'.[29] The legitimacy of State actions therefore depends on a perception that they are fair and just. Social contract theory argues that the public will only cooperate with the criminal justice system if it is believed to be performing justly.

Beetham suggested the legitimacy of an authority which exerts powers over others comes not just from people's consent to the use of that power but also from perceptions about the authority's conformity to rules and whether those rules are justifiable in terms of societal shared beliefs.[30] Legitimacy can rely on both perceptions by individuals where said authority is legitimately empowered to restrict their rights as well as whether that authority perceives itself to have a legitimate entitlement to do so. This book focuses on society's perception of the legitimacy of the State's authority to restrict individual rights by restraining or detaining individuals as part of a criminal justice system. Establishing legitimacy of this aspect of a State's authority has been linked to whether people believe the police operate within an ethical framework similar to their own.[31] This is particularly relevant to the inquest system which scrutinises the actions of police and prison against a legal framework.

The legitimacy of the actions of State authorities is particularly pertinent in relation to exercising control over an individual by police or the prison service, as increased perceptions of a process being legitimate has been shown to correlate with an individual complying with the process.[32] Tyler's research has shown that positive perceptions about the fairness of a court process correlate with perceptions about the legitimacy of authorities, and subsequently increased likelihood of compliance to the outcome.[33] In contrast, Sunshine and Taylor showed that positive perceptions about the effectiveness of a process did not necessarily produce a corresponding correlation with compliance.[34] It is therefore important to understand what aspects of a process are likely to increase perceptions of whether the process is fair, as well as whether it is effective.

---

[28]Richardson (1993, p. 28–30).
[29]Sunshine and Tyler (2003, p. 513).
[30]Beetham (1991).
[31]Jackson and others (2012, p. 1052).
[32]Tyler (1990), Jackson and others (2012), Paternoster and others (p. 163).
[33]Tyler (1990).
[34]Sunshine and Tyler (2003).

8.3 Procedural Justice in the Inquest System

This section will consider how the procedural justice theory introduced above relates to the inquest system, specifically complex inquests which are looking at deaths in custody. This book sets out the perceptions of those who have participated in such complex inquests, so it is very important to understand how those perceptions might impact on the perceived legitimacy of the system. If State failings contributed to a death, the outcome of the inquest can be important in both holding the State to account for its actions in detaining individuals and ensuring lessons are learned so future deaths can be prevented, so the legitimacy of the system is vital.

8.3.1 Intrinsic Value of Ensuring Legitimacy at Complex Inquests

An inquest is often the primary way State actions in restraining or detaining an individual who dies are scrutinised and therefore linked to ensuring accountability. The legitimacy of the system is therefore very important. This book focuses on the participation of bereaved families and how this relates to the fairness of the process. As discussed previously, a fair process can be argued to optimise the potential that a fair outcome is reached as well as impact on perceptions of legitimacy on the process itself. The legitimacy of inquests considering deaths in custody is important in two ways. Firstly, the legitimacy of the inquest system itself as a process which adjudicates whether human rights obligations are being fulfilled. Secondly, the inquest system holds the authorities to account and can provide public scrutiny of their actions.

The first aspect involves whether the inquest system itself is seen as a legitimate process. When considering deaths in custody, the inquest acts as a body adjudicating whether human rights are being respected; it is of central importance that people affected by any decisions perceive the process by which those decisions were reached as just and fair.[35] In reference to procedural requirements, a body performing an adjudication function must act fairly by ensuring a fair hearing (which includes the right for parties to access the evidence and be heard) and unbiased decision-making.[36] It is important that bodies that are adjudicating human rights violations should include procedural fairness as a fundamental aspect of the process simply because they are set up to protect human rights and must apply fair principles themselves.[37] Fair treatment from a human rights adjudicating body can also have a large impact on the psychological recovery of an individual who has suffered a human rights violation.[38] Chapter 5 set out the impact an inquest can have on a grieving family, and where inquests are discharging Article 2 duties to investigate a death, the lack of procedural fairness during the inquest could constitute a harm to a grieving relative. Systemic

[35] Brems and Lavrysen (2013, p. 182).
[36] Richardson (1993, p. 18–19).
[37] Brems and Lavrysen (2013, p. 184–185).
[38] Tyler (2007, p. 26), Brems and Lavrysen (2013).

concerns might be taken into account when the ECtHR is assessing whether a violation has occurred.[39] Research has argued that procedural justice at the ECtHR is important in part due to the authority that an ECtHR judgment has beyond the case under consideration.[40] This could also be argued to be true in relation to inquests, where one of the stated purposes is to set out any reforms needed to ensure future deaths are avoided. The legitimacy of the inquest system can therefore have a wider impact on systems and institutions in the justice system.

Second, an Article 2 inquest provides scrutiny of the authorities and therefore has a direct impact on the public understanding and trust in the police and prison systems. The public's feeling of security relies on the belief that they are protected by authorities who will treat them with consideration.[41] This is why it is so vital that authorities' actions are accountable to the public; so people can trust those in power. The criminal justice system is based on consent; as Cooper says, 'The criminal justice system works because it is understood and respected by the people it serves'.[42] Police officers enforce laws and protect the public but they are also the authority directly responsible for social control.[43] Perceptions about police legitimacy can impact on wider compliance with the law and justice system.[44] Prison officers represent the same authority within a prison society. The role of the criminal justice system overall is to protect the public but in order to fulfil this role, law officers are empowered to restrict the rights of some individuals (for example, arresting and detaining them).[45]

The rule of law requires public agencies to act 'within the law' when using powers delegated by Parliament.[46] This requires police and prison officers to act fairly and consistently towards all individuals when carrying out their duties.[47] If their actions are perceived as illegitimate, their authority may be challenged and individuals are less likely to comply and cooperate with criminal justice authorities. This was illustrated in the study by Tyler and Sunshine which showed that, as individuals' perception of police legitimacy increases, their willingness to empower officers with wider discretion also increases.[48]

The criminal justice system relies on public support: controlling behaviour through compliance to law is far more effective than requiring a permanent physical presence of authoritative officials to ensure good behaviour.[49] This is as

---

39 Brems and Lavrysen (2013, p. 185).
40 Brems and Lavrysen (2013, p. 186).
41 Tyler (1990).
42 Cooper (2011, p. 1).
43 Wolfe and Piquero (2011, p. 332).
44 Jackson and others (2012, p. 1062).
45 Walsh and Conway (2011, p. 70).
46 Richardson (1993, p. 17).
47 Walsh and Conway (2011, p. 71).
48 Sunshine and Tyler (2003).
49 For example, the expectation is that the public do not break the law even if there are no police officers present.

true within a prison as in wider society as, if order is maintained through compliance, prisoners do not have to be locked in cells 24 hours a day but can freely associate, work and attend education programmes. Tyler's research has illustrated procedural fairness contributes to increased perceptions of legitimacy but another contributing factor is trust. Good governance and accountability of law officials can impact on public trust by maintaining democratic values and protecting human rights.[50] Trust relies not just on an expectation that those in the criminal justice system will act in a fair manner, it requires transparency and acknowledgement if mistakes or failures do occur.

The comprehensive work by Tyler on the impact of improving the legitimacy of the police force and the criminal justice system in general is arguably straightforward. The role of the police within society requires empowerment to infringe the rights of any citizen suspected of breaking the law and therefore perceptions of legitimacy are important. Police legitimacy comes from both an acceptance of the obligation to obey authority and a perception that the power given to authority is justified.[51]

However, the prison service involves only a minority of the public: those who have either been found guilty of a crime or who a judge has determined should be detained on remand. Within the autocratic, closed system of a prison, the necessity of democratic values of legitimacy is more questionable. Although democratic systems fundamentally need legitimacy to continue, autocratic systems can find it easier to bypass legitimacy. Prisons are, by definition, autocratic systems where power is exerted in order to detain and control prisoners who are generally held against their will.[52] However, the prison disturbances in the 1980s and early 1990s show what happens when prisons have a problem with legitimisation.[53] It may seem contrary to talk about the legitimacy of an autocratic prison system which detains people: however, it is detrimental for order and security to be maintained in a prison using force and coercion alone. Controlling and maintaining safety among an unwilling population without using force and coercion alone is an ongoing problem in the penal system.[54] There are not enough prison officers to have complete control over all the prisoners all the time.[55] This was recognised in the Prison Rules published in 1964, with rule 2(2) stating that prison officers should seek the 'willing co-operation' of prisoners.[56]

Scraton argues that prison is an expression of imposed authority that is not legitimate; with order being achieved purely through coercion and force.[57] However, this author disagrees, as there is little evidence to suggest that order is

---

[50]Walsh and Conway (2011, p. 63).
[51]Jackson and others (2012, p. 1054).
[52]Sparks and Bottoms (1995, p. 49S).
[53]Cavadino and Dignan (1992).
[54]King (1985, p. 187).
[55]Sparks and Bottoms (1995, p. 50).
[56]UK Government, *Prison Rules 1964* (1964).
[57]Scraton, Sim, and Skidmore (1991, p. 63).

only achieved through use of coercion and force.[58] Sykes suggested that it was precisely because authority in a prison was imposed without the consent of the prisoner that officers had to find a way of legitimising their authority in order to achieve cooperation and compliance.[59] Legitimacy is not an all or nothing concept; Beetham argues that it is created partly by comparison against social norms so there can be gradations along a scale from legitimate to illegitimate authority.[60]

It is clear that compliance with authority is a very important concept in prisons. Prison officers can gain some form of legitimacy in the eyes of the prisoners if they treat prisoners fairly, and administrative decisions are not perceived as arbitrary. Sparks and Bottoms' research indicates Tyler's procedural justice theory translates into the prison service.[61] They showed that harsh regimes could be countered by officers treating prisoners fairly and with respect, while more relaxed regimes might actually have little prisoner perception of legitimacy if decisions were seen as arbitrary and general security in the prison left prisoners feeling unsafe.

Giddens argues that legitimacy relies on 'standards external' to the authority wanting to claim legitimacy.[62] Following on from this, Beetham's use of shared societal beliefs to justify legitimacy suggests that the legitimacy of the criminal justice system in general (as the process that put a prisoner in detention) can influence compliance and acceptance of prison officer's authority.[63] It has been shown that perceptions of treatment by State agencies do not just affect the understood legitimacy of that agency by the individual receiving the treatment but also by others watching.[64] This could be extrapolated to suggest that the perceived fairness of the inquest system (as the main investigation into deaths in custody that is open to public scrutiny) can also impact on prisoner perceptions of the legitimacy of prison authority. If there is a fair system in place that can be trusted to hold the prison system and officers accountable, this will impact positively on the perceived legitimacy of prison in general. When deaths occur in prison, there will often be uncertainty amongst the prisoners as to the details of what happened: this should be dealt with by transparently investigating all the circumstances so any questions are answered.

As Tyler has shown, it is not just about whether an outcome holds authority to account but whether the process followed in reaching that outcome is procedurally fair. Ensuring the dignity of the deceased is maintained as much as possible will impact on prisoner perceptions, and any investigation that disrespects either the deceased or their family will likely be perceived as procedurally unfair. The fact that perceptions of those observing a process (even if not participating) will

---

[58]Sparks and Bottoms (1995, p. 51).
[59]Sykes (1958).
[60]Beetham (1991).
[61]Sparks and Bottoms (1995).
[62]Giddens (1977).
[63]Sparks and Bottoms (1995, p. 59).
[64]Bierie (2013, p. 15).

influence their understanding of legitimacy underlines the importance of investigating a death in custody fairly as this can impact on wider public confidence in the criminal justice authorities.

8.3.2 Role of a Coroner in Achieving a Fair Outcome at a Complex Inquest

Decision-making processes are often classified as either adversarial or inquisitorial, although in reality many legal procedures are an amalgamation of the two. Kessler summarises the differences between adversarial and inquisitorial models as whether the court or parties were in control of initiating the process, gathering the evidence and setting the remit and nature of the proceedings.[65] The inquest system is described as inquisitorial but when complex inquests occur, the process often takes on many adversarial aspects, including having a jury and legal representatives cross-examining witnesses and the evidence.

Adversarial models are defined as contested procedures with the adjudicator generally having no prior information of the case and taking a passive role during the process.[66] Adversarial processes normally have two opposing sides gathering the evidence for lawyers who then take decisions on how to present and scrutinise the evidence.[67] The main purpose is to adjudicate between two parties rather than focusing on finding the truth: one party instigates the proceedings and both parties govern the presentation of the evidence.[68] An adversarial procedure is framed by strict rules which govern the process including what evidence is allowed to be presented and what questions can be asked of witnesses.[69] In adversarial processes, the decision-maker is usually unable to question any aspect of the facts unless it is brought up by either of the parties before them; their role is to provide an unbiased arbitration throughout the process. If there is a jury present, then it is vested with the responsibility of determining the outcome. This is the case with complex inquests, with the law requiring juries for any death in custody.[70]

Conversely, in inquisitorial procedures, the decision-maker is responsible for initiating the process, gathering and presenting the evidence.[71] In addition, there are officially no opposing parties. Non-adversarial procedures often prioritise the process above the outcome, with the aim of repairing relationships and communities by privileging the position and the voice of the victim.[72] The procedure is directed by more discretionary rules allowing flexibility to ensure the truth is established.[73] The decision-maker in an inquisitorial procedure is responsible for deciding what evidence is brought before the proceedings and therefore must have

---

[65] Kessler (2004, p. 1187).
[66] Warwick Inquest Group (1985, p. 45).
[67] Lynch (1997, p. 2117).
[68] Warwick Inquest Group (1985).
[69] Warwick Inquest Group (1985).
[70] Coroners and Justice Act 2009, Section 7.
[71] Kessler (2004).
[72] Jamieson and McEvoy (2007).
[73] Warwick Inquest Group (1985, p. 46).

prior information about all aspects of the case before them.[74] This active role of the decision-maker which necessitates prior knowledge means they will have pre-conceived ideas about the case which may influence the way they use their discretion to govern the process, including what evidence is relevant.[75] Also the decision-maker may be more receptive to information that confirms their pre-conceived hypothesis and the outcome may therefore be influenced by confirmation bias.

An inquest is officially an inquisitorial process and certainly the coroner is responsible for initiating the procedure and requesting the collection of evidence. The coroner also decides what evidence will be presented but all parties are allowed to make representations as to what evidence and which witnesses should be involved in an inquest. In practice, the evidence is often gathered by the parties following a death in custody, with the investigatory body report being the central source of information presented before the court.[76] In addition, the remit of complex inquests is restricted by the law which provides limitations on the evidence that can be presented, similar to adversarial processes. In an inquest, the coroner is responsible for both deciding what evidence is presented and also for questioning the witnesses, as is expected of an inquisitorial process.[77] However, in complex inquests, many coroners will leave the questioning to the different parties (or more commonly, their legal representatives). This means the process becomes adversarial with contested parties presenting different narratives. It has therefore been argued that coroners must be held to the same standard of bias as that set out for criminal procedures.[78]

Millar argues that fair outcomes are achieved through the different parties striving to prove the other side wrong, which ensures the evidence is tested and the truth ascertained.[79] Where opposing parties are allowed to question the evidence provided by the other side, the scrutiny of the evidence is seen as a vital part of reaching a correct outcome.[80] Fuller suggested that presenting the evidence through an adversarial model appeared to be 'the only effective means' of compensating for the tendency of human beings to judge in line with their own preconceptions.[81] Although the independence of an arbiter is often a requirement of a fair system, it is difficult to ensure any decision-maker does not have pre-conceived ideas but the scrutiny of evidence by different parties (as discussed in the previous chapter) can be an important element of ensuring fairness.

The coroner does begin the inquest procedure with a good understanding of the evidence to be presented (as they will have seen all documents, including

---

[74]Damaška (1975, p. 1088–1089).

[75]Damaška (1975, p. 1092).

[76]This is mostly the IPCC and PPO.

[77]*Mack, R (on the application of) v Coroner for Birmingham and Solihull & Ors* (2011) EWCA Civ 712.

[78]Cooper (2011, p. 14).

[79]Millar (1923, p. 1).

[80]Damaška(1975, p. 1094–1095).

[81]Fuller (1961, 1971).

witness statements), which does allow for pre-conceived ideas, if not the pre-existence of bias, to influence the process. Therefore, the adversarial presentation of the evidence is important in restricting the impact of this prior knowledge on the behalf of the arbitrator. Although inquest procedures are classified as inquisitorial and interested parties are not designated into opposing sides, in practice, the process following a death in custody is adversarial in nature with contestation of the evidence and witness statements. All parties are empowered to involve themselves in the process of a complex inquest by suggesting evidence to be presented and directing the questioning of witnesses. However, the coroner has discretion over these opportunities, so is key in ensuring the effective participation of parties and that the process is fair. The independence of the coroner, as well as perceptions of the decisions they make, will therefore impact on perceived legitimacy of the system.

8.4 Intrinsic Impact: Family Participation Impacts on Perceived Legitimacy of System

The last section in this chapter looks at how the views of participants relate to perceptions about the legitimacy of the process and wider system. Family experiences of how independent, fair and transparent they found the inquest process to be impacted heavily on their perceptions about how legitimate the process was, as well as their confidence in the outcome. Certain aspects are highlighted here in relation to whether they improved family perceptions about the process in respect to whether they saw it as independent, fair and transparent. In line with the research described above, participants generally felt families being able to participate in an inquest could lead to them perceiving it as legitimate and having more confidence in the system. However, it was clear that it was only where families were able to participate fully and effectively that they perceived the process as fair. Important factors identified by participants to ensure fair and effective participation are set out in Chapter 10.

8.4.1 Independence of System

Independence was identified by participants as a key issue relating to both confidence in the inquest system and its legitimacy. Two participants (LA2 and LA6) both thought family confidence in the system relied in part on their perception of whether the process was completely independent and not biased to 'the other side' (LA2). IPCC noted they had to be very careful to be sure they were not perceived by any parties to be biased.

Participants stated that a perceived lack of independence left families feeling very unsatisfied with the process and less confident in the outcome. Concerns were raised about a perceived lack of independence in relation to both investigations and coroners themselves. One issue mentioned was the fact IPCC investigations were not perceived as independent of the police for two reasons; firstly, because they relied on police to carry out investigations and secondly because a high proportion of IPCC staff were ex-police officers. One lawyer (LA1) thought although there were high hopes when the IPCC came in, lack of independence (as exemplified by almost all officers being recruited from the police) and transparency had led to 'a fundamental lack of trust' and 'fairly wide acceptance [that the IPCC] is just not fit for purpose'. Another (LA6) gave the example of the Duggan case where a witness went to the BBC with relevant evidence instead of the IPCC because they did not trust either the police or IPCC.

It was agreed that it was challenging for the IPCC to be seen as independent when they were so reliant on police resources for carrying out investigations. Two participants (ESP2 and LA6) pointed out the IPCC had a lack of resources, so often had to rely on the police to carry out parts of the investigation; specifically in securing and searching the scene of death. One family member (FA5) remembered feeling dismayed to find the IPCC relied on the police (who were not independent of those involved in the death) to carry out the investigation and consequently lost confidence in the whole investigatory process.

The second issue raised as important by participants was the fact that IPCC staff were ex-police themselves. Two participants (ESP1 and LA6) said some people did not have much confidence in the independence of the IPCC as they often have ex-police working on investigations. A family member (FA5) said once they realised how the IPCC was made-up, they did not consider it to be properly independent, which left them with 'absolutely no faith in the IPCC, whatsoever'. Another (FA2) agreed, saying that when they realised IPCC investigators were predominantly ex-police, it left them questioning the independence of their investigation.

Some participants (ESP1, CO2, CO3, CO4 and FA3) noted that a lack of confidence in investigating bodies only reinforced how important perceptions about coroners were to maintain confidence in the whole system. One ex-police officer (ESP1) thought the inquest process could provide independent scrutiny and transparency which 'adds a layer of legitimacy'; they believed the public had more confidence in the inquest system than the IPCC and therefore saw it as more legitimate. Three coroners (CO2, CO3 and CO4) all said families' perceptions of whether the inquest process was independent was very important; with one (CO4) saying they were careful to do nothing that 'could be said to [be] compromising your judicial independence'. A family member (FA3) was very concerned about the lack of independence of the hospital investigation but was satisfied with the final inquest outcome as they believed the coroner was independent of the original investigation (for example, instructing a new expert witness). This was even though the jury actually agreed with the hospital expert, not the independent witness.

Problems were still identified which negatively affected the perceived independence of coroners; the first being that they were sometimes seen to be biased towards the State. One coroner (CO1) suggested an 'open channel of communication' between coroner and State parties could ensure a good working relationship but acknowledged this might be perceived to impact on the independent decision-making of the coroner. One lawyer interviewed (LA2) thought families lost confidence in the system if the coroner appeared to be biased and sympathetic towards State parties. Another lawyer (LA3) said coroners sometimes treated families (especially unrepresented ones) as a nuisance, but were more positive towards State parties. A family member (FA1) felt 'the coroner was on the prison side' in their inquest. Another (FA4) felt the same, saying it was obvious the coroner was biased to the State party as 'he accepted the police thing word for word'.

Another concern raised by participants was due to links between coronial staff and local police: regardless of whether that police force was involved in the death. One coroner (CO4) acknowledged that both their coroner's officers were retired police officers. An ex-police officer (ESP2) explained their local coroner's officers were serving police officers: and noted this had a large impact on the process as, in practice, a lot of initial decisions were made by coroner's officers.[82] For example, coroner's officers will often decide who to ask to carry out the post-mortem as well as being the point of contact for families. One family member interviewed (FA5) made a distinction between the two coroner's officers, one of whom was a police officer and the other, who was not: saying they felt more comfortable with the latter. Another (FA2) said they were concerned when they realised the coroner's officer was not just ex-police but friends with one of the officers whose actions were under scrutiny. In fact, they felt the officer in question was given preferential treatment: for the example the officer was able to sit through the whole hearing before giving evidence, whereas other witnesses were unable to sit and observe the hearing until they had been questioned. In all these cases, the perceived lack of independence of coroner's officers was linked to overall concern about how independent the inquest process would be, and therefore led to less confidence in the process.

A closely related issue raised was the fact coroners relied heavily on police or other investigating bodies to gather evidence and investigate the death. Three participants (FA3, FA4 and LA6) all thought this limited the capacity of the coroner to oversee an independent process. Two of them (FA3 and LA6) were clear this decreased the legitimacy of the inquest. One family member (FA3) thought this was particularly relevant in relation to deaths in secure hospitals, where investigations carried out before the inquest were not independent at all.

Participants suggested a perceived lack of independence in the system led to families having little confidence in either the process or the outcome. Three participants (PPO, LA1 and LA2) all linked perceptions about the independence of the process with how confident families were that the correct outcome was reached. One family member (FA2) found their confidence in the inquest was damaged when they felt the coroner's staff were biased to the police. The discretion left to the coroner and their staff means their impact on the process is huge, therefore perceptions about their independence will always be important.

Overall, perceptions about independence were linked to the confidence that families had in the system's ability to find out the truth and reach an accurate

[82]Detached to the coronial staff but still actually police employees.

outcome. This was understood by all participants, although two lawyers said that in their experience, families often felt the system was biased in favour of the State. A clear distinction was made between perceived independence of investigatory bodies and of coroners themselves. In particular, questions were raised about whether the IPCC was independent of the police that they were required to investigate. Participants felt that the fact IPCC investigators were often ex-police, as well as the fact they often had to rely on existing police officers to carry out some investigatory duties (such as collecting evidence or interviewing witnesses), all influenced perceptions of bias. (It should be pointed out that the PPO rely on the police in the same way, but this does not impact on perceptions of bias in the same way as the PPO are investigated prison staff, not police officers.) However, it was acknowledged that the inquest process (although reliant on reports drafted by investigatory reports) could improve confidence in the independence of the process, if coroners were perceived to be unbiased.

Some coroner participants felt an important part of their role was to be independent of not just the State bodies they were investigating but also the investigatory bodies themselves. However, family and legal representative participants felt coroners were not always seen as independent; especially when coroner's officers were either ex-police or current police officers. The fact coroners rely on investigatory body investigations and reports was another issue raised, as it was questioned whether a coroner could be truly independent and impartial if they only received evidence produced by an investigation that was perceived to lack independence. Two participants (CO1 and SP1) highlighted the difficult position coroners could find themselves in, as if they were perceived to be biased towards families, they were seen as not protecting State agents sufficiently. Most participants felt that perceptions about whether the investigation or process was not independent resulted in the family having little confidence or trust in either the process or the outcome. People expect a decision-maker to act impartially when adjudicating between parties.[83] So the importance of a coroner acting in a way that is seen as independent from State parties and investigatory bodies, by acting in an unbiased way, has a significant impact on confidence in the system.

8.4.2 Transparent Process

Another aspect identified as important to influencing perceptions of legitimacy was the transparency of the process: in particular, whether families perceived State parties as being honest and upfront with them. Negative examples were given where families felt State parties were not being honest, so they lost confidence in the system or struggled to accept the outcome. One family member (FA4) said they lost confidence in the prison when they lied to them about details and gave them inconsistent information about important facts. One example related to the cell where their loved one had died. FA4 Father was taken to one cell to pay their respects following the death but when he went back to the prison

[83]Leventhal (1980).

to take photographs (as requested for the inquest), they took him to a different cell and initially pretended it was him that was confused, before admitting the mistake. The prison also kept changing the story in relation to who was present when the deceased was found and what time they were found. All these 'mistakes' left the family feeling the prison were not being honest with them.

One participant (CO1 – in their role as legal representative for State agencies) thought that if State agencies were open with families from the start, then families had greater trust and confidence in the State as they perceived them as being transparent. One family member interviewed (FA3) also thought State parties acknowledging mistakes not only increased families' confidence in the authorities but also improved public confidence in, and therefore the legitimacy of, the State agency. Another (FA5) said immediately following the death of their loved one, they implicitly trusted State officials but when they started being evasive, FA5 lost confidence in them. A third family member (FA4) felt the same, saying they started by wanting to trust the State officials but in the end concluded they could not, as they seemed them to be hiding things from them.

Most concerns mentioned related to the State agencies involved in the deaths, but as with the previous section, a transparent investigation or inquest process could also impact positively on perceptions about the legitimacy of the process. One family member interviewed (FA5) made a distinction between the State officers involved in the death and those investigating the death: their confidence in the investigation remained strong as they thought the two officers were thorough and kept the family well-informed, as well as responding promptly to questions; so they felt they were being open with them. Similarly, another family member (FA3) made a distinction between the State agencies and the coroner; they lost confidence in the former when they became aware the State were only providing them access to the evidence 'under duress' but were confident the coroner wanted a transparent process. It is therefore clear a transparent inquest process could lead to families accepting the outcome and feeling the system was legitimate, although this would not necessarily change perceptions of State officials involved. Similarly, participants thought where families were supported to effectively participate in the inquest process, this left them feeling the whole process was transparent. Two participants (IPCC and LA1) thought effective participation for families had a big impact on whether they found the system transparent and therefore accepted the outcome and could be confident in the legitimacy of the system.

Participants' perceptions about how transparent officials were with families during the process were linked to how confident the families were that the right outcome was reached. Family participants said they felt if State officials were not being honest and upfront in sharing details about circumstances surrounding the death, they lost confidence in the whole process. Although again a distinction was made between State officials who were present or in some way involved in a death and the coroner. If families only received information after the coroner compelled the State to produce the information (maybe by relying on legal rights for families), then families might not feel the State officials were being transparent. This could result in families having confidence and trust in the coroner and the inquest system as a whole, but less confidence in, and distrust of, the State agency or officials involved in the death. It is important to note, though, that if coroners were perceived as being open with families throughout the process, families would be more confident in the process and therefore the outcome reached.

8.4.3 Fair Process

The perceived fairness of the process was also very important to families and could lead to increased satisfaction and acceptance of the outcome. One lawyer (LA4) said in their experience, families were always satisfied if the coroner had been fair throughout the process. Another (LA5) thought there were intrinsic complexities involved with most custody deaths which meant fairness during the inquest process was incredibly important. Two coroners (CO1 and CO2) said, regardless of the outcome, the most important thing was for all parties to feel the process had been fair.

Family participation was seen as an opportunity to allow families to assess the fairness of the process and ensure they perceived the inquest as distinct from State agencies and other investigations which could help their acceptance of the outcome. Another coroner interviewed (CO3) said the bereaved family could start by feeling antagonistic to the coroner but by allowing them to engage fairly, by the end of the process they could be satisfied and even grateful to the coroner.

One family member interviewed (FA2) were worried when the process appeared unfair, even when it was other parties who were being treated unfairly. They gave the example that the press had reported two police officers had lied about what happened, which the coroner said the jury were not to be informed about, but then a barrister for another party 'accidentally' showed the jury the press report. Although the family thought the jury should have been told about this, they were unhappy with the way it had happened as 'things like that shouldn't really be going on'. Another (FA4) agreed, saying they were convinced the correct processes should be followed, not because it might have changed the outcome but because 'that is only fair and proper'. Perceived unfairness left the family with no confidence in the outcome or in the inquest system. A different family member (FA3) also thought the most important thing was to have a fair process with balanced evidence, regardless of whether it changed the final outcome. A legal representative (LA2) thought families did not mind other parties protecting themselves as long as ultimately the process was fair.

In general, a number of participants linked perceptions about how fair the inquest system was to whether families accepted the outcome and felt satisfied at the end of the inquest process. It should be noted, however, that coroners are obviously in a difficult position to ensure fair treatment to all parties and it must be acknowledged that certain rights of State actors must be protected by a process which can sometimes lead to either civil or criminal cases. Participation is key, as it ensures families are able to judge for themselves the fairness of the decision-making: including hearing explanations from the coroner as to why particular decisions were made. Even in situations where families were concerned about lack of independence, if they believed the correct process was followed by the coroner as 'is only fair and proper' (FA4), they could trust the outcome. Families having the opportunity to positively engage in the process was suggested to ensure they ended up with positive perceptions about how fair the process was, allowing any concerns they had to be resolved. Participation was argued not just to influence perceptions of fairness but result in increased trust in the process and therefore the outcome. Research has indicated that decision-makers providing parties with justification for any decisions that might be perceived as negative can negate perceptions that the process is unfair.[84] So even if a family are concerned about the validity of the process, a coroner who explains their decision-making can improve perceptions about the fairness of the process.

8.4.4 Legitimacy of Process

Family participation impacting on the legitimacy of the inquest system was seen as key by participants, partly due to the purpose of the system of investigating deaths in custody which involved both closed (and therefore non-transparent) institutions and potentially contentious issues in terms of duty of care. One coroner (CO1) explained inquests into custodial deaths were distinct as there was always an understanding, not that the deaths were necessarily controversial but that potential criticisms of the State could be investigated. Another (CO3) said one of the reasons they encouraged legal representatives (for all parties) to be involved in questioning was because it provided a perception of legitimacy for all parties to be engaging with the process. A family member interviewed (FA2) felt very strongly that as the State duty of care was under scrutiny, it would not be legitimate for State bodies to participate without ensuring equitable participation for families.

Some participants (LA6, FA1, FA3, IPCC and SP1) linked the general reform of the system and increased family participation with increasing legitimacy of the system via increased public confidence. One lawyer (LA6) said in their experience, the reform of the inquest system over the last 30 years ensuring greater family involvement in the process, had increased legitimacy in the eyes of the public. A family member interviewed (FA1) felt that if families could participate fully (with Government funding for legal representatives) in inquests following prison deaths, the penal system would be improved and therefore public confidence in the system would increase. Another family member (FA3) thought what was 'damaging to the public confidence and legitimacy' was when State parties were defensive and did not treat families fairly or respectfully. A senior police officer (SP1) was clear that the perception of an inquest being independent, transparent and open to the public was vital to the legitimacy of the system; even if the public did not attend or know much about the process, 'it's the symbolic nature'. So ensuring fair participation for families was seen as vital to ensuring an inquest was legitimate, which was itself seen as very important due to the purpose of an inquest to hold the State to account.

The interviews therefore illustrated that perceptions about the independence, transparency and fairness of the process directly impacted on whether the process

[84]Bies and Shapiro (1988).

was seen as legitimate. This related to both beliefs about the legitimacy of the State actions under scrutiny, and the inquest process itself. If the State bodies involved in the death were seen as being open with families, and treating them fairly, families were more likely to see them as legitimate, and be confident in what they were saying. However, even where there was a lack of confidence in the legitimacy of the State bodies under scrutiny, if the inquest process (and particularly the coroner themselves) was seen as independent, transparent and fair, then the process was seen as legitimate, and the family were more likely to have confidence in the outcome. Some participants also linked the requirement that the process ensured an opportunity for the family to participate in the inquest with the public's perception about the legitimacy of the process.

8.4.5 Trust in the Process

Participants believed a benefit of family involvement was that it allowed them to judge the process for themselves, which could result in them trusting both the system and the outcome. Two coroners (CO3 and CO4) acknowledged that perceptions about the coronial system could be negative to start with, but engaging with the process allowed families to feel more positive. One of them (CO3) noted families sometimes saw the system and coroners in particular as 'archaic, old-fashioned', but participating in a fair process could change their minds. The other coroner (CO4) thought if families could participate effectively, they saw an inquest as a 'living investigation[s] to come [……] to answers, to help people come to terms with [the] death'. When one family member (FA3) realised their coroner was happy to challenge the State and stick to the law, they trusted they were going to get 'a proper inquest'.

Three family members interviewed (FA3, FA4 and FA5) all thought they could only trust in the outcome when they had been able to assess the evidence presented themselves and understand the process. Two participants (LA2 and ESP2) agreed that trust came from fair participation, and families being 'able to go through the process' (LA2).

It should be noted that sometimes family participation led them to challenge the legitimacy of State agencies, even if the inquest system is seen as fair and therefore legitimate, as evidence highlighted during the process led them to distrust the actions of the State. One family member (FA4) felt the inconsistencies and mistakes made after the death meant a fair inquest was unable to make up for the failings in the investigation. It should also be acknowledged that if families participated in an inquest process they did not feel was fair, independent or transparent, they would be likely to mistrust the process and see it as illegitimate.

8.5 Conclusion

A fair process can be shown to maximise the opportunity of reaching a fair outcome, as discussed in the previous chapter, but it also has intrinsic value, regardless of whether it has an instrumental impact. There is intrinsic value in a

State ensuring a fair process, as this is the way they can ensure a fair outcome, and in addition, there is moral value in a fair process for all. It can help ensure fair treatment for all, which is particularly important in relation to the criminal justice system, where there are current issues relating to disproportionality. The legitimacy of State actions which involve restraining and detaining individuals (as in relation to the criminal justice system) relies on those actions being carried out in line with established principles, and ensuring there is a fair process to scrutinise those actions can be linked to public confidence in the State. The inquest process is particularly important in relation to establishing the legitimacy of State actions, and the fairness of the process is therefore vital. Procedural justice theory has illustrated a clear correlation between perceptions about how independent, transparent and fair a process is and the perceived legitimacy of the process, and consequent confidence in the outcome. This research proved this correlation in relation to family perceptions about the inquest process, and their perceptions about the legitimacy of the process, and confidence in the outcome. This final section has described participants' views on why family participation is so important to the legitimacy of a process and how ensuing fair and effective participation in a transparent and independent investigation process can ensure legitimacy. It indicates that in order to maximise family confidence in the system, State parties should be encouraged to be as open as possible with families and treat them fairly during the inquest process. However, it is also clear that even where families have ongoing concerns about the State parties, as a result of participating in an inquest, if they perceive the inquest itself to be independent, transparent and fair, then they will ultimately see the inquest as legitimate and have confidence in the outcome. The role of the coroner was seen as key in ensuring families had positive perceptions following their participation in inquest: making sure they are seen as unbiased, as well as being transparent both in relation to ensuring families have access to all relevant information and explaining all decisions are vital, as is ensuring the inquest process is seen as fair to all parties.

This chapter focused on the intrinsic value of families' participation, but families can also ensure accountability of the State and any actors in relation to restraining or detaining individuals. The different ways family participation can benefit accountability will be considered in the next chapter.

Chapter 9

Family Participation Benefits Accountability

This chapter introduces the author's views on how family participation benefits accountability; referencing how the empirical evidence affirms established theories which cover both the instrumental and intrinsic value of fairness. Chapter 7 covered how ensuring families' participation can have an instrumental benefit to both the outcome and the wider legitimacy of the system. Families scrutinise the evidence, bring balance to an adversarial process as well as introducing vital evidence about the deceased – all of which help an inquest to reach a fair and accurate outcome. Beyond influencing a single inquest, families are often the ones pushing for positive change to encourage further learning to prevent deaths as well as encourage accountability through punishing those responsible for a death. By increasing dissemination of outcomes, they also make the system more transparent and therefore improve public confidence. Chapter 8 explained the importance of public confidence in a system that scrutinises deaths in custody as a vital part of our democracy which empowers State agents to detain and restrain individuals. Ensuring State agents are not above the law, and use those powers fairly underpins public confidence in the legitimacy of the State. Procedural fairness also means that ensuring families' can participate in an inquest increases the legitimacy of the system. This does not just impact on families' perceptions about legitimacy but wider societal understanding about the system. This chapter explains the added value that family participation brings to achieving accountability as well as identifying limitations in the current system linked to a failure to scrutinise change following inquests and restricted publication of outcomes.

9.1 Accountability via the Inquest System

The interviews linked the role of a bereaved family participating in an inquest to ensuring State accountability in a number of ways. Firstly, participants suggested families have an instrumental effect by optimising the likelihood an inquest would reach a fair and accurate outcome. Secondly, families were argued to play a key role in disseminating the inquest outcomes, which is particularly relevant where media interest is either non-existent or inconsistent. Thirdly, families were argued

Death in Custody, 139–149
Copyright © 2020 Jo Easton
Published under exclusive licence
doi:10.1108/978-1-83909-025-720201014

to drive through positive change; both in calling for any necessary reforms to prevent deaths and improving the inquest system itself. Fourthly, family participation was linked to the legitimacy of the process, especially when it was perceived as a fair process.

The instrumental effect of families was argued by participants to have two main aspects. The first involved cases where the family either provided or uncovered evidence relating to the death.[1] One example given was the case of Sean Riggs; his family, along with their legal representation, identified important CCTV evidence which had not been presented to the IPCC and therefore not investigated. The CCTV evidence was then presented at the inquest hearing, where it helped establish the circumstances surrounding Sean Riggs' death. It can also be important where families ensure the deceased is seen by the coroner and jury as a rounded individual (as discussed previously), which means they can better understand the deceased as an individual and therefore interpret the facts of the case more accurately. The second way families' participation has an instrumental effect is via the scrutiny they can provide during an inquest hearing. The coroner can question witnesses but a number of participants argued that the best way of establishing the truth was through cross-examination; which is most appropriately carried out either by the family or on their behalf, as they are likely to be sceptical of the evidence.

In England and Wales, the inquest system is the primary route by which non-criminal State actions relating to protecting the life of individuals are scrutinised in a public hearing.[2] An inquest hearing provides two aspects which are vital to discharging the procedural obligation of Article 2 which are not always ensured by investigatory bodies. The first is the opportunity for public scrutiny, not just of the conclusions to any investigations but of the evidence itself. The second is an opportunity for families to scrutinise the evidence provided by any investigation. Case law indicates that both these elements are vitally important to ensuring compliance with *Jordan*.[3] Participants agreed that participation of families is key to ensuring accountability through scrutiny of the evidence.

The instrumental effect provided by families participating in the inquest system arguably leads to improvements in how the State detains or restrains individuals. Fair participation for families allows them to provide evidence as well as scrutinise and question evidence provided by the State; this maximises the likelihood of an accurate outcome and the more accurate the outcome, the more likely it is to identify any systemic failings. Any failures identified in part either due to the assistance of families or via their scrutiny of the evidence can lead to changes which provide greater protection for people in custodial settings or interacting with police. An example of this would be the issue of positional

[1]The *O'Brien* case is another example where predisclosure allowed the legal representation for the family to scrutinise the evidence and realise vital forensic evidence was missing. Referenced in Section 2.2.6.3.

[2]*R. (on the application of Middleton) v HM Coroner for Western Somerset* (2004).

[3]*Jordan v United Kingdom* (2003), *McCann v United Kingdom* (1996), para 161, *McKerr v United Kingdom* (2002), para 70, *Letts v Lord Chancellor* (2015), para 70.

asphyxia which has been identified in a number of inquests over the last 10 years. Positional asphyxia is the name given to a condition that can lead to a severe risk of death when an individual is restrained for any length of time by being bent over forwards with their arms secured behind their backs. This method of restraint was previously sanctioned for use in youth custodial settings but the official guidance was changed after it was shown to severely restrict an individual's breathing, leading to a risk of asphyxia.[4] This risk was identified during the inquest into the death of Gareth Myatt, who was restrained in this way.

Participants felt that ensuring families' fair and effective participation in an inquest could improve the accuracy of the outcome, and therefore the likelihood that failings were identified. However, concerns were expressed that the current system did not provide adequate accountability for two reasons; firstly because of a failure to identify culpability and secondly because there was no assurance that further deaths would be prevented. Participants felt the inquest system was not always able to sufficiently identify any State culpability, particularly as it is not possible to name a particular individual as being culpable in a death. It was pointed out, however, that the scrutiny provided by an inquest could be key to identifying those cases where further investigation, and possibly prosecution, should be considered. Participants also felt that it was a problem if, even where inquests produced clear evidence of culpability, there was a lack of will to prosecute such cases, which did ultimately limit accountability.

Participants indicated that holding the State to account was not solely concerned with securing prosecutions of State agents. Finding the truth could be sufficient, even in cases where there was perceived immunity for State agents. This supports research suggesting that victims of police brutality or their families can be satisfied with acknowledgement of the truth.[5] However, it was clear that participants thought establishing the truth was only sufficient when it ensured necessary changes were subsequently made to prevent future deaths. Whether participants felt prosecutions were needed to achieve accountability, or whether establishing the truth could be sufficient, it was clear that both were linked to what participants saw as the fundamental priority for achieving accountability, which was to identify failings and ensure changes were made to prevent future deaths.

Participants were not confident that this happened in practice, due to the lack of follow-up after individual inquest verdicts made recommendations on necessary reforms. Further concerns related to the lack of a framework by which institutional learning could be guaranteed, beyond any specific institution involved in a particular death. The problem of national learning is illustrated by the example of positional asphyxia, as the issues were identified in 2007 by the inquest into Gareth Myatt's death but systemic learning did not occur. This meant that privately employed individuals acting on behalf of the State to deport Jimmy Mubenga were still using the dangerous hold which resulted in his death

---

[4]INQUEST (2007), UK Government Ministry of Justice (2010).

[5]Walsh and Conway (2011, p. 67).

in 2010.[6] Some participants pointed out that the newly appointed role of Chief Coroner would hopefully be putting in a place a system to allow national learning from any systemic failings identified at an inquest.[7]

The views of participants that the inquest system has a key role to play in ensuring accountability reflect the importance of the inquest system in identifying failings of the State. Accountability requires independent investigation into State actions which allows identification and punishment of individuals culpable for any deaths. Criminal and civil courts are one framework for achieving this, with the judiciary usually seen as independent in Western liberal societies.[8] However, there are disadvantages in utilising the adversarial criminal court system to hold police or prison officers to account. Particularly in relation to the police service, it is argued there can be a negative impact internally on police morale and respect for those managing the service in imposing legal liability.[9] In addition, it has been illustrated that adversarial procedures can intensify differences between parties rather than resolve them.[10] An inquisitorial system can be a mechanism for allowing the truth to be identified and published, instigating a change in policy and behaviour without punishing individual officers. The inquest system can therefore play a part in ensuring accountability by finding the facts surrounding a death and identifying any State failings, without some of the negative effects of an adversarial process. In addition, participants understanding that accountability means going beyond finding the truth and ensuring future potential violations are prevented fits with potential benefits to family participation established in case law.[11]

There are established principles that a fair justice system must ensure equal treatment for all people before the law. The rule of law demands that each individual should be treated equally and fairly by the law, regardless of race, gender or economic status.[12] Fundamental to human rights is the principle that all humans must have access to the same rights and be considered equal before the law. Article 2 of the Universal Declaration of Human Rights states that, 'Everyone is entitled to all the rights and freedoms set forth in this Declaration, without distinction of any kind'.[13] Democratically, it is important that everyone believes they are equal before the law, otherwise they will not have equal vested interest in complying with the law as a full citizen.[14] Therefore, individuals must be confident that State actors will be held to the same laws as ordinary citizens.

---

[6]INQUEST *Updated briefing on Jimmy Mubenga* (2013).
[7]The Office of the Chief Coroner has committed to publication of PFD reports, and some summary findings from inquests, which does facilitate some national learning but there is still a lack of enforcement associated with the changes that need to be made.
[8]Walsh and Conway (2011, p. 66).
[9]Walsh and Conway (2011, p. 64).
[10]Richardson (1993, p. 63).
[11]*Letts v Lord Chancellor* (2015).
[12]Principe (1999, p. 371).
[13]United Nations, *Universal Declaration of Human Rights* (UNG. A. Res 1948).
[14]Fuller (1969, p 210).

Another important aspect of equity is described by Simmel, who says the unwritten contract between Government and citizen sets up an expectation that the authorities will abide by their own laws.[15] Fuller argues that authority is internally legitimated by its own compliance to the laws when exercising its own power.[16] The inquest system is where State actions are scrutinised to ensure they are lawful; other procedures such as prosecutions are required where actions are deemed unlawful but identifying legality is often part of an inquest following a death in custody. In order for the public to be confident that State actions are lawful, there must be confidence that the inquest system is a fair and rigorous process, which is able to adjudicate the legality of State actions.

It has been argued that inquisitorial systems as a method for achieving accountability partially depend on the will of the authorities to not just acknowledge failings but to act on findings to prevent further violations.[17] This is relevant in respect of the limitations of inquests which do not establish legal liability. The system by which coroners must produce reports identifying actions that have to be taken by institutions to prevent further deaths was discussed in Chapter 4. Concerns were raised by participants that these Rule 43 reports did not always ensure suitable learning across institutions; although the Chief Coroner is working to improve this.[18,19] In addition to the new system publicising PFD reports, which allows all public agencies to learn from inquest findings, media campaigns can be successful in highlighting failings. Media interest can result in public pressure being placed on key stakeholders to ensure necessary changes are made. Case law is also important in sign-posting relevant agencies to unlawful practice. Participants suggested that bereaved families have an important role to play in both instigating, or encouraging, media campaigns and bringing important legal cases. In addition to assisting with the identification of specific systemic failings causal to deaths, family involvement can also lead to wider systemic changes in the investigatory processes, thereby improving investigations into deaths in custody and increasing accountability. The next section will look at how media reporting can impact not just on ensuring accountability but also increase public confidence in the legitimacy of the system.

9.2 Public Confidence via a Transparent Inquest System

Participants all agreed that the fact an inquest process is open to the public could have a positive impact on public perceptions about the legitimacy of the system. However, it was also pointed out that there is little public understanding of the inquest system which, it was suggested, impacts negatively on perceptions of the

---

[15]Simmel (1950).

[16]Fuller (1969, p 211).

[17]Walsh and Conway (2011, p. 68).

[18]Now called PFD (Preventing Future Death) Reports but the old name of Rule 43 reports has been used throughout this book.

[19]The Chief Coroner publishes most PFD Reports: https://www.judiciary.gov.uk/related-offices-and-bodies/office-chief-coroner/pfd-reports/.

legitimacy of the system. A number of legal representative and coroner participants felt the public nature of inquests was very important but admitted that the public rarely attended hearings, so thought the press were vital in ensuring the public was informed about the process. Questions were raised about the accuracy of the press reporting, though, especially as participants felt it was rare for reporters to attend the whole inquest hearing, and that usual practice was for them to witness only the verdict being given. Participants said all parties could feel dissatisfied when only verdicts or snippets of a hearing were reported, without the media providing a detailed context. Although it was acknowledged that families were likely to be present for the whole hearing, because families have a unique interest in the death, participants did not feel families could be said to represent the wider public in this situation. However, participants felt families generally wanted a true account of what happened to be in the public domain. It is likely that press departments for State institutions often prefer verdicts that found no failings to be disseminated to maintain public confidence, but are not keen for critical outcomes to be publicised. In these cases, a family desire for publicity can be vital for ensuring media interest.

It is a core principle of Anglo-Saxon legal systems that justice is carried out transparently so everyone can see that a judgment is reached in a fair and understandable way.[20] The expression 'justice must be seen to be done' means that, in general, processes as well as judgments are accessible to all so they can validate the legitimacy of the decision.[21,22] The public nature of inquests is therefore vitally important. However, with evidence that public attendance at hearings is negligible, media reporting becomes key.[23] It could be argued that if the family are the ones publicising cases, this will only happen where the State authorities have acted wrongly or negligently. Two participants were concerned that if the public only heard about the negative actions of State agents, they may have skewed or inaccurate perceptions about State use of detention and restraint; and that if the public only know about negative examples, it would reduce public confidence in the legitimacy of State. This has been supported by research illustrating there can be an effect of lessening public confidence in the police in response to a well-publicised direct conflict between the police and a private citizen in court.[24]

---

[20]Jaconelli (2002, p. 5).

[21]*R. v Sussex Justices; Ex parte McCarthy* 1 KB 256, para 259.

[22]Important exceptions include in the interests of security and privacy for vulnerable individuals such as victims or children.

[23]Following the implementation of the Coroners and Justice Act, the Chief Coroner now published 'Prevention of Future Deaths' reports written by individual coroners following the conclusion of inquests. These reports focus on the changes that should be made to prevent future deaths: a brief description of the circumstances of the death are included but they are not detailed records of the inquest process. See https://www.judiciary.gov.uk/subject/prevention-of-future-deaths/.

[24]Smith (2001).

However, this author argues the opposite view that it is positive for transparency to be assured in those situations where State actions are considered questionable, as transparency shines a light on any poor behaviour. In addition to the role the inquest system plays in holding the State to account, a fair system is important in maintaining public confidence in the legitimacy of State actions. It has been argued that procedural requirements for legal processes overseeing actions of public agencies 'promote the rule of law' in ensuring that such agencies act fairly and consistently.[25] Public confidence is linked to perceptions about the legitimacy of State actions and inquests can illustrate State compliance with two important principles which relate to holding State agents to account; equality for all before the law and transparency. Equality before the law is a fundamental principle that does not just describe the fact that all citizens must be treated the same but also ensures that no one is above the law, including State officials. Transparency allows citizens to understand the laws in place but in relation to legitimising authority, it can go further in allowing public scrutiny of their actions (from law making to use of power to detain or restrain individuals). Public confidence in the existence of a robust system which complies with rule of law principles, by ensuring State officials actions are accountable and scrutinised for any actions which may have caused or contributed to a death, is therefore vital. It can be argued that if the public are aware of critical outcomes identifying any State failings, they can be confident that there is a robust system scrutinising State actions in relation to detaining or restraining individuals, therefore ensuring the legitimacy of State actions. This, consequently, raises a concern. Given that the current system relies on families to liaise with media to disseminate inquest outcomes, critical verdicts will only be brought to the public's attention when there is family involvement. Cases with no family involvement may therefore remain hidden.

9.3 Increased Perceptions of Legitimacy via Procedural Fairness

Participants all explained that enabling family participation increased the legitimacy of the process but families' perceptions about how fair the process was impacted on their own understanding of whether they felt the process and consequentially the outcome were legitimate. Perceptions about legitimacy were then linked to whether families expressed confidence and trust in the system. The main aspects identified as influencing families' perceptions of legitimacy were the independence, transparency and fairness of the process.

Where families perceive the inquest as independent, especially of State bodies, then they have more confidence that the process will reach a fair and accurate outcome; identifying any failings that are relevant to the death. It is clear that families often feel the process is biased towards the State. This can begin with the investigation carried out following any death – there are many concerns about the independence of the IPCC from police (which ultimately resulted in a new organisation being introduced). Even where the investigatory bodies might be seen as

[25]Richardson (1993, p. 18).

independent, the fact they often rely on the police to carry out much of the investigatory duties (such as collecting evidence, and interviewing witnesses) leaves families worrying that the investigation is not fully independent. It therefore becomes vitally important that the inquest system is seen as independent. Especially where the process relies on investigatory bodies to provide evidence to be considered at the inquest. Even where families feel an investigation was not fully independent, if it is clear that the coroner is unbiased, and willing for everything to be fully scrutinised, this results in families seeing the final outcome as independent.

Transparency of the process was highlighted during the interviews as another key factor influencing families' confidence in the outcome. Again, families often feel State bodies are not open with them, often hiding evidence, and only releasing it to the coroner and families' when forced to do so. Similarly, investigatory bodies are not always seen as being fully transparent about the investigation. It is obvious that any indication that there is not full transparency leads to suspicions of why things are being kept hidden. These suspicions lead to a lack of confidence in the State bodies, and sometimes investigatory bodies as well. Where a coroner ensures full transparency – not just in securing evidence for the families' to scrutinise but also by explaining the process and decision-making to families as they go along – then families are more confident that the outcome achieved was fair.

It is clearly important for families to feel they have been treated fairly during an inquest process. Participants mentioned a number of aspects that could be considered as unfair to families, including bias by coroners (or their staff), inequity with State parties having access to all the evidence and being represented by teams of specialist lawyers throughout the process, whereas families struggle on both counts. It was also clear that families sometimes felt they were disadvantaged due to lack of knowledge about the process. In these situations, coroners need to ensure sufficient advice and support is in place for families, often through their officers. It is likely that to perceive a process as fair, families would have to receive support and advice from the coronial team. This could be argued to leave a coroner open to suggestions of bias towards families. It is a complex situation if, by remaining unbiased, coroners allow the process to be unfair to families. Any perception by parties that the decision-maker has acted improperly will lead to concerns that the process itself is invalid, even if parties have been able to participate effectively.[26] Coroners therefore have to balance unbiased and transparent decision-making with ensuring families are able to participate effectively.

Participants clearly identified the benefits of families being treated respectfully through a complex inquest, including positive perceptions relating to increased confidence and trust in the outcome and therefore legitimacy of the process. Positive engagement with families from the earliest point of contact was identified as fundamentally important. This should include not just ensuring families are informed about the process and their rights but also appreciating that families are bereaved and therefore should be treated with patience as well as respect. Family participants were clear that respect should include taking the time to talk to them

[26]Lind and Lissak (1985).

and explain the process as it was going forward. Simple acts such as acknowledging families and offering condolences to them at the start of a hearing were suggested to have huge and positive impacts. Additional examples of good practice mentioned were coroners keeping the process as informal as possible, avoiding complicated legalese and checking with families to make sure they understood the process. Participants pointed to two factors which were unique to families compared with other interested parties, firstly that they had no experience of inquests or even the processes relating to detention, so they struggled to understand what was happening or being discussed if care was not taken to explain things properly. Secondly, it is the families who had the personal connection to the deceased and therefore were grieving. Family participants mentioned how important it was for everyone else involved in an inquest to remember that for them it was a very emotional experience, not just another day in the office. Some participants identified challenges for coroners in treating families differently from other interested parties without influencing the process unduly and opening themselves up to accusations of bias (see above). However, coroner participants suggested that treating families respectfully could ensure they had positive perceptions about the process without interfering with the fairness of the process or the outcome. An example was given of a photograph of the deceased being placed on the bench during the inquest hearing; it was suggested this could be beneficial for the family as they could be sure the deceased was central to the proceedings but it did not influence the process itself.

The views of participants followed procedural justice theory as perceptions about the procedural fairness of a process were shown to impact on perceptions about the legitimacy of the process and consequently the confidence in the outcome.[27] Tyler and Blader proposed a four-component model involving four criteria by which people evaluate the procedural fairness of a process.[28] The criteria put forward were general and specific; with the general being the rules governing both the decision-making and the established rights of parties and the specific relating to how decisions are made and parties treated in specific instances. Aspects of participation raised in Chapter 8 which impacted on perceptions of legitimacy, confidence and trust correlated with the four-component model. Participation in the inquest system ensures families have the opportunity to assess the independence, transparency and fairness of the process; which was linked to increased perceptions about the legitimacy of the system and the outcome of the process. In terms of the general criteria, the transparency, equity and independence of the process can all be related to how parties might perceive the fairness of the rules governing the process. Both the transparency and independence of the inquest system can correlate to perceptions on the fairness of the rules governing how decisions are made during inquests. Similarly, whether the system ensures equity of parties can be seen as an illustration of whether the rules ensure parties are treated fairly. The other aspects raised by participants can be linked to the

[27]Sunshine and Tyler (2003) Tyler (2003), Tyler (1990).

[28]Blader and Tyler (2003).

specific criteria of the four-component model by looking at how decisions are made in practice and how families perceive they are treated during the process. The independence of the coroner as it is perceived to relate to unbiased decision-making can influence perceptions about whether decisions are fair to all parties. Also, how families perceive they are treated by a coroner and their staff during the process directly correlates with the last criteria of the four-component model. Where families perceive the inquest system to be independent of State bodies, transparent and fair, then they believe the system to be legitimate; which ensures they have trust and confidence in the outcome.

It was argued by a few participants that family participation did not just influence their own perceptions about how legitimate the investigation was but also perceptions of the public. This supports research which says that watching others being treated fairly in a process will increase your understanding that said process is legitimate.[29] Again, perceptions about legitimacy were linked to confidence and trust in the system. So the public will perceive the process as more legitimate if families are seen as being able to participate fairly, leading to the public having more confidence in the process. The converse is also true, with one family participant believing that when families were not treated fairly and therefore unable to participate fully, public confidence in the system was diminished. This is supported by Richardson, who asserts that, even though common law protections tend to rely on the instrumental benefits of fairness in traditional adjudicatory processes which involve disputing parties, to infer rights on parties who have substantial interests which could be affected by the process can also guarantee decisions 'reflect the public interest'.[30]

Another aspect of whether fair participation for families might impact on public perceptions on the legitimacy of the system is linked to whether families can be argued to be representing the public. Research has shown if the public can be confident that a party is representative of the public voice, then the fair participation of that party can have a positive impact on the public's perceptions about the procedural fairness and therefore confidence in the legitimacy of the process.[31] Where families take on the role of scrutinising State actions and therefore holding the State to account, this is arguably in line with public aims. Concerns have even been expressed about whether it is in the public interest for resources to be targeted towards funding complex and lengthy inquests or whether other processes are more appropriate for learning lessons.[32] However, the author believes the importance of ensuring accountability and public confidence in any system which scrutinises the actions of the State successfully rebuts such concerns. So where families are benefiting the accountability achieved in relation to ensuring State actions are fully scrutinised, this can be seen as in the public interest.

---

[29]Bierie (2013).

[30]Richardson (1993, p. 35).

[31]Nonami and others (2015).

[32]For example, see discussions around the Bloody Sunday Inquiry and the inquest into the Hillsborough disaster. Rolston and Scraton (2005), Elliott and McGuinness (2002).

9.4 Conclusion

This chapter has set out the potential wider benefits to the system that can result from the fair and effective participation of bereaved families in an inquest following a death in custody. The evidence shows that family participation can impact on the capacity of an inquest to hold the State to account in relation to any actions that may be linked to a death. Accountability comes from any failings being identified, and appropriate action being taken to punish anyone culpable for a death, as well as ensuring changes are made to prevent future deaths. Family participation can benefit this in a number of ways, including through maximising the opportunity for a fair outcome to be reached by scrutinising the evidence presented at an inquest, and directly pushing for change.

The importance of ensuring State accountability for any deaths that occur in custody is linked to the legitimacy of State actors who are empowered to restrain and detain individuals for lawful reasons. The legitimacy of their actions relies on them complying with established legal and moral norms, including principles such as everyone being equal before the law. The public can be confident in the legitimacy of State actions, if they can be confident in processes scrutinising those actions. There is intrinsic value in such processes being seen as fair and legitimate. This chapter has illustrated that procedural justice theory is relevant in relation to inquest processes, and specifically the perceptions of families in relation to how independent, transparent and fair an inquest process is can be linked directly to whether they perceive the process as legitimate, and have confidence in the outcome. Wider perceptions about whether the process treats families fairly by allowing them to participate effectively are also linked to whether the public see the process as legitimate.

This chapter was the last using the empirical research to illustrate the different benefits offered by ensuring a bereaved family is able to participate fairly and effectively in an inquest process following a death in custody. The next, final part of this book looks at the practical aspects of achieving a system that maximises the opportunities for this participation.

Part 5
Achieving Fair and Effective Participation

This book has explained the existing challenges with the law, policy implementation and differing practice around England and Wales in relation to family participation in an inquest following a death in custody. The previous two parts of the book have set out the benefits offered when families are able to participate fairly and effectively: this last part sets out both the main challenges to ensuring such participation and proposed solutions to combat those challenges.

The specific issues identified by the author reflect those previously highlighted by organisations and academics working to support families in these situations. Firstly, although the law ensures each family has the right to be legally represented, the lack of equity in funding for said representation is a gap in the law that leaves families struggling to find and pay for adequate legal support. Secondly, policy directives to relevant police and prison investigative agencies require them to provide families with access to all relevant evidence related to an investigation; but in practice there can be delays before families are given the documents, if they even receive them at all without the intervention of their legal representation forcing disclosure. Thirdly, although family access to the inquest process is legally protected, in practice lack of information about the process as well as a lack of support provided to families prevents them participating fully. This problem relates as much with the approach taken by individual decision-makers as any lack in legal protections. Access to information depends on decisions taken by coroners, their officials and other State agencies; and although there are examples of good practice, many decision-makers do not take a process value approach which would ensure positive engagement with families. Even where families are able to participate effectively with the support of INQUEST and legal representatives, they often feel they have had to fight for their rights, which leaves them with negative perceptions about the process as well as the State actors involved. Some great work has been done to challenge existing laws and policies to bring in change to increase a families' opportunity to participate effectively and fairly. This has improved legal protections as well as requiring decision-makers to follow certain policy directives in a top-down approach attempting to force good practice from a central governance structure. This author takes an alternative approach by starting from the ground up, looking at why participation is important, what benefits are possible to families and the wider system and how these benefits can be achieved. The author believes if decision-makers understand why participation is important, they will be more likely to change their approach and make decisions by framing how to support or maximise participation. Chapter 10 relies on the experiences gathered during the interviews to describe the practical challenges.

Chapter 10

Practical Challenges to Effective Participation

10.1 Introduction

The previous two parts of the book presented the reasons why it was important for bereaved families to be allowed to participate in an Article 2 inquest. This chapter summaries participant views on what is required for participation to be effective. As discussed previously, families have different reasons for wanting to participate in an inquest, so they might require different things to ensure their participation is effective in fulfilling their needs and protecting their legitimate interests. Some participants (CO1, IPCC and PPO) also pointed out that not all families wanted to participate fully in the process. Both IPCC and PPO said families all wanted to engage on different levels during investigations; some wanted to know everything and have a lot of input, while others did not want to comment or even see information. This was also said to be true during the inquest process, with one coroner (CO1) pointing out that each family was unique so levels of participation during a hearing consequentially differed. IPCC felt the amount of contact the family had with the deceased prior to the death was a determining factor in relation to a families' desire to engage with the process; saying in their experience, families who were in close contact with the deceased were more likely to want to be involved in the process.

Family participants (FA2, FA3, FA4 and FA5) felt the biggest challenge for families who wanted to engage was that the system did not recognise families had varied needs and might want to 'deal with things differently' (FA5). It was also clear that the emotional state of a family could impact on whether they felt able to engage. One family member (FA2) said they were initially very depressed after the death of their loved one which left them with little motivation to engage with the investigation process. But other families (FA5) felt they needed to be involved in everything from the start.

Another factor raised by participants was that family structures influenced how involved families wanted to be in the process. One family member interviewed (FA2) thought engagement without a large family was difficult as it was time consuming and emotionally draining. They reported that as next of kin they had to not just be point of contact with official agencies but also coordinate the

Death in Custody, 153–179
Copyright © 2020 Jo Easton
Published under exclusive licence
doi:10.1108/978-1-83909-025-720201016

different needs of family members. Another family member (FA5) had a similar experience and felt their engagement was more complicated as each member of their large family wanted to participate on different levels and at different times. A lawyer (LA4) agreed that they often saw families whose members wanted to engage on different levels.

This chapter identifies generalities as to what can assist participation for those families that do want to engage; allowing for the fact each family is unique and therefore there will always be some aspects that are more important than others for different families. It should be acknowledged that lawyer and family participants' views relate to families that wanted to engage, and although coroners and investigatory bodies may have come into contact with families who did not want to engage, generally most of their experiences are of those families who participate actively. By definition, those families who do not want to engage will not have come into contact with many of the participants for this research.

10.2 Right to Participate

10.2.1 Right to Be Heard: Voice of the Deceased

Chapters 5 and 6 illustrated that an important aspect to families' participation in an inquest is to ensure they are able to represent the deceased through the process. This chapter begins by considering how this can be achieved. Three coroners (CO2, CO3 and CO4) gave examples of how they allowed families to ensure the voice of the deceased was present throughout the process; including putting a photograph of the deceased on the bench, asking the family how the deceased should be referred to (such as should they use their first name, for example) and allowing a statement about the deceased to be read out. One family member (FA5) was allowed to tell the inquest about their memories of the deceased and found this helpful. Two other family members (FA3 and FA4) felt there was not sufficient space in the process for them to represent the voice of the deceased, but they did explain that small things could make a difference. One family member (FA3) gave the example that it felt like the coroner brought the focus back to the deceased by concluding all hearings by expressing condolences to the bereaved family. Another (FA4) said that when one of the days of the inquest fell on the anniversary of the deceased's death, the coroner held a minute's silence, which they appreciated.

It is clear that small actions can be taken, which ensure the deceased as a person is not forgotten through the process. These do not have to divert from the legal process, but can sit outside the main formalities. Even just ensuring that everybody present at an inquest remembers the process involves a death and the deceased is treated respectfully throughout can have a positive impact. Obviously, it is important that coroners involve families in discussing how the deceased should be respected, as they are the ones most likely to be taking on the responsibility to represent the deceased.

10.2.2 Right to Influence: Access to the Process

Fundamentally important to allowing effective participation is ensuring families have access to the inquest process, which includes making sure they are fully informed about the process (including their rights) as well as practical issues that can impact on attending the hearings themselves. The first step in ensuring families are kept informed about the process is for them to be identified as interested parties.[1] One of the primary ways coroners identify who should be the interested party for families is to look to the next of kin (or their representative if they are minors). Some participants (LA1, LA4, LA5, CO3 and IPCC) said coroners sometimes restricted interested party status to the one individual identified as the next of kin, which could cause problems. Both IPCC and CO3 had seen cases where the coroner refused to deal with more than one identified next of kin and nobody else in the family was allowed interested party status; which was technically within the rules but they thought was not very helpful. Three lawyers (LA1, LA4 and LA5) said they similarly found coroners preferred to designate one family member as an interested party which meant only this individual could access their legal rights.

Participants pointed out a complication from this approach was that the individual designated as interested party had to represent the needs of the whole family, which was noted as being a huge strain. One family member (FA2) said in their case they had a large family so had had to deal with a lot of people who were ringing them constantly and putting their own viewpoints across. They gave the example that at one point in the process, the press had reported family connections inaccurately, and members of the family expected them to deal with it: they were 'ringing me up of a night and having a go'. This was not an uncommon situation with other participants saying they had seen participation in complicated inquests tearing families apart. IPCC said they had experienced families turning on each other. Three legal representatives (LA1, LA5 and LA6) had all worked with families who fractured under the pressure of the process. Two of these (LA5 and LA6) had experienced cases where families had come to disagree with the family member initially identified as the point of contact, which made it very difficult. One lawyer (LA5) pointed out there were practical difficulties if families wanted to change who was their point of contact because the original person had been officially designated as the legal representative's client.

Another problem mentioned was that it could sometimes be difficult to identify the next of kin; particularly in large or broken families. One ex-police officer (ESP1) agreed it could sometimes be very difficult to identify one next of kin; giving the example of a deceased having been married to one person but living with somebody else. Two participants (ESP1 and LA1) had seen coroners ask the family to identify a single point of contact even if different family members (for example, parents and partners) were not on speaking terms. One lawyer (LA4)

---

[1]A coroner must identify anyone who has a legitimate interest in the outcome of the inquest; which includes not just family members but other parties such as prison or police officers involved or representatives of insurance companies.

said where families were split, with parents having new partners, expecting them to work together as one interested party with one lawyer was unrealistic if not impossible in some cases. Another (LA5) pointed out that designation of a single point of contact had a negative impact on funding, as even where families were split, legal aid was only available to the person identified as next of kin. Access to funding and legal representation will be discussed further later.

A number of participants pointed out that although it was within the rules to identify only one point of contact as an interested party, it was possible to give more than one family member interested party status. Two participants (ESP1 and IPCC) said if families were split, the police would designate multiple Family Liaison Officers (FLOs) so different parts of a family could be dealt with separately. They pointed out that this could be beneficial if different members of a family did not talk to each other. A coroner (CO4) said whenever the family was split, they made sure everyone who was a properly interested person was able to participate. Two family members (FA3 and FA4) both thought it was important for all family members to be involved, with FA4 father saying there was a benefit in family members who were not grieving the most being involved in the process as they could be less emotional. A family member (FA3) said in their case, other family members were allowed to ask questions, although they were not the next of kin and not legally represented so were not able to participate fully. It is clear the system allows sufficient discretion for multiple family members to be given interested party status, and therefore participate, but this flexibility is not always utilised effectively. It is unfortunate that coroners do not take a more proactive approach in giving as many family members interested party status as is necessary to ensure that different viewpoints are reflected.

10.2.2.1 Information about System

One of the primary difficulties mentioned during the interview that prevented families participating in an inquest was a lack of understanding about the process. Participants pointed out that inquests were unique processes and little understood, apart from those who engaged with the system regularly; which meant families needed basic information in order to understand the process. Two lawyers (LA3 and LA5) said the inquest process was alien to most people so families generally did not 'have an understanding of what it's supposed to be'. Two participants (LA3 and CO1) thought the title 'coroner's court' led families to believe the process would be similar to criminal hearings. More participants (LA2, LA3, LA5, PPO, ESP1, ESP2 and SP1) all thought it was very helpful for families to have the inquest process explained to them as it prevented misunderstandings and helped manage expectations. A lawyer (LA2) said, in their experience, if families understood from the beginning what was likely to happen during the process, they found it less frustrating. A coroner (CO3) agreed that managing families' expectations from the start led to them being more satisfied with the process. An ex-police officer (ESP2) said it was only natural to be more satisfied and accepting of something you either expected to happen or at least were prepared for in advance.

Three coroners (CO2, CO3 and CO4) all agreed that good coroners should (either themselves or through a member of staff) speak to families directly early on to make sure they understand the process and know what to expect. None of the family participants had experienced such a personal process and all suffered from a lack of initial information about the inquest process. Family members interviewed (FA1, FA2, FA3 and FA5) all received little information from the coroner's office and said one of their biggest worries was they had no idea about the system or what to expect. One (FA5) said they felt 'very, very at sea' and another (FA1) felt like they had been 'thrown in a big hole' without any advice on how they could get out of it.

All family participants wanted better information about the system from the coroner's office but also thought there should be better signposting to organisations like INQUEST, which could provide impartial advice. One family member (FA5) said they had only found support by Googling 'inquests', and another (FA3) felt it was only through 'incredible good fortune' that they were directed to INQUEST. Although IPCC said families should receive signposting information from the outset from IPCC officials, one lawyer (LA2) said in their experience the PPO were far better at signposting families to either INQUEST or specialist legal representatives. Family participants (FA2, FA3 and FA5) indicated signposting did not always happen, and often they struggled to find anyone to advise them on who to contact.

Another issue to consider is how information should be provided to families. As discussed earlier, families are all unique and therefore have different views on how much information they want to be given at any one point and in what format. One family member (FA1) said they wanted to have simple, straightforward hard copy information, whereas others (FA2 and FA5) said they did not understand the hard copy information they were given and wanted to have people to contact to answer questions. It should be remembered that immediately following a death, next of kin may be too distraught to retain information given to them, which is why different approaches should be available. One of the family members (FA5) said that when they first met with the police, they struggled to retain and understand what they were saying. One solution is to ensure families are signposted to support organisations and also provided with basic facts about the inquest system in multiple formats (such as hard copies, websites and point of contacts).

In order for families to engage with the process, it is important they are aware of their rights. Participants explained that a failure in families being informed about specific rights limited their participation. One family member (FA5) said they were not given any information about what their rights were. Another (FA3) said they had not realised at the start that they had a right to be informed about what was happening at all. In fact, they were told they could not be told anything about the investigation while it was 'an ongoing inquiry'. A different family member (FA4) said they did not know they could appoint someone to attend the post-mortem on their behalf and 'were kept in the dark about things like that'. The rules require the next of kin to be informed about when the post-mortem will take place and allows them to nominate a representative to attend on their behalf, but families are not necessarily aware of this. Unfortunately, current rules do not require families to be told they have a right to be represented by a lawyer and to have access to evidence gathered during the investigation. A legal representative (LA2) said often families only realised they could have a solicitor by reading about other cases in the press; other families were only signposted by INQUEST. A coroner (CO1) explained the current rules for disclosure to families stated 'if they ask, you have to give it to them', but if families were not told about their rights, they did not know to ask. One family member (FA2) said they were not sent any information about the process and later realised this was because they had not asked for it. Requiring families to be proactive would be challenging enough if there was a good level of understanding about the process, but if you do not know anything about the process, or what your rights are in relation to it, it is next to impossible to ask for what you are entitled to.

Participation in an inquest process starts soon after the death has occurred, so early provision of information and support is the first step to ensuring fair participation for families.

10.2.2.2 Access to Engagement during the Hearing

In addition to families not being given relevant information from the start of the process, participants identified problems associated with access to the inquest hearing itself. One of the problems identified was the lack of details provided about the inquest hearing. Three family members (FA2, FA4 and FA5) all said they had been given little or no information about when and where the inquest would take place. One (FA2) said their biggest worries about participating were practical ones: 'where will I go, and who'll be there and where will I sit and will I have to sit on my own?'

Additional worries identified by families were practical ones related to having to take time off work for weeks to attend the inquest, find childcare for the same time frame, travel the distance to the courtroom and then find convenient parking. One family member (FA2) said the practicalities of attending the first inquest 'were just a nightmare'; they had to drive 60 miles every day for six and a half weeks as well as finding childcare for that period. Another family member (FA5) suggested it would be incredibly helpful if coroners provided families with details of how to find the location and possible places to park. In their case, the only parking FA5 found was £15 a day. This does not seem an unrealistic ask or something that would be that challenging to provide in all cases.

Coroners were aware of practical difficulties some families had in attending inquest hearings, but two coroners (CO4 and CO2) both said that in their respective areas, there were a limited number of suitable locations that could be used for inquests. They pointed out complicated inquests could take weeks, and it could be difficult finding courtrooms free for such a long period; which meant sometimes families had to travel considerable distances. One of these coroners (CO4) said if they were aware there would be difficulties with the family attending a particular location, they would try to find an alternative but that it was not always possible.

Participants identified further difficulties with finding suitable spaces: local halls often did not have adequate facilities but courtrooms could be intimidating for families. One family member (FA5) said their inquest was held in a Town Hall, which did not really have enough room for all the attendees. However, two other family members (FA2 and FA4) said their inquests were held in criminal courtrooms which they found very formal and intimidating. One lawyer (LA5) said they had seen positive examples where coroners had been 'very mindful of the family' and rearranged the courtroom layout so either all parties were on the same level or families were invited to sit alongside the coroner on the raised bench. Regardless of the space used, separate waiting rooms were suggested as very important. Two family participants (FA2 and FA5) were approached informally during breaks at the inquest by other parties whose actions were under scrutiny, which they both described as 'awful'. They suggested a space set aside for families to sit in peace and discuss things with their legal representatives 'should be standard' (FA2) and 'like a little bit of a refuge' (FA5).

The challenge posed by the formality of the process is not just due to the space used for a hearing, but some participants (CO3, CO4, LA3, LA5 and SP1) felt the process was inherently formal. Some of these (CO3, CO4, LA3 and SP1) said it was difficult to make the process user-friendly as it was 'a court at the end of the day' (CO3). One lawyer (LA5) agreed that some families found the process incredibly formal, which negatively impacted on their participation. For example, the use of technical or legalistic language was seen as an impediment to families understanding what was happening. Two coroners (CO2 and CO3) said they tried to minimise the terminology used as it was difficult to follow and encouraged all parties to use 'reasonably user-friendly language' (CO2). A family member participant (FA2) said this would have been helpful for their inquest as it had felt like the process was being run in 'a foreign language'.

Another aspect raised as impacting on access to the process was the delays which often occurred before inquest hearings were concluded. Some participants (FA2, FA5, CO2, CO3, PPO and IPCC) all said delays were likely following deaths in custody, with families having to wait five or six years before the inquest hearing. Chapter 5 illustrated the negative impact delays could have on the grief process. One family member (FA5) said another problem with the whole process taking so long was that it meant multiple meetings and hearings, which were both practically difficult and traumatic for families to attend. Although two other participants (PPO and LA4) acknowledged delays were a problem, they pointed out that inquests could not be held before the report by the investigatory body was complete as the evidence was not yet compiled, so some delays were necessary.

It is clear that the current system poses challenges for families accessing the process, but support and advice can certainly minimise the difficulties faced by families by managing expectation and reducing worry about the unknown. Some of this information is purely factual and should be provided by coroners (or their staff) as a matter of fact. Advice can also be provided by coroners, but families should be referred to specialist legal representatives for independent advice, as soon as possible.

10.3 Fair and Respectful Treatment

10.3.1 Respectful Treatment

Part 4 of this book set out why procedural fairness towards families during an inquest system is important. One aspect of that is respectful treatment and the next section sets out what participants thought that entailed. All participants were clear that the general approach of the coroner and other decision-makers towards families should not be underestimated in how much of an affect it had on family participation. Some of these interviewed (LA4, LA5, CO1, CO2 and CO3) all agreed it was very important for coroners to ensure respectful treatment of families, as it improved the families' experience of participating but could also provide a benefit for the process.

As discussed above, participants were clear about the benefits of coroners or their staff engaging with families early on in the process to make sure they understood what was happening. Some participants (FA1, FA2, LA2 and CO4) all said if coroners allowed time to meet with families before the hearing began, it helped make the process seem less daunting and encouraged families to participate more fully. One family member (FA5) said although the coroner did not meet with them, the coroner's assistant had met with them and been very welcoming. Participants pointed out if it was not possible for coroner's to meet with families, then a simple way to ensure families felt involved in the process was to welcome them at the start of the hearing. These participants (LA2, FA1, FA3, FA4 and FA5) all thought it was beneficial if coroners simply acknowledged families and referenced their grief at the start of the process: 'it's such a small thing but it's just not done, incredible' (LA2). One family participant (FA1) said in their case, the coroner ignored the family completely and a lawyer (LA2) said unfortunately they often saw coroners who did this.

As mentioned previously, participants pointed out that families were often the only parties involved in an inquest who had no experience of the system. Participants said because families were often at a disadvantage to other parties, as well as having an emotional reaction to the process, coroners had to ensure families felt at ease. Some participants (LA3, LA5, CO2 and CO3) felt families had to be given certain leeway in how they participated as they were not professionals, as well as grieving, and therefore had to be treated sensitively and compassionately. One coroner (CO3) said coroners needed to have 'more tolerance, more patience, just more sensitivity' to ease the process for families. Two participants (LA3 and FA1) thought coroners should take the time to ensure families did not feel like a nuisance or a 'lesser class' (FA1) than other parties so they felt comfortable and positive about participating in the process.

Participants identified ways in which coroners and their staff could ensure families felt they were being treated respectfully. Two of those interviewed (CO1 and LA3) suggested one approach was for coroners to take into account that families might need more breaks than other parties, as inquests were physically and emotionally draining for them. A coroner (CO2) said they positioned the family at the front of the court so they could 'maintain eye contact with them'.

One lawyer (LA5) said they had seen positive examples of coroners doing 'simple day to day things' such as ensuring there were enough seats for family members at the inquest.

It was also pointed out that it was not always in the power of coroners to ensure a respectful environment; one coroner (CO1) said all parties had to act in a reasonable and measured way in order for there to be a positive collaborative approach. A lawyer interviewed (LA5) agreed that it was the actions of State parties that could be disrespectful to families. Three family participants (FA2, FA4 and FA5) raised concerns that they felt other parties seemed to forget the purpose of the process was to look at the circumstances of someone's death, with one (FA2) saying 'it was so insensitive'. All of these family members said they had been hurt by certain behaviour of the other parties, including officials that were laughing and joking during the inquest process and on one occasion actually celebrating a State officer's birthday with a cake in the courtroom during a break.

It is clear that respectful treatment for families can be provided in simple ways without conflicting with the rules and regulations governing the inquest system. The impact of simply politely welcoming families at the start of a hearing should not be understated, but it should also not be overstated. One family member (FA3) pointed out respectful treatment only goes so far if it is not backed up by ensuring families are treated fairly as well.

10.3.2 Fair Treatment

The importance of fairness and why it is relevant for parties to perceive that they were treated fairly throughout the inquest process was discussed in Chapter 8. Some participants (LA1, LA2, LA4, LA5, FA1, FA2, FA4 and FA5) all said families often felt the process was unfair and biased towards the State parties. Factors which lead families to feel the process was unfair include the fact that other parties were better represented, funded and supported to participate in inquests. Equity as it relates to equality of arms in terms of legal representation is discussed in the next section, but other disparities between families and other parties were raised. Three family participants (FA1, FA2 and FA5) said it felt very unfair to them that State parties were supported to attend the inquest, whereas families struggled to cover the costs of participating. Two family participants (FA2 and FA5) both noted all the other parties attended as part of their jobs so they were effectively paid to attend, whereas the family had to take unpaid leave to be there. One of these (FA2) said 'it was like really rubbing salt in the wound, the fact that I knew [the officer under scrutiny] was getting paid to attend'. Another family member (FA1) thought the most unfair thing was that all the other parties were 'taken care of [....] it didn't matter what it was costing', whereas families were left 'out on a limb'. Generally, concerns expressed by participants that the inquest process did not appear to be fair related to the lack of equity between the support available to different parties; with the main issue being legal representation.

10.3.3 Equity of Legal Representation

All participants thought equity between parties was beneficial in ensuring a fair inquest. Two coroners interviewed (CO2 and CO3) both thought this was particularly important for inquests looking at deaths in custody as there should always be equality of arms if you are dealing with something as serious as a sudden or unexpected death involving the State. Another coroner (CO1) said, in their experience, it was rare for parties involved in inquests into custodial deaths to not all be legally represented. However, all the legal representative participants said in their experience, there was 'almost exclusively in these cases a complete lack of equity' in terms of access to information and legal representation (LA1). They all identified the inequality of arms in relation to legal representation, with State parties always being fully represented but families struggling to find funding to pay for one lawyer. One lawyer (LA4) said not just State parties but all other interested parties (such as private security or insurance companies) were always represented by legal teams. Almost all the family participants (FA1, FA2, FA4 and FA5) felt it was incredibly unfair that they had to pay for their own lawyers but the legal representatives for other parties were paid for by the State. One (FA4) pointed out it did not seem right that State parties had experienced legal teams from the start but families were left 'to fend for themselves'.

An important issue raised by a number of participants (LA1, LA4, LA5, CO3, FA4 and FA5) was that because each different State party was legally represented, this resulted in 'an array of lawyers' for the prison, police or hospitals (LA4). Two participants (LA1 and CO3) said in most cases, State parties had multiple legal teams, as each official had their own lawyer; as did the overall police force or prison as well as the national service, senior officials and maybe the Ministry of Justice: 'there can be a load of different people' (CO3). One family member (FA5) said in their case, 13 State parties were individually represented. Two lawyers interviewed (LA1 and LA5) said in their experience, legal representatives for different State parties usually worked together so families definitely felt 'ganged up on' (LA1). Two other lawyers (LA2 and LA4) had similar experiences and were concerned that multiple representatives for State parties could all argue a particular view point, which might bias how the evidence was perceived. Two family members interviewed (FA4 and FA5) both felt very strongly that all the State parties worked together in their respective cases. Two lawyers (LA1 and LA5) both pointed out multiple legal representatives for State parties were especially concerning in relation to equity as families are generally designated as one interested party (as discussed earlier).

Lack of equity was also raised in respect to the quantity and quality of legal representation available to different parties. This linked to funding (see next Section 10.4.2.3.) but is also mentioned here as participants talked about differences in the number and seniority of legal representatives as an issue of equity. Some participants (CO3, LA1, LA2, LA3, LA5, FA1, FA4 and FA5) all said generally families were represented by one solicitor, while other parties had large legal teams, including barristers. Three of these (CO3, LA1 and LA5) said families were often not legally aided, whereas State parties appeared to have 'a bottomless pit of resources to put into representation' (LA1). Two lawyers (LA2 and LA3) said the State was always legally represented by experienced barristers. It was pointed out by a senior police office (SP1) that State officers needed to be well represented as it was their actions which were under scrutiny.[2] This author would argue that instead of limiting the representation for State parties, equity could be achieved by ensuring families are sufficiently funded to have similar representation in terms of quality, if not quantity.[3] This is especially important as equity was linked to family perception of fairness; therefore, it can lead to lack of confidence and trust in the process and outcome.

10.4 Legal Representation

All participants raised the issue of legal representation for families being linked to ensuring effective participation in an inquest process. It was mentioned in relation to fairness and equity (see previous section), but participants identified other reasons why legal representation for families was vital. This section will look at the aspects which were put forward as benefits of legal representation, and what is important in ensuring families have access to legal support.

Almost all participants (CO1, CO2, CO3, CO4, LA1, LA2, LA3, LA4, LA5, LA6, PPO, IPCC, FA2, FA3 and FA5) said that in their opinion, legal representation for families during the inquest process was the most important factor affecting participation. Two coroners (CO2 and CO3) said families should be ably represented in all custodial death inquests 'in an ideal world' (CO3); with a lawyer (LA1) saying it was 'beyond important'. Both PPO and IPCC said they always preferred families to be well represented; as unrepresented families could struggle to participate in the process which left them feeling 'outside of it' (PPO). Two lawyers interviewed (LA4 and LA5) said families could only participate effectively if they had a lawyer representing them. Three family members (FA2, FA3 and FA5) all thought they would not have managed to engage with the process without legal representation.

Most of the lawyers interviewed (LA2, LA2, LA4 and LA5) all thought the primary benefit in them supporting families was to ensure their legitimate interests were protected. This included ensuring families could defend themselves and the deceased during the process, with two of them (LA2 and LA3) pointing out families were often attacked or smeared through the process.

---

[2]It should be noted a recent case found that an individual who had been acquitted of arson (relating to a fire which resulted in a death) did not require funding for legal representation at the subsequent inquest into the death. The decision was challenged as breaching their Article 6 rights, but it was judged there was no breach as an inquest was not a criminal proceeding. *R. (RJ) v Director of Legal Aid Casework* (2016) EWHC 645 (Admin).

[3]Attempts have been made to introduce legislation that ensures parity of funding for families in cases involving scrutiny of the police. An amendment was introduced in the Police and Crime Bill, see House of Lords Debates on the Bill through 2016 and 2017, and the Public Authority (Accountability) Bill or Hillsborough Law was introduced as a Private Members Bill by Andy Slaughter on 29 March 2017.

Participants generally agreed that grieving families were in a vulnerable position during the process, which made it even more important that they had support and assistance from legal representatives. Most lawyers interviewed (LA2, LA4, LA5 and LA6) felt the fact that families were dealing with a very emotional situation meant it was too demanding to ask them to participate without having legal representatives. Two of these (LA5 and LA2) both said that even with their expertise, if one of their loved ones died in custody, they would want their own legal representative to support them through the process. Two family participants gave examples of how their emotional state affected their participation. One (FA4) said it was difficult to remain calm while engaging with the process (especially State officials) when you were grieving and found themselves becoming upset or angry. The other family member (FA2) said immediately following the death they did not feel in a 'fit state to do anything': this included making an official complaint.

Most participants (CO1, CO2, CO3, CO4, IPCC, PPO, LA1, LA2, LA3, LA4, LA5 and SP1) agreed that legal representatives were vital in supporting families, as although certain family rights were set out in law, a lot of decisions about the inquest process were left to the discretion of individual coroners. They all said the coronial system was hugely variable because so many decisions were left to the coroner, who all had 'very different ways of doing things' (CO2). Two participants (IPCC and LA1) said some coroners were not aware of the complexities of Article 2 law, which could limit them ensuring the protections put in place to ensure family involvement were proactively followed. Two lawyers (LA2 and LA4) both thought there was unfortunately a large disparity between the approaches taken by different coroner's in relation to engaging with families. Other lawyers (LA4 and LA5) agreed that legal representatives could negate the disparities in the way coroners treated families. This was reflected by two family participants, with one family member (FA5) saying they felt they 'would have been at the mercy of the coroner' without legal representation. A family member (FA2) also thought unrepresented families would never know they had the right to influence the process and challenge coroner's decisions. This leads on to the next section which looks at why legal representatives for families are so important in ensuring their effective participation. Just some of the more important factors in relation to legal representation are set out.

10.4.1 Benefits of Legal Representation for Families

10.4.1.1 Early Access to Legal Representation

Participants were clear families needed to have legal representation early on in the process for full beneficial effects. Three coroners (CO2, CO3 and CO4) said it was very important for families to have good representation from the beginning; with one (CO4) saying they would 'very strongly encourage' families to find representation as soon as possible in the process. Three participants (CO2, CO3 and PPO) all thought it was very difficult if families found legal representation late on in the process; with one coroner (CO2) saying they found it 'profoundly unhelpful'. Three lawyers interviewed (LA2, LA3 and LA5) all agreed it was more beneficial to represent families from an early stage, as it allowed families to be both fully involved and able to influence the process. One participant linked early access to equality and fairness with a family member (FA1) saying they had wanted legal representation as soon as possible when they realised the State parties had representatives in place immediately following the death.

10.4.1.2 Explain Inquest and Custody Processes

It was discussed earlier that families were at a disadvantage in not understanding the inquest system and family participants mentioned finding legal representatives helpful in explaining the process to them. Two family members (FA2 and FA3) said before they found lawyers, they had not known what an inquest entailed, what to ask or when to ask it. Three lawyers interviewed (LA3, LA4 and LA5) all thought part of their role in representing families was to make sure they understood the inquest process. It was pointed out by some participants (CO2, CO3, PPO and IPCC) that if families were unrepresented, other officials had to step in and make sure they understood the process. Three participants (CO2, CO3 and PPO) all said it was coroners who had to explain the aim and scope of the inquest to unrepresented families during hearings. IPCC said they had been involved in cases where they had to 'do a fair bit of work' explaining the process when families were not legally represented. Two participants (PPO and CO3) both said the main difficulty for coroners was to make sure families knew how they could be involved in the process. An example given by one coroner (CO3) was that it could be difficult to allow questions that families had as they might be outside the scope of the inquest.

Some participants (LA4, PPO, FA2 and ESP1) pointed out it was not just the inquest system that families did not understand but usually they had little knowledge about custodial systems. Three of them (LA4, PPO and ESP1) said the terminology used by professionals working in custodial institutions was very hard for families to follow, if it was not explained to them. This was supported by one family member (FA2) who said, before they met their lawyer, everything had seemed to be in a foreign language. PPO was also concerned that without legal representatives providing context for families, what they heard about custody processes during an inquest might be misunderstood and appear very cold and harsh.

10.4.1.3 Legally Complex

In addition to assisting families with understanding the process itself, another important factor to be considered when looking at whether legal representatives are required is whether parties need assistance understanding the law governing the process. Most participants (CO3, LA1, LA2, LA4, LA5, PPO, SP1, FA1, FA2, FA3 and FA4) all said any inquests into a death in custody involved complex points of law and legal arguments were common, which required experienced legal representatives supporting families to ensure they were not excluded from participating. Three lawyers interviewed (LA1, LA3 and LA5) all mentioned the preparation that had to be done before an inquest hearing, including legal submissions. One of them (LA5) pointed out that the level of legal preparation for a custody inquest was complex in terms of both the law and the medical or forensic evidence. A senior police officer (SP1) agreed that inquests covered complex legal matters, so it was understandable legal representation was needed for all parties. PPO said legal complexity was one reason coroners found it difficult to involve unrepresented families. Three family members interviewed (FA1, FA2 and FA3) all said they found the whole inquest process very legal and would have struggled to understand without legal representatives.

The issue of coroners not always fully understanding the legal complexities was mentioned earlier, but even where this was not a problem, participants were very clear that State parties would always put legal objections forward. Two lawyers (LA1 and LA2) said they found they had to battle the State parties on issues including disclosure, the scope of the inquest, what verdicts could be left to the jury and what constituted neglect or culpability. It was pointed out by two participants (LA2 and FA4) that lack of legal representation for families could also have a negative impact on the outcome if it meant coroners only heard the legal opinions of State parties, which could bias any decisions they made.[4] This issue also links with a point raised earlier lack of equity where State parties had large legal teams but families may only have one representative.

Another aspect raised was the issue of legal strategy which was noted by a few participants (CO1, LA4, LA5 and SP1) as being particularly relevant for custody inquests where juries were present. One lawyer (LA5) said even if coroners were able to assist families with the complexities of inquest law, legal strategy was still very important in building a case and bringing out the evidence you wanted. Two participants (CO1 and SP1) both pointed out inquest processes were structured differently from other legal processes which meant legal representatives had to consider very carefully how to get their message across to the jury within the limited rules. A senior police officer interviewed (SP1) thought this involved legal representatives learning 'to behave in a different way'.[5] Again, the emotional state of families was an issue with two lawyers (LA4 and LA5) both pointing out it was very difficult for them to objectively strategise, even if they had the skill or experience. One very specific way legal representatives can help families relates to ensuring their legal right to access to documents is followed.

10.4.1.4 Assist in Getting Access to Documents

The importance of families having access to all the documents in a case will be discussed later, but the role that legal representative's play in assisting families in achieving access was raised by a number of participants. LA2, LA3, LA5 and IPCC all said families having legal representation made a 'significant difference'

---

[4]The importance of families bringing balance to any decisions was discussed in Part 4.

[5]This links to the need for legal representatives to have specialised experience to be discussed later.

(LA2 and LA5) to the amount of documents that were disclosed to families before the inquest hearing; especially when families had to battle State parties to get full disclosure. Three family members (FA2, FA3 and FA4) said this reflected their experiences, as State parties withheld evidence from them until their respective legal representatives managed to fight for full disclosure. One (FA2) said they were prepared 'to fight tooth and nail' for disclosure but they felt very dependent on their solicitor. Another family member (FA4) said their lawyer 'basically had to force things out of [the State]'. It was pointed out by two lawyers (LA4 and LA5) that, in addition to being able to fight State bodies, experienced legal representatives also had the advantage of knowing what documents should be available, whereas families did not know what to ask for. Another lawyer (LA6) said ultimately unrepresented families had to rely on State parties 'being vaguely honest' and disclosing everything. Once families get access to all the evidence, the next step is to be able to understand it.

10.4.1.5 Assess Evidence

The fact families usually lack understanding about custody processes mentioned earlier was also referenced in relation to being able to assess any documents disclosed to families during the process. Some participants (LA3, LA4, LA5, IPC and PPO) all said legal representatives had to go through all the evidence on behalf of families before the inquest, as specialist knowledge was needed to be able to assess it. Two lawyers (LA3 and LA4) pointed out that families did not know what to look for when given access to documents but expert legal representatives understood the language and practice referred to in official documents so could pick up things families might not. Two family members interviewed (FA2 and FA5) agreed, saying that without knowing or understanding custody procedures they had found it impossible to piece all the evidence together, identify any gaps in documents or whether an action discussed represented correct or incorrect practice. Three participants (LA2, LA4 and PPO) said experienced legal representatives were not just useful in assessing the evidence before a hearing but being able to follow the evidence as it arose during an inquest hearing. Assessing the evidence as it was disclosed was linked as a vital step in families providing scrutiny through questioning at the inquest.

10.4.1.6 Asking Questions

The importance of families scrutinising the evidence presented at an inquest by questioning witnesses was discussed in Part 4 in relation to the impact on families' influencing the outcome of the process. Participants (LA1, LA2, LA3, LA4, LA5, LA6, PPO, FA2, FA3 and FA5) were clear that unrepresented families struggled to ask questions and challenge State evidence. PPO said without legal representation during the process, questioning was a very frustrating experience for families. LA6 said good cross-examination by a legal representative was the only effective way of 'teasing out what really happened'. Three family members interviewed (FA2, FA3 and FA5) said they did not think they would have been able to question the evidence at all without the support of their legal representative. Different reasons were given as to why legal representatives were vital in assisting families in questioning the evidence; including their emotional state, the need for skilled cross-examination and their lack of knowledge about custodial practices or the inquest system.

Firstly, the emotional state of families mentioned previously was thought by some participants (LA2, LA4 and LA5) to leave them at a distinct disadvantage in being able to question witnesses. They all pointed out that attending inquests was traumatic for grieving families, and it was 'simply not possible [for them to] take an objective stance and to be able to question those people' (LA2) without support from legal representation. Secondly, the fact that legal representatives were more skilled at cross-examining witnesses was mentioned as being important in finding the truth. Three lawyers (LA2, LA4 and LA6) all said in their experience, State parties did not want to admit anything if they could avoid it, so legal representatives had to question them in a way that would bring out 'all the facts' (LA4). One family member interviewed (FA4) said their barrister 'basically had to force things of the witness', which ultimately introduced evidence not previously mentioned in their witness statements. Thirdly, the lack of understanding about custodial practices was raised (as discussed above in relation to identifying and assessing relevant documents). Three participants (PPO, LA2 and LA3) said unrepresented families struggled to understand the evidence given at an inquest which left them unable to fully question anything presented by State parties. One of them (LA3) said this meant issues relating to fault or neglect were not always identified. Fourthly, the fact families did not understand the inquest system was raised by a number of participants, who pointed out the scope of hearings was limited by law so only certain questions were permitted. Some participants (CO1, CO3, CO4 and IPCC) all said families often wanted to know the answer to questions which were outside the scope of the process and legal representatives could help explain this to families as well as advising them which questions were permitted. Three family members (FA2, FA4 and FA5) all said their respective legal representatives had taken the family concerns and crafted them into questions that were allowed. They all thought this approach had been very effective in helping them participate, as it had allowed the issues they wanted to be raised during the inquest.

It was suggested by one coroner (CO3) that coroners could take on the role of questioning on behalf of unrepresented families; so if families wanted to raise issues, the coroner could turn them into appropriate questions and put them to the witnesses. In fact, they thought it was not necessarily a problem if families asked questions that were outside the scope of an inquest as the coroner could just ensure any out of scope issues are not put to the jury. Two participants (CO3 and LA3) pointed out that some coroners could be relied upon to make sure all the necessary questions were asked to get to the truth, even if unrepresented families were not able to ask the questions themselves. Two legal representatives interviewed (LA2 and LA4) expressed concerns that most coroners did not have the necessary skills or experience to question parties, but even if they did, it would prevent families' views being put forward. If coroners take on the role of questioning where families are not able to raise issues themselves, although the outcome may be the same, families' participation in this part of the process would be severely limited. One solution was proposed by one lawyer (LA4), who said when they were unable to represent a family during an inquest, they would always ensure the coroner was aware of any questions the family had and ask for them to be put to witnesses by the coroner. This is one way that families' questions can still be put, where they are not legally represented during the hearing, but it does open up coroners to charges of not being independent. It is also likely that unless they have legal representation asking the coroner to take on this role, families will be at a loss as to whether it is even something they can ask for.

10.4.1.7 Support

In addition to assisting families with the legal nature of inquests, good legal representatives were also noted to perform a role akin to liaison officers by supporting families through the process. Three participants (PPO, IPCC and ESP1) all referenced how important it was for families to have FLO's to assist them through the inquest process (this links to the need for families to have the system explained to them mentioned earlier). Two of them (ESP1 and PPO) both said FLOs should explain the scope of the inquest system to families; specifically what aspects relating to a death would be investigated. However, a number of participants (ESP1, ESP2, FA2, FA4 and FA5) pointed out that for deaths where State bodies' actions were under question, FLOs provided by the State struggled to provide independent support to families. Two ex-police officers (ESP1 and ESP2) both agreed police FLOs were first and foremost police officers, who took on an investigatory role while with families. One of them (ESP2) did not think this prevented them also supporting families but acknowledged families might be concerned if they knew FLO's were there as investigators rather than to support them. This was reflected by some family participants (FA2, FA4 and FA5), who felt that when FLO's began acting like investigators, they could not trust them to support them. One family member (FA4) found their prison FLO was not independent as they worked with other prison staff in trying to intimidate the family. Two other family members (FA1 and FA3) felt the system did not seem to acknowledge how emotionally shattered families were and how necessary it was for them to have support from people who knew the process. Both IPCC and PPO said it was understandable that families were frustrated during the process but that there was a gap in support available, as victim support did not get involved following deaths in custody as they were not usually investigated as criminal matters. A family member (FA2) thought families should have access to witness support schemes reflecting the service available in criminal courts.[6]

A number of participants (IPCC, LA1, LA5, FA2, FA3 and FA5) said good legal representatives could fill the gap in the system, by providing families with

---

[6]The Coroners' Court Support Service does provide a service akin to victim support at some coroners' court, but it is staffed by volunteers with no specialist knowledge or understanding of complex inquests.

support as well as legal advice and assistance. IPCC said they had seen good legal representatives act as case workers for families; which was beneficial for everyone involved in the process. Two lawyers interviewed (LA1 and LA5) both said families needed support and advice from legal representatives; someone 'holding their hand through it [the process]' (LA1). Three family members (FA2, FA3 and FA5) all said their legal representatives provided them with both practical and emotional support during the inquest process. One (FA2) said, their legal representative went 'way beyond [their] role' and 'wore many hats in the process'. They gave examples of how their lawyer had supported them including sitting with them every lunchtime, going over everything with them each evening and even liaising with journalists on the families' behalf. Two other family members (FA3 and FA5) said supportive and kind legal representatives made a wonderful difference and helped them feel at ease. If families feel well supported, the process is less stressful for them and therefore participation easier.

10.4.1.8 Benefit the Process

The main points raised during this section relate to how legal representatives can assist the participation of families during the inquest process, but participants also identified two ways in which families being legally supported benefited the process itself. Firstly, it was suggested legal representation for families improved the process by making the role of the coroner easier. Three coroners (CO2, CO3 and CO4) all noted if families had good legal representation it 'makes the coroner function easier' (CO2) as well as making the process smoother because coroners had to give more time and support to unrepresented families. Both PPO and IPCC agreed legal representation for families was positive in assisting the process; with PPO saying the whole process could be negatively affected when coroners had to work hard to involve unrepresented families. One lawyer interviewed (LA2) also felt they assisted coroners by making the process smoother when they represented families.

The second suggestion was that by assisting families in challenging the State narrative and putting alternative views forward, legal representatives helped ensure a fair outcome (as discussed in Part 4).

10.4.2 Challenges to Legal Representation for Families

10.4.2.1 Adversarial

One argument used against the necessity of families having legal representation is that the inquest process is in principle inquisitorial rather than adversarial. Most participants who worked in the inquest process acknowledged the system was meant to be inquisitorial but said in practice inquests looking at deaths in custody became adversarial. All the lawyers interviewed (LA1, LA2, LA3, LA5 and LA6) said although an inquest was fact-finding and not a court of blame, for controversial cases (such as deaths in custody), 'the reality is that the Coroner's Court is adversarial' (LA3). One lawyer said inquests became 'remarkably like a criminal court' (LA6), and another thought 'it is a complete anomaly that there is this fallacy that it's an inquisitorial process' (LA1). Another lawyer (LA2) noted that when you were fighting for the truth about what happened to a loved one, 'it was not a nice and fluffy situation'. Two participants (ESP2 and PPO) both agreed inquest processes following a death in controversial circumstances always became adversarial.

Two participants thought it was the presence of legal representatives themselves which caused the process to become adversarial. The two coroners (CO1 and CO2) both said although the inquest process was set up to be inquisitorial, it was 'the rare custodial death' (CO1) inquest that did not have legal representation for all parties, which meant it was unavoidable the process became adversarial. However, other participants pointed out it was not just the presence of legal representatives but the fact the process was deciding responsibility for deaths in controversial situations which meant 'people were going to be defensive' (SP1). Most of the lawyers interviewed (LA1, LA2, LA5 and LA6) all said State bodies were always on the defensive and trying to limit criticism, which automatically meant inquests became adversarial. One coroner (CO1) said that (when acting as a legal representative for NHS Trusts) they had to try and avoid shortcomings being identified, which inevitably meant taking an adversarial position. Two family members (FA1 and FA3) both thought State parties would do anything to protect their image, which made it unrealistic to think you were not going to get opposing sides. This provided context of why participants felt legal representatives for families was important in ensuring equity, which is a vital principle for a fair adversarial process. As introduced in Section 7.1.2.1, participants generally agreed that scrutiny was an important part of holding the State to account, and the process becoming adversarial can be consequential to the need to cross-examine evidence.

Although participants acknowledged inquest processes became adversarial, they did not necessarily think this was beneficial to the process. One senior police officer (SP1) said in their opinion, when inquests became adversarial this did not contribute to understanding why a person had died. Three coroners (CO1, CO2 and CO4) all raised concerns about situations where families wanted to use an inquest to put the police or prison on trial; which was not the purpose of the process. One family member (FA3) said they would have preferred a more collaborative approach, but in their case, it was the State party who had taken an adversarial stance. An ex-police officer (ESP2) said regardless of which parties led to an inquest becoming adversarial, once that situation had arisen, it meant State parties did not engage in the process fully as they were preoccupied with fighting to protect their interests. It has to be acknowledged that even if the system is set up to be inquisitorial, when deaths in custody are being considered, the scrutiny required to ensure full accountability of State actions leads to the process being adversarial. Currently, this is not acknowledged by policy directives, which puts families at a disadvantage when applying for legal aid funding.

10.4.2.2 Specialist Legal Representation

The complexity of these inquests means that, without specialist knowledge, legal representatives cannot navigate the system or support families. Participants indicated that it could be difficult for families to find legal representatives with experience and expertise in complicated inquests. Some participants (CO3, CO4, SP1 and IPCC) all said inquests were a specialised process, so legal representatives had to be experienced in order to assist families. One coroner (CO3) thought 'thank goodness for that' when they realised good legal representatives were supporting families. Three lawyers interviewed (LA1, LA2 and LA3) all agreed that inquests were unique legal process and that non-specialist lawyers struggled to prepare families. One of them (LA3) said they needed to know custody processes and rules as well as inquest case law. They also said that, as a barrister, they had to provide families with a lot more information and support if their solicitor was not an inquest specialist. Three family members (FA3, FA4 and FA5) all said it was obvious to them that inquests were unique proceedings requiring legal representatives with relevant experience. Two of them (FA4 and FA5) both had to change legal representatives as they struggled with inexperienced solicitors with no understanding of complex inquests. One of these family members (FA4) said they experienced both specialist and non-specialist support as their first solicitor was very knowledgeable but their second solicitor struggled to help them at all as they did not know the inquest system. Two coroners (CO2 and CO4) thought it caused problems if families were represented by non-specialist legal representatives who were not experienced in inquest law; with one coroner (CO2) saying it was 'worse [for them] than being unrepresented'.

A number of participants (CO2, IPCC, FA1, FA2 and FA5) pointed out that geography was an important factor in finding specialist legal representation. Three of them (IPCC, FA2 and FA5) all thought the legal representatives with the most experience were based in London, with IPCC pointing out State parties were usually represented by legal teams from London (wherever the inquest was being held). Two other participants (CO2 and FA1) said in their respective rural locations there were no specialised legal representatives; with one (FA1) saying it had been impossible to find any solicitor local to them who would take them on as clients.

All family participants pointed out it was not just geography which made it difficult to find legal representatives but, unless advised by either coronial staff or an organisation like INQUEST, it could be difficult to know who had the necessary expertise. One family member (FA5) said that without being sign-posted, the most obvious way of finding a solicitor was to use Yellow Pages, which is how they initially ended up with someone who did not know anything about inquest law, let along custody deaths. A senior police officer (SP1) pointed out it was not just families who needed specialist representation, and that the process could be negatively affected if any parties had inexperienced lawyers. A family member interviewed (FA3) agreed, saying the legal representative for one of the other non-State parties involved in their inquest appeared to have no experience in complex inquest law, which made it difficult as both the coroner and the families' legal representative had to keep reminding them of legal restrictions. Generally, though, as other parties do not have the same financial constraints as families, they are supported by specialist legal representatives. The difficulties of finding specialists put additional strain on families, as well as leading to situations where they inadvertently get legal advice from those without the necessary expertise which not only affects their ability to participate fully but also can cause delays in the process.

10.4.2.3 Funding for Legal Representation

The aspect most commonly raised by participants as important in ensuring families had adequate legal representation was funding. This was discussed above in reference to fairness and equity, with participants raising concerns that State parties were well-funded, whereas families often struggled to get funding for legal representatives. Three participants (CO2, CO3 and IPCC) all said families were 'not likely to be legally aided' (CO2), which meant most families were either unrepresented or had to find a legal representative who would work pro bono.[7] Four participants (LA1, LA3, FA1 and FA2) all mentioned the emotional impact on families if they struggled to get legal aid funding. Three of them (LA1, FA1 and FA2) pointed out the cost of a single experienced legal representative for custodial inquests ran into tens of thousands of pounds. One family member (FA1) said they were so worried about how they would find this money, they contacted the Ministry of Justice and were told that they would just 'have to sell something'. Some participants (CO2, CO3, IPCC, LA1, LA4 and FA2) explained that trying to get legal aid funding was an incredibly complicated process. One lawyer (LA4) said the process to apply for legal aid was so noxious that some families did not see it through. This reflected the experiences of a family member (FA2), who said applying for legal aid had taken months and involved filling in 'endless forms' about their wages, outgoings and bank account details.

One of the ironies pointed out by a number of participants (LA4, LA5, LA6, FA2 and FA3) was that applying for legal aid was so complicated that most families needed the assistance of legal representatives to complete the process. Three lawyers (LA4, LA5 and LA6) all said legal expertise was needed to secure sufficient legal aid funding; with two of them (LA5 and LA6) saying solicitors had 'to fight for every single hour of work' (LA5). Another lawyer (LA4) said they probably spent 'half my time writing to the Legal Aid Agency'. Two legal representatives interviewed (LA4 and LA5) both said they often had to take the case and put resources into assisting a family without knowing whether they would be recompensed by the LAA. Two family members (FA2 and FA3) both said their legal representatives had been vital in helping them with the legal aid application.

In addition to the need for legal support in dealing with the LAA, other factors introduced as impacting on funding were the inquest being categorised as an Article 2 case, the next of kin being willing to engage with the process and the fact the LAA tended to challenge the adversarial nature of complicated inquests. Firstly, three lawyers (LA2, LA3 and LA4) all said families getting legal aid funding relied on coroners identifying the inquest as engaging Article 2; with one lawyer (LA3) pointing out that before the HRA, public funding was almost never available for even the most complicated custodial inquests. Secondly, another

---

[7]IPCC pointed out that this was a particular issue for foreign nationals.

lawyer (LA4) said there were two issues relating to the family dynamics which impacted on legal aid funding; the first being that usually only the next of kin was considered for funding, so if they did not want to engage but someone else in the family did want to, they might not get funding. The second issue raised by this lawyer (LA4) was that the LAA needed financial details of all family members, so one person may be refused legal aid because they had a parent or sibling who had sufficient funds but did not want to use them to engage in the process. Thirdly, another lawyer (LA1) thought the biggest challenge for families trying to get legal aid funding was the fact the LAA said inquests were inquisitorial, not adversarial, which was both very unfair and 'naïve'.

The lack of equity between the State parties' legal representatives (in the form of well-funded, experienced teams) and families' legal representatives (in the form of one legal representative) was discussed earlier. A couple of participants (LA1, LA5, FA2 and FA5) said they thought this lack of equity was due to the legal aid funding being so poor. Two family members (FA4 and FA5) only had a solicitor to represent them at their respective inquests (and no barrister) as they had no legal aid funding and had to pay the costs themselves. One lawyer interviewed (LA5) said they 'cannot do many inquests on public funding' as LAA funding would not cover the full costs because the complexity of custody inquests was not recognised so they did not approve sufficient hours of legal work needed to support families. Two family members (FA2 and FA3) both said that even though they managed to get legal aid funding, it only covered a proportion of the legal bill, not the full costs. One lawyer (LA5) noted that sometimes, even if there was a successful civil case, families did not recover the costs incurred in participating in an inquest, let alone receive compensation.

Two participants (CO2 and LA1) both said a common effect of families struggling to get funding was that they did not have legal representation from the start of the process and both experienced cases where the inquest hearing started before families managed to get legal aid funding. LA6 pointed out that families found it almost impossible to get legal aid funding to judicially review any decisions or request an inquest to be reopened, which impacts on the effect of family participation on holding the State to account as discussed in Part 4 of this book. This creates situations that without legal support, families are unlikely to be successful in either of these endeavours, but they cannot get funding for legal support unless they had already been successful.

The conclusion is that for whatever reason, complex inquests do become adversarial and although it might be preferable for families not to have to take the scrutinising position, in reality, this is what happens and to ensure the process is fair and equitable, families should have experienced legal representation.

10.5 Access to Documents

This section will set out the importance of a families' right to access documents, illustrate how this right is not fully enforced and look at how full implementation to the right should ensure families have access to information in a timely manner which allows them to digest material, assess and scrutinise it to prepare for the inquest.

Access to documents was raised as particularly important in impacting families' participation in relation to deaths in custody, as it is only through the documents that families are able to find out the facts surrounding a death. Two lawyers interviewed (LA1 and LA5) pointed out the State held the information about what had happened and it was unfair not to share it with families. Three family members (FA1, FA3 and FA4) all said they relied on the reports from the investigatory bodies to inform them about what happened; with one (FA1) saying the report was 'where I found out about everything'. Another family member (FA4) felt that families were at a disadvantage as they could not collect any evidence themselves but had to wait for the State to provide it. Three family participants (FA3, FA4 and FA5) said it was only through accessing the documents that they realised what they had been told originally had been incorrect. This disparity between what families were told by officials and what they later found out will be looked at later in relation to providing families access to documents in a timely manner.

The legal requirement under Article 2 for all documents to be disclosed to families was noted by a number of participants (LA3, LA6, CO1, FA3 and FA4) as vitally important. Two lawyers interviewed (LA3 and LA6) said full disclosure to families should be automatic in Article 2 cases. Two participants (LA3 and CO1) both said some coroners would not even contemplate giving families' disclosure unless it was an Article 2 inquest. Two family members (FA3 and FA4) both said they had to rely on the law to get full access to documents before the inquest hearing. However, one coroner (CO1) considered disclosure so important to participation that they always gave families full access, even if Article 2 was not engaged. One lawyer (LA3) agreed that this was good practice as it ensured 'a full and fearless enquiry'.

Even with the legal right, families do not always obtain full access to documents for a number of reasons. A couple of participants (CO1, LA6, FA3 and FA4) said there was a lack of knowledge about the law, which was frustrating. Two participants (LA6 and CO1) both said there were still coroners who were not clear on the rules, which was why there were inconsistencies on families getting access to documents. IPCC said some coroners would not allow families to have a copy of the investigatory report before it was presented at the inquest. Two family members (FA3 and FA4) both experienced officials not knowing the law in relation to disclosure, with one (FA4) having to contact the Home Office to force the coroner to give them access to all documents. The other family member (FA3) found the coroner had to use the law to demand the hospital trust provided the family with all the witness statements collected during the investigation.

Some participants (LA1, LA2, LA3, LA6, FA1, FA2, FA3 and FA4) all said it was a struggle for families to get full access to documents in a timely manner and that it was rarely given proactively by State parties. Most of the lawyers interviewed (LA1, LA2, LA4, LA5 and LA6) said they were usually caught up in lengthy arguments with the authorities about material being disclosed to families. One (LA6) said it still happened 'time after time', and another (LA1) said they could not 'think of an inquest [...] where there has not been a battle for disclosure'. Three family members (FA1, FA2 and F3) all said it had been difficult to get access to the evidence (including witness statements); with one (FA2) saying it felt like 'a real closed door policy'.

A further problem identified related to how much access families were given. Some participants (LA1, LA6, ESP1 and FA3) said that even where authorities agreed to disclose documents to families, disclosure was not full and exhaustive. Two participants (ESP1 and LA1) were both concerned that unused material was not disclosed to families, even though this was normal practice in criminal cases. One family member interviewed (FA3) said in their case, some witness statements were relied on at the inquest hearing which they had not seen previously. One legal representative (LA1) said they had been involved in situations where either the family had been given a list of documents but not the documents themselves or even where access had only been via LA1 themselves viewing documents at the State offices but being unable to copy or take away documents. This latter approach would obviously severely limit participation of families, who would not see the documents at all but rely on their legal representatives to assess, scrutinise and feed back to them all the relevant details.

Even where State parties did provide families with access to all the documents in a case, the time taken for this to happen was identified as a common problem. Some participants (LA1, LA4, LA5, FA1, FA2, FA3 and FA5) all said that even where there was disclosure, there were often lengthy delays before families were given access to documents. Two of the lawyers (LA1 and LA4) said it could take months or even years, with State parties often coming up with different excuses to delay disclosure. Another (LA5) said sometimes families only got access to documents just before the inquest hearing started; this was the experience of all the family participants. One family participant (FA5) said the IPCC kept making excuses about why they could not provide the family copies of the CCTV evidence and eventually only handed it over three or four days before the inquest. When they were eventually provided with the CCTV, it was in an inaccessible format so the family had to rely on the police supplying a different copy the morning of the inquest.

Participants summarised the importance of families having access to documents in a timely manner for three main reasons: firstly, that they needed to be able to prepare for the inquest hearing, secondly, that they needed to be able to scrutinise the documents and, thirdly, that they had to be able to digest the information. Some participants (IPCC, LA1, LA3, LA4, LA5, FA2, FA4 and FA5) all said there should be an expectation that families would have access to all the evidence gathered to help prepare fully for the inquest. Three lawyers (LA1, LA3 and LA5) all thought families and their legal representatives were 'handicapped' (LA3) or prevented from engaging, if not given access to the evidence to be considered by the inquest. One legal representative (LA4) said if they were only given the draft investigation report on the day of the inquest, it made it impossible to prepare properly. One lawyer (LA3) said the evidence had to be assessed so that lines of enquiry could be identified and fed into the investigation. A family member (FA2) felt left in the dark and unable to engage because they had not had sight of the evidence in time. Another (FA4) said in their case, it was difficult to go through all the evidence just before the inquest and it would have been much easier if they had been given access to all the documents earlier.

Most family members and lawyers interviewed (FA1, FA3, FA4, FA5, PPO, LA1, LA2, LA3, LA4 and LA6) thought families must be allowed to scrutinise and challenge the evidence presented at the inquest; and that disclosure must be made sufficiently early to allow this to happen. PPO said one of the purposes behind ensuring families had full disclosure of the evidence was to ensure they were able to ask questions during the hearing 'in an informed way'. Two family members (FA2 and FA4) both said it was only by going through all the files that they realised 'things don't tally' (FA4). If families do not get disclosure early enough to fully scrutinise the evidence, it might only be after the inquest that inconsistencies were identified or the inquest itself might have to be adjourned. Another family member (FA3) said they were given an adjournment by the coroner for the inquest as 'clearly it was out of order to hold an inquest' before they had had the chance to scrutinise the evidence. One lawyer (LA3) agreed, saying coroners had to be patient and wait to hold the inquest hearing if State parties were slow to disclose.

Another point raised by this lawyer (LA3) was that if full disclosure was not made in a timely manner, it meant any lawyer representing the family might waste time looking into issues that were not necessarily relevant. This links to the point raised earlier in Chapter 5 about families not being provided with accurate information at an early stage, leading them to create a narrative around misapprehensions. This has a negative impact on their grieving process, as it is difficult to reconstruct an alternative narrative after a period of time. One lawyer (LA4) said when families were presented with evidence at a late stage in the process which turned 'everything on its head', they struggled to adjust the narrative they had created to explain the death. This is one reason why it is so painful for families to hear new evidence or facts at the inquest hearing, years after the death happened. Some participants (CO2, CO3, CO4, IPCC, LA2, LA4, FA2 and FA5) all said how important it was for families to have time to digest the information about a death. IPCC recognised 'it has gone wrong if the first the family know about something is at the inquest'. Three coroners (CO2, CO3 and CO4) all thought it was important for families to have time and space to assimilate evidence which was likely to be painful to hear. One of them (CO4) said one reason they held pre-inquest hearings was so they could go through the more complex or potentially painful evidence with families. A lawyer interviewed (LA2) agreed, saying allowing families' access to evidence in good time before the inquest ensured they had time to take on board potentially painful facts. Two family members (FA2 and FA5) both said delayed access to information left families misunderstanding what had happened which could be very painful. One of them (FA2) said they were grateful they had seen the evidence before the inquest as it gave them 'the chance to digest it a bit'. Alternatively, another family member (FA5) said they were only able to watch CCTV footage of circumstances surrounding the death the morning of the inquest, which was 'really, really hard' as they had not had time to digest it before the hearing started and the footage was shown. In fact, when the footage was shown they had to leave the courtroom a few times because it felt horrible; 'so sad and quite cruel'.

Some explanations were introduced as to why families were not always given access to documents in a timely manner. Three participants (IPCC, FA2 and FA4) said a balance had to be achieved between giving families access to information as early as possible and making sure the information was correct. IPCC agreed families had a right to information but said they had been criticised for passing on information to families before it had been verified. Two family members (FA2 and FA4) both agreed with this in principle, saying they wanted to be kept informed but only wanted the facts, not speculation. Two family participants (FA1 and FA4) both had been provided with documents in a piecemeal way, without any context, and found this was more of a problem than a benefit. It was discussed earlier that legal representatives could help families go through the evidence, but without legal representation, families can be inundated by documents they do not understand. Two participants (IPCC and ESP2) said one reason disclosure might be delayed was if there were good reasons why information should not be in the public domain and there were worries families could not be trusted to keep material to themselves. One coroner (CO2) was very clear that even if there were legal reasons why evidence could not be made public, families should always be provided with full access and could be trusted as long as it was carefully explained why material had to be kept confidential.

It is clear that families' rights to access all relevant information are vital to ensuring fair and effective participation; but families struggle to access this right fully, especially without the support of legal representation. This book has identified that ensuring families can fully access the process and have sight of all the documents in a timely manner are often reliant on having support early on in the process from specialist legal representatives. This makes access to legal aid funding fundamental not just to ensuring fairness but for all aspects of effective participation.

10.6 Conclusion

This chapter set out the challenges identified through the empirical evidence in relation to families participating and the factors necessary to assist families. The issues identified cover the following:

- Practical access to the inquest process, including information about the process (inquests are unique legal processes that are rarely understood), how families can engage and practical support attending meetings. etc.;
- Influencing the outcome through the investigation, questioning the evidence and being involved in framing the narrative verdict by asking the jury questions;
- Families have a right to be given access to the evidence, but there are challenges in relation to ensuring access is timely, all relevant evidence is disclosed and families understand the evidence once they have been given access to it;

- Although families have a right to be legally represented, there are challenges in families not being given legal aid. Legal representation is vital in helping families understand the process, engage with it, ensuring families have access to the evidence and playing an important role during the inquest process itself which often becomes adversarial.

The next chapter puts forward some practical solutions as to what can be done to support fair and effective participation to ensure the benefits described in the previous two parts of the book can be optimised.

Chapter 11

Practical Solutions

The previous chapters of this book have looked at the existing legal frameworks governing family participation in an inquest following a death in custody and then considered the various benefits that can flow from ensuring that participation is fair and effective. Chapter 10 then described some of the main challenges to maximising participation, and this chapter provides recommendations to resolve those challenges.

11.1 Access to the Process

The first step for families participating in a complex inquest is ensuring they have access to the process. This can include fundamental aspects such as families being informed about the process itself, especially what their rights are in relation to participating, and practical issues such as how to communicate with important decision-makers (for example, the investigatory bodies) and attend meetings or hearings. A coroner must identify interested parties, who are then entitled to participate in the inquest process.[1] The next of kin will often have been identified before being designated as an interested party, as they will usually be the first person informed about the death. The rights of the next of kin include being able to either be present themselves or represented at any post-mortem examination, so it is important they are identified soon after the death.[2] The coroner will generally declare the next of kin as an interested party automatically if they can easily identify who they are, but there can be problems either with identifying who is the next of kin or with split families who all want to participate but separately instead of as one interested party. The rules state the next of kin should be designated as an interested party, but coroners can also designate as many different people as interested parties as they think necessary. It was clear from some of the family experiences that even in the most cohesive family, it could be difficult for them to be designated as one interested party.[3] For families that are split, it is sometimes

[1]Coroners and Justice Act 2009, Section 47.

[2]Coroner's Rules 1984. No 552, Rule 7.

[3]The Guide to Coroners Services encourages families to nominate one next of kin; Ministry of Justice, *Guide to Coroner Services.*

Death in Custody, 181–200
Copyright © 2020 Jo Easton
Published under exclusive licence
doi:10.1108/978-1-83909-025-720201017

impossible for them to work together as one interested party through a designated next of kin or point of contact. It was pointed out by both ESP1 and IPCC that good practice in the police was to designate multiple FLOs in situations where the family is split. It is important that coroners similarly allow families to be represented by multiple interested parties so that it not only relieves pressure within the family but also improves equity as it is common for State officials to be identified individually as interested parties. (For example, after a prison death, the prison as an institution, the prison governor, National Offender Management Service and individual officers will all be designated as separate interested parties.[4])

An additional challenge for families is that it can be very difficult to get legal aid for anyone other than the next of kin. This means that, even if more than one family member is designated as an interested party by the coroner, they may struggle to participate effectively unless they can afford to cover the expense of an experienced lawyer to represent them. This is another aspect leading to a lack of equity as all State interested parties will be legally represented individually.

The inquest system is unique and distinct from other legal or quasi-legal processes. Although inquests are officially structured as inquisitorial processes, complex inquests (including Article 2 inquests after a death in custody) often become adversarial, creating a unique hybrid process which is neither completely inquisitorial nor adversarial. Public knowledge about the inquest system in general is poor; and as most inquests are very straightforward, even less is known about complex inquests such as those following a death in custody.[5] This lack of prior knowledge about the system is a huge problem for families, as they often feel out of their depth and 'at sea' (FA5) in relation to the process without expert advice and information about the system. INQUEST is a great organisation that can provide families with basic information, as well as providing a case worker system; and they will also help families find specialist lawyers to support them. It is also true that coroners, with their staff, can give families information about the system or signpost them to organisations like INQUEST, but it is clear this is usually not happening. It should be seen as priority to make sure families are given information (including the detailing of their legal rights) as soon as they are contacted by the coroner to prepare them for the process.

While it should be pretty straightforward for basic information to be provided relatively easily (see the INQUEST handbook or toolkit), it is also clear that it is useful for families to have someone to speak to them in person, who can offer them advice.[6,7] It must be remembered that families are grieving, and straight after the death they may also be in shock, so giving them a point of contact, who can answer their questions, is vitally important. But it should be recognised that the liaison officers provided by State agencies may not be the most appropriate

[4]Renamed as Her Majesty's Prison and Probation Service in April 2017; https://www.gov.uk/Government/organisations/national-offender-management-service.

[5]Raised by CO1.

[6]INQUEST (2011).

[7]See http://info.inquest.org.uk/toolkit/.

point of contacts for families, especially where those agencies were in contact with the deceased prior to the death and will therefore be under scrutiny during the inquest process. For example, you cannot expect families to trust police FLOs if they know that first and foremost, they are a police officer, and their primary responsibility is always to the investigation, not to the family. Similar concerns were raised about some coroner's officers, who are often police officers themselves. So while early engagement with families is very important and can lead to more positive experiences for families, it is most successful when provided by someone seen as independent from any other parties involved in the case. This means that it should either be a support worker (INQUEST does have case workers who can work with families) or specialist legal representatives to provide families with advice.

In addition to being given general information about the system and how it works, more specific information such as what rights families have is also very valuable in helping families access the process. It is obvious that without specialist support or advice, families are not always informed about their rights in relation to participating in the inquest. This can start from the earliest point, when families are often not told about their right to either witness or send a representative to witness the post-mortem, as well as not being aware of their right to be involved in the investigation. Where families are not told about their rights, it will lead to them losing confidence and trust in the process. In particular, where families find out later that they should have had access to the process earlier, it leads to them being suspicious about everyone involved. Access to this information is fundamental not just for families to be able to engage but also to ensure they retain trust that the process will be fair. And in order to ensure that trust is maintained, information about a families' legal rights should come from, preferably, the coroner or their staff.

Access to the process goes beyond being given all relevant information and support but also includes ensuring families can physically attend meetings and hearings. Again, families are particularly vulnerable as they are grieving, and asking them to navigate the complexities of multiple meetings and hearings, often in places a long way for them to travel, makes it practically challenging for them. Everything from getting time off work or organising childcare arrangements through to parking availability at the location can be additional worries for families during an already stressful time. Again, advice or information from either coronial staff or good legal representation can help families feel more confident and relaxed about attending hearings. In the most complex cases, families may have to attend multiple meetings or hearings over years if they wish to participate fully. As mentioned previously, there is a support service for coroners' courts, which tries to provide a similar service as the witness support scheme in criminal cases, by attending inquest hearings with family members. However, unfortunately, as a service provided by volunteers, it only covers 30 out of 92 coroner areas.[8] The volunteers are also only trained to support families at the majority

---

[8]http://www.coronerscourtssupportservice.org.uk/about-the-ccss/index.html.

inquests, which are nothing like the lengthy and complex inquests which follow a death in custody, so they do not necessarily have the expertise or capacity to support families in these latter cases. Again, useful information about attending hearings can be provided in writing or on a website, but families also need a point of contact to speak to in person, so their questions can be answered.

As identified in Chapter 10, one of the most important aspects to ensure families can fully access the inquest process is support from legal representation. Again, the problem of families not understanding the process (and therefore how complex it is likely to become) or their rights means that families are often not told that it is their right to have legal representation or how important this can be to assist them participate. When taken in conjunction with how beneficial it can be for families to have good legal representation at an early point in the process, failure to inform families of this right can be very damaging. It should therefore be included in the basic information provided by coroners when they first contact families.

11.2 Participation Allowing Families to Influence the Outcome

The theoretical framework set out in Chapter 4 explained that the right to participate required a party to be heard and have a real opportunity to influence the outcome. The three most important aspects in ensuring families can influence the outcome in relation to complex inquests following a death in custody are by being able to influence investigations before the inquest hearings, by asking questions during the hearing and influencing the questions to be left to the jury to answer as part of their narrative verdict.

In order to influence the outcome of an inquest, it is important for families to be able to participate in the investigation, as the investigatory reports often frames the evidence heard at the inquest. Although some coroners may hold inquests before the investigatory report is completed, generally they rely on the detailed investigations by police, IPCC or PPO to determine witnesses and evidence to be heard at an inquest. This is partly because coroners do not usually have the resources to carry out thorough investigations themselves, so they rely on investigatory bodies who, in turn, usually rely on the police to carry out most of the investigatory duties such as collecting evidence and taking witness statements. The investigation process is the most important point of influence for the outcome – decisions about whom to interview and what to ask them will influence what evidence is available at the inquest, which will obviously determine the likely final outcome. Therefore, for families to be able to influence the outcome, they must have input into the investigation itself. This could be by suggesting witnesses or possible lines of enquiry. Generally, the investigatory bodies are trying to involve families more in the investigation; taking family views and incorporating them into their investigation where possible. However, it is clear that this is still not happening in all cases, and sometimes attempts to involve families are little more than a tick box exercise, rather than a meaningful opportunity to influence the process. Of course, all investigatory bodies must be careful to ensure they are independent of all parties, and they have to therefore put limits on families being given undue influence in an investigation. And currently the law does not necessarily protect a family's right to participate in the investigation, with recent case law stating Article 2 requirements are discharged by the inquest hearings themselves not any preceding investigations.[9] However, this author argues this is an example of the law not reflecting the theoretical understanding about what the right to participate should encompass as allowing participation in an inquest but not the preceding investigation fundamentally limits the opportunity to influence the final outcome. Investigatory bodies should understand the importance of involving families in an investigation and ensure this good practice is followed in all cases.

The need for family participation in the investigation process is not just necessary to ensure their right to participate is fully embodied but also because currently there are concerns about the lack of independence from the police or prison authorities of the relevant investigatory bodies. In particular, the IPCC links to the police led to concerns that investigatory bodies biased the inquest process towards the police by controlling the evidence presented. One example is the failure of the IPCC in the Rigg case to investigate obvious lines of enquiry such as collecting and watching the CCTV evidence from the police station where the death occurred.[10] Family opportunity to be involved in the investigation not only ensures there is a lack of bias but can also ensure that obvious lines of investigation are not missed. This therefore not only benefits families but also the process itself.

At the moment, as a family's right to participate in investigations carried out looking at deaths in custody is not protected by law, participation in the inquest process is even more important, as it is often their only opportunity to both represent the deceased and influence the outcome. Families have an established right to participate in the inquest itself, which means they must have an opportunity to influence the outcome, by scrutinising and questioning the evidence produced by the investigation for the inquest hearings. The opportunity for families to be able to ask questions during the inquest process is very important for a number of reasons. Firstly, for families to feel involved and that the process is fair, they should be able to have their questioned answered. Secondly, if one of the objectives for the process is for families to be able to understand what happened to their loved one, they have to be able to ask questions to clarify any queries they have. This is particularly important following a death in custody as families are not necessarily going to understand either the police or prison processes involved in any interactions prior to the death. They may well therefore have many questions about normal processes, as well as specific details relating to their loved one.

---

[9] *Antoniou, R (on the application of) v Central and North West London NHS Foundation Trust & Ors* (2013) EWHC 3055 (Admin) (England and Wales High Court (Administrative Court)).

[10] The importance of factors such as access to documents and legal representation in ensuring families have an opportunity to input into the investigation will be discussed later.

Another route by which families can be offered the opportunity to influence the outcome of an inquest relates to the narrative verdicts produced by the jury. Article 2 or similarly complex inquest verdicts include both a specific verdict (such as unlawful killing) and a narrative verdict that includes relevant details about the circumstances or failings which contributed to the death. The narrative part of the verdict is normally created by the responses given by the jury to a number of questions put to them by the coroner. It is common practice for interested parties to propose questions to the coroner who makes the final decision as to which questions should be put to the jury. Although it can be challenging for coroners to ensure families questions are appropriate (especially where families are unrepresented), as they may have queries that are outside the remit of the inquest, this is an example of good practice that should be followed by all coroners. It ensures the different views of all parties can be represented, as well as making sure families feel they were able to fully participate by being offered a real opportunity to influence the outcome.

A more contentious issue is whether families (or other parties) should be able to influence what stand-alone verdicts are available for the jury to choose. Again, the coroner decides which stand-alone verdict options are to be left to the jury, so this can limit the outcome considerably. For example, if the coroner does not allow the verdict 'unlawful killing' to be left to the jury, they are unable to choose it as a final verdict. It can be argued that this final verdict is the most important outcome of the inquest, and therefore all parties (including families) should be able to influence what is available. And certainly, where parties are legally represented, they can provide coroners with legal opinions about the different options. However, it is also important that these final, stand-alone verdicts can be relied upon to be reached consistently – so the public can be confident that, for example, "unlawful killing" is only reached when a certain legal standard is proven. This is particularly true where the consistency of verdicts can be very important in identifying patterns; for example, the high incident of suicides in a particular institution might suggest systemic failings.[11] The inquest system only looks at an individual case, and therefore it can be difficult to indicate systemic failings without analysing a series of verdicts, over a period of time. One concern is where coroners are unduly influenced by families who may not want a death to be labelled as a suicide if they feel their loved one did not intend to die but acted as a cry for help, thus making the death accidental.[12] It is also important that certain verdicts may have impacts beyond the inquest; for example, in a civil case or even linked to the requirement that the Director of Public Prosecutions (DPP) must re-examine any decisions not to prosecute following an unlawful killing verdict.[13] It is therefore important that appropriate verdicts are left for the jury to consider.

---

[11]For example, the suicides at Scottish YOI Glenochil or Styal women's prison in 2002–2003, Liebling (2001), Corston (2007, p. 14).

[12]Biddle (2003).

[13]Crown Prosecution Service, Prosecution Policy and Guidance: Deaths in Custody (2004).

However, it must be acknowledged that the current system leaves the decision to the discretion of the coroner, which may not produce consistency in practice. In fact, it can be argued that to ensure consistency, there should be very few circumstances where a coroner should be able to restrict the verdicts being left to a jury. It could still be helpful if interested parties (especially where represented by specialist lawyers) provide the coroner with legal arguments if they believe there is a legal need for certain verdicts to not be left to a jury. In those rare cases where there is a valid legal reason why the juries are not able to consider a specific verdict, it is important coroners explain this decision to families, who may not appreciate the legal nuance. However, in general, if all verdicts were left to all juries, who then considered the evidence before deciding the appropriate verdict, there would be no perception of unfairness or of one party trying to restrict the outcome in any way. This is particularly important in relation to the "unlawful killing" verdict, as where this is not left to the jury, it can leave families feeling frustrated that it was not even an option. It is therefore an important part of a coroner's role to ensure there is transparency of decision-making, which can help families perceive the outcome differently.

11.3 Access to Documents

In comparison to some of the challenges to participation discussed above, the families' right to be given access to documents or evidence during an inquest is established in law. However, it is evident that there are still a number of problems with how this is working in practice. Difficulties mostly revolve around families having to fight to get full access to all relevant evidence in a timely manner. One of the issues is that families are only being given access to documents which they specifically ask for, which relies heavily on a good knowledge of both the law and custody processes themselves. It is also clear that access is not given in a timely manner; in some particularly bad examples, documents are only provided to families at the start of, or even during, an inquest hearing. It is important for families to have access to documents as early as possible for two main reasons. Firstly, families need to know what happened to their loved one as early as possible so their grief process is not negatively affected. Secondly, families must have access to the evidence while the investigation is still ongoing, so they can ask questions and influence both the investigation and the inquest itself (as discussed above). The role of families in scrutinising the evidence as described in Part 4 relies on families getting access to information all the way through the process and having knowledgeable legal representation to assist them. One of the benefits of families being supported by knowledgeable legal representation (to be discussed later) is that they can assist families in scrutinising the evidence, once it has been disclosed, as families often do not understand the processes or terminology in official, State reports.

While it should always be a priority for State parties to ensure families are given access to all the documents they have a right to in a timely manner, it is also important that they only share information which has been confirmed as credible.

Bearing in mind the reasons why families should be given access to this information, it is clear that providing families with inaccurate or uncorroborated evidence can be very damaging. It can mean they create a narrative based on false information or waste time assessing and scrutinising evidence that is not valid. Of course, even when it is accurate, sharing evidence can be potentially damaging if families struggle to understand or assimilate the information correctly. Isolated bits of information given to families out of context can cause additional and unnecessary confusion. This is another benefit to families being represented by specialist lawyers, as they can help talk through the evidence with families. It is also clear that, if, in trying to find the right balance, State parties attempt to protect families by hiding information from them, this can be seen negatively. It is generally very important for families to see all the evidence for themselves so they can make their own judgement about what happened. For those families that are wanting to be involved in the process and offered the opportunity to influence the investigation, they do not want to be presented with edited, contextualised evidence setting out a particular scenario but given all available information so they can assess and analyse it for themselves. So while every effort must be made to ensure families are only given information which has been corroborated and assessed as accurate in a structured way, State parties should avoid trying to provide a clear, tidy picture before passing information on to families. The added benefit of being open with information is if State agencies are seen as being open and transparent with families, it can foster positive and trusting relationships.

Another issue related to access to documents for families is that, although it is a legal right, families often have to fight to get full access. Even where families are supported by good legal representatives who ensure they get full access to documents in a timely manner, families can feel very negatively about State parties and the coroner if full access was not offered freely. Families generally feel suspicious of State parties if they only provide documents when forced to; and similarly if coroners are not seen to be proactive in ensuring State parties comply with the law by providing access to documents, families are likely to perceive the process as biased against them. It is therefore important that all decision-makers involved in deciding what information will be shared with families, and when, must take a proactive approach and not wait to be forced to make disclosure.

State bodies sometimes argue that they cannot safely share some information with families, as they cannot trust they will not put it in the public domain, and some information needs to remain confidential. This is not the correct interpretation of the law, as families' right to disclosure is not restricted in relation to what can be made available to the public. It is clear that if there are concerns about families not disclosing information in the public domain, this is best dealt with by explaining to families clearly why it is necessary to keep some material out of the media. When linked to the earlier issue of families' trust and confidence in a fair process as explained by procedural justice theory, it is clear that being open and transparent with families is the best approach to optimise a positive outcome in any situation. If families perceive the process as fair and trust the coroner to reach a fair outcome, they are far more likely to comply with directions relating to restricting what information can be shared with the public or media. It should also be noted that inquests are public hearings, so in saying there are issues about information not being put in the public domain, it is usually the timing of when that information should be made public which is considered sensitive, as ultimately the evidence will be presented during the inquest hearing and therefore in the public domain. There are therefore no reasons why the legal requirement for families to have a right to information is not fully embraced, and perhaps if decision-makers understood the positive impact of being seen as open and transparent with families, they would ensure full disclosure to families in a timely manner.

11.4 Legal Representation for Bereaved Families

The previous chapter sets out that one of the most important aspects in ensuring families can fairly and effectively participate in an inquest is having access to specialist legal representation. It is clear that families' legitimate interests cannot be protected unless they are legally represented: it not only provides families with the information and advice necessary for them to access the process but also ensures they can influence the outcome and secures access to documents in a timely manner. But good legal representation for families also benefits the process itself. It can ensure all the evidence is fully scrutinised, which leads to a fair outcome and it is also a matter of equity and therefore an important aspect of ensuring the process is fair.

It is sometimes suggested that because the inquest system is inquisitorial, there is no need for families to have legal representation, as it is argued that the coroner can ensure their legitimate interests are protected. However, asking coroners to support, advise and assist families puts them in a difficult position in terms of remaining independent. This book has shown that all parties (not just families and their lawyers) including State bodies and coroners themselves believed it was beneficial when families were represented by good lawyers.

This is for a number of reasons. Firstly, because during a complex inquest, key decisions about the process are left to the discretion of the coroner, which makes it even more important that they are not seen as being biased towards any parties. Secondly, families are at a disadvantage in comparison with other parties, as they have no experience of the inquest system or knowledge of custodial processes, as well as the fact that they are grieving, so it can be very difficult for them to engage objectively in an inquest. Thirdly, although the inquest system is set up to be inquisitorial, it is generally agreed by everyone with any experience of inquests following a death in custody that these processes become adversarial.

There are a number of reasons why a complex inquest becomes adversarial in nature. Firstly, emotions will always be heightened when there is a death at the centre of a process. Secondly, families will nearly always have many questions where a loved one has died in custody, especially when there were contentious aspects to a death. Thirdly, ensuring accountability for State actions to restrain and detain individual's means that State parties should have their actions closely scrutinised, and any actor whose actions are being questioned will want to defend themselves robustly. Although inquests are not allowed to identify culpability, it is undeniable that underlying the whole process is an attempt to find out who, if anyone, might be responsible for a death. It is therefore inevitable that the process will become adversarial. An adversarial process involves different parties robustly scrutinising the evidence, and although families (as an interested party) have the have the right to question the witnesses giving evidence at an inquest hearing, without legal representation this is almost impossible for a number of reasons.[14] Firstly, some questions can be disallowed if the coroner decides they are irrelevant, due to the limited scope of an inquest.[15] Secondly, families are vulnerable during hearings as emotional and upsetting issues are being discussed, so the ability to calmly and objectively assess and question is very challenging, even if they had the knowledge and skill to do so. Thirdly, the scrutiny needed to reach fair and correct outcome requires skilful cross-examination, not something that families can be expected to carry out effectively. Therefore, legal representation for families assists not only the families themselves but also the process by optimising a fair outcome.

It is sometimes argued that in addition to being inquisitorial, inquests are straightforward processes in which families can participate without legal support. However, it is clear from this book that inquest law as it relates to death in custody is complex and therefore it is impossible for families to participate effectively without specialist support. Legal support for families can also assist coroners in deciding complex legal matters as it ensures different interpretations and viewpoints are put forward. It is worth noting that the Government acknowledged the legal complexities of even "normal" inquests when they changed the law so only legally trained individuals could become coroners, excluding medically trained individuals who were previously able to act as coroners.[16] When Article 2 requirements are also engaged, the process becomes even more legally complex, as European as well as domestic case law becomes relevant. Without specialist knowledge, it is impossible for a lawyer to adequately represent a family. Specialist lawyers do not need to just understand the complexities of inquest law, but they must also have good understanding of law and processes governing detention. It is important for lawyers to understand the terminology used by custodial institutions and the police as well as the rules governing detention practices to be able to assess and scrutinise all the documents. For example, in order to assess whether actions are in compliance with expected standards, a lawyer must have an understanding of those standards.

State parties are legally represented for the duration of an inquest process, often with a team of lawyers representing each different State actor and agency. It is therefore common for State parties to have numerous lawyers representing different individuals or agencies who appear to work together with the same objectives, leading to perceptions amongst families that there is a lack of equity as

[14]The Coroners (Inquests) Rules 2013, Section 19.
[15]The Coroners (Inquests) Rules 2013, Section 19.
[16]Coroners and Justice Act 2009.

they are usually just identified as one interested party. Families' often feel outnumbered or "ganged up on" (LA1). The lack of equity leaves families feeling the process is unfair, as it appears to be biased towards the State, as with numerous lawyers working together, there are numerous opportunities for them to present or question evidence in line with an agreed viewpoint. But as families are only one interested party, with one lawyer (if they are lucky), they only got one opportunity to present their viewpoint.

Lack of equity relates not just to the fact that State parties are identified as multiple interested parties but also that each one will have a team of experienced legal representatives supporting them. However, where families are able to fund legal representation, this will usually only be one solicitor, who they rely on to both assist them in preparing for the inquest and during the hearings themselves. It is rare for families to have a barrister alongside the solicitor during the hearing, which puts them at a disadvantage. In fact, families often struggle to get legal aid funding for any specialist legal representation and if they do receive funding, it is unlikely to cover anywhere near the costs of even one specialist solicitor for the whole process, let alone a team. In general, all aspects relating to costs leave families perceiving the process is unfair. (Additional costs for families relating to participating include taking time off work, travel costs and finding childcare, whereas for State actors, all these costs are obviously covered for them.) In terms of equity, it is undeniable that in order for the process to be perceived as fair, families must have legal representation to represent their interests, as State parties will all be legally represented.

Funding for legal representation is incredibly important both in respect to ensuring fairness and equity for parties (with State parties being funded) and also due to access to justice issues with specialist legal representation being expensive. Due to the complexity and duration of inquests following a death in custody (it can commonly take years for all the hearings to be complete), the cost of one experienced legal representation can be tens of thousands of pounds for the duration of an inquest process. However, because the law does not automatically grant families legal aid funding for these inquests, families struggle to get funding via the LAA. Guidance on exceptional funding for legal aid for inquests has been updated following the *Letts* case, and this book sets out the experiences of participants under the previous guidance, but the majority of the issues identified will continue to be relevant.

The three biggest problems faced by families in accessing legal aid funding are that the inquest must be categorised as Article 2 inquests, family members who were applying for the funding having to be the next of kin and the complexity of the application process. It is clear the Human Rights Act 1998 has had a positive impact on achieving funding for Article 2 inquests, but this does depend on a coroner clearly identifying the inquest as engaging Article 2 at an early stage. Some coroners prefer to wait until the later stages if it is not clear whether Article 2 is engaged, whereas others take the position that if there is doubt, Article 2 can be presumed to be engaged, allowing full investigation but verdicts can subsequently be restricted if it becomes apparent Article 2 is not engaged. This, of course, relies on coroners having a clear understanding of Article 2 case law, as well as appreciation of the impact of their decision on families accessing funding.

This is why getting legal aid funding is still a difficult, if not impossible, situation for many deaths in secure mental health institutions. It would be preferable for all coroners to take a more open approach and presume Article 2 to be engaged whenever it is possible – thus ensuring families can access legal aid funding. Then, if it becomes apparent Article 2 is not engaged, the process can be restricted at a later stage.

The LAA also only generally funds representation for the next of kin, which can be very difficult in a split family or if a particular member of a family who is the next of kin does not want to engage with the process (for example, a parent may not wish to engage but a sibling may wish to). A recent case in 2015 found the law had been correctly applied when funding was refused for a relative due to the fact one member of the family had already been granted funding.[17] In addition, strict criteria about financial assets are in place governing who is eligible for legal aid. These criteria do not just relate to the individual applying for funding, but the financial details of an individual's close relatives are examined to ensure family funds are not available.[18] Of course, just because a relative has sufficient funds does not mean they would be happy to release them to fund participation in a complex inquest. In split families, it can put people in an impossible situation of having to ask relatives they are not close to or they are distanced from for financial details. If the law was changed, so that any family member who could show a close connection to the deceased was eligible for funding, without the existing strict financial criteria being in place, it would ensure that those family members who wanted to participate were able to access the legal funding to do so effectively.

The third problem faced by families is the complexity of the legal aid application process. It is ironic that experienced legal representatives are actually very important in assisting families with negotiating the legal aid process and getting funding for legal representation. A recent report by the Law Society highlighted how challenging it could be for lay people to complete applications through the Exceptional Case Funding (ECF) without legal assistance.[19] The complexities of the legal aid process as well as the legal arguments around Article 2 engagement which are needed to achieve funding create a situation where families without experienced legal representatives are unlikely to get legal aid. This contradiction means either there are delays before a family can get legal representation while they are struggling to get funding or lawyers have to agree to work on a case without being sure whether the family will legal aid funding (which often requires a lawyer to be willing to work pro bono or at a low rate). A recent case highlighted the difficulties a delayed decision in respect to receiving funding can have in relation to family participation, with the inquest going ahead in this example before the LAA had considered the application for funding.[20] This can leave

[17] *R. (on the application of Joseph) v Director of Legal Aid Casework* (2015) EWHC 2749 (Admin); (Queen's Bench Division (Administrative Court)).

[18] Legal Aid Agency (2013, p. 6).

[19] Law Society (2017).

[20] *R. (on the application of Wiggins) v HM Assistant Coroner for Nottinghamshire* (2015) EWHC 1658 (Admin) (Queen's Bench Division (Administrative Court)).

either the family or the lawyer (or both) out of pocket at the completion of an inquest. If families only get legal representation late on the process (for example, near the inquest hearing but months or years after the death), it is actually frustrating for other parties, including coroners, as it can mean the whole process is delayed. Looking at all the benefits that legal representation can bring to families, including managing expectations about the process; making sure families understand both the process and the evidence; assisting families to assess and scrutinise evidence and providing overall support to families, early access to this representation is incredibly important.

Participants pointed out that even when legal aid funding was granted, it was unlikely to cover the full costs of experienced legal representation for a complex inquest, partly because the LAA did not understand the complexities, the preparation necessary and the number of pretrial hearings or meetings required to support a family to participate effectively.

The problems associated with legal aid funding are mostly due to the fact that the decision on whether to award legal aid funding is mostly left to the discretion of the LAA and individual staff members. The fact that these decision-makers do not understand the complex, adversarial nature of inquest following a death in custody or fully appreciate all the benefits associated with families having specialist legal representation (not just to families but the wider process as well) means they are refusing legal aid applications without understanding the implications. It would be helpful if those making decisions about legal aid applications understood all the benefits for the families and the process of granting legal aid. However, another solution would be to change the law so there is a presumption that families get legal aid in cases where the State parties are funded.[21]

Even if legal aid funding was guaranteed for all families, there is still an issue due to the lack of specialist lawyers outside of London, leaving families struggling to get the necessary support from people with the appropriate expertise. However, it should be remembered that State parties outside of London will usually be adequately funded so they can employ experienced, specialist lawyers who usually travel from London. So, as long as equitable funding is provided for families, this should not be an insurmountable problem.

Automatic access to legal aid funding would go a long way to resolving some of the problems identified in this book. The positive impact cannot be underestimated. However, even with support from good legal representatives, many of the challenges families face remain. And even where their lawyers manage to ensure fair and effective participation, the fact that this is usually only due to the intervention of their lawyers and not something easily facilitated by the process and key decision-makers has a negative impact on the perceptions of the families.

---

[21]Organisations like INQUEST are continuing to campaign on this issue, and the Labour Party is now supporting such a change in law.

11.5 Impact of Families Struggling to Participate

The importance for families to be treated respectfully during an inquest process was described earlier and this is one aspect of participation that legal aid funded legal representation does not necessarily improve. It was mentioned previously that if State agencies are seen to be acting obstructively to families, for example, requiring intervention by coroners or family lawyers to ensure families have access to the process and documents, this damages family confidence and trust in those agencies. In addition, to ensure families perceive the process to be legitimate, they must feel respectfully treated by coroners and their staff. If families feel they have to fight or argue to be able to participate fairly and effectively, they do not perceive decision-makers to be respecting their rights fully and freely. Good legal representation can support and assist families but the responsibility to ensure families' rights are fully exercised should not be devolved to their legal representative. It is clear that support offered by experienced legal representatives is vital in ensuring bereaved families are able to effectively access the process and be appropriately informed about their rights, the process and the evidence, all of which is necessary for participation. However, for families to perceive the process as legitimate, their access to the process and relevant information must be given by the decision-maker freely, not only in response to strong and compulsive arguments put forward by their lawyers. Coroners and investigatory bodies should ensure families know their rights and, along with State parties, provide aspects relating to participation, such as access to documents, freely to ensure families' rights are fully exercised. If it is perceived by families that it is only through the good work of their legal representative that their rights are being respected, they might be able to effectively participate but still have negative perceptions about the legitimacy of the process.[22]

The Government have published a guide which sets out the process for interested parties.[23] However, it was disappointing that while the Government initially intended this charter to focus on bereaved families, in the end, although the guide is primarily for bereaved families, it did not set out expectations for families above any other interested parties.[24] This book has clearly set out why the bereaved families are in a distinct position to other interested parties, in particular due to their grieving and also due to the fact they are often the only ones without previous experiences or the necessary support to be able to understand the process. It was also unfortunate that the guide did not cover the specific complexities of inquests following deaths in custody, as these inquests are so unique and different from other inquests. This author would call on the Government to produced updated guidance that clearly sets out the special needs of bereaved families, in particular in relation to complex inquests following a death in custody.

---

[22]Gau (2014).

[23]The Chief Coroner's Office (2013).

[24]House of Commons Constitutional Affairs Committee (2006, p. 11), INQUEST (2011).

11.6 Conclusion

This research came about because the author understood from first-hand experience how bereaved families often struggle to participate in the inquest system following the death of a relative in custody, even though their right to participate is established in law. A debate in the House of Lords discussing family participation in complex inquests highlighted this struggle with Lord Rosser stating, "Many bereaved families can find themselves in an adversarial and aggressive environment when they go to an inquest".[25] In the same debate, Lord Paddick explained that his experience was that, for bereaved families, '[...] a search for the truth turns into a bruising adversarial encounter'.[26] The right of families to participate is established as a human right in law, but the implementation of that right is not fully achieved as families struggle to access it. Human rights must be accessible to be real and practical, so this author wanted to look at not just what the challenges were but provide a road map to improving access. It is obvious that individual decision-makers (especially coroners and LAA officials) have a huge impact on family participation, so the author wanted to produce evidence to change the approach taken by decision-makers to promote as well as protect the family's legal right to participate.

In order to improve participation in the inquest process, the author started by re-evaluating why participation is so important and then went on to establish important criteria that should be in place to ensure fair and effective participation for families is secured in practice. This book explores the legal framework which governs a bereaved families' right to participate as well as considering theoretical explanations for why participation is important. In addition to this legal and theoretical work, the research has drawn on a unique series of interviews with stakeholders who have experience of being involved in inquests following a death in custody in order to collect their detailed views and perceptions of the processes involved. Two main research questions were asked: firstly, what are the benefits of family participation in an inquest (to families themselves, to the outcome of the inquest and the wider inquest system)? Secondly, what factors need to be incorporated to ensure fair and effective participation which could optimise the achievement of those benefits?

The interviews sought to identify why the different stakeholders thought family participation was important and what such participation should involve in practice. These views were collated, analysed and interpreted by the author with reference to relevant legal and theoretical frameworks, as well as real-life examples. The process undertaken for this book has therefore identified the reasons why families should be able to participate in the inquest process and what is needed in terms of participation to achieve the identified benefits.

In relation to bereaved family participation in the inquest system following a death in custody, the legal framework establishes a right to participate in order to protect the legitimate interests of families. Early judgments focused on financial

[25]House of Lords Committee Stage Policing and Crime Bill (2016), Column 756.
[26]House of Lords Committee Stage Policing and Crime Bill (2016), Column 759.

benefits to a family via a civil case or compensation as their primary legitimate interests but the recent *Letts* case provided a wider understanding of a family's interests, including finding out the truth, identification of State culpability and knowing further deaths will be prevented.[27] This book showed that while families might have unique reasons for participating in an inquest, generally their main reason is to find the truth and identify failings, which then impacts on them receiving redress in the form of an apology, obtaining a commitment that lessons have been learned, seeing individuals culpable for the death punished or a public record of any identified failings. In addition, this research identified the important role a family has in representing the deceased throughout the inquest process. This can be particularly relevant following a death in custody where there is potential for the deceased to be stigmatised due to their interaction with either the police or prison services. Effective participation for families can ensure the voice of the deceased is heard through an inquest, which provides a rounded picture of them as an individual beyond the circumstances surrounding their death.

Recommendation 1: The voice of the deceased can be represented by allowing a bereaved family sufficient support and space to represent the deceased throughout the inquest process.

It is also important to recognise the impact participation can have on a families' grief process. Complicated grief theory states that extending a grief process can have negative impacts on an individual; and there are a number of reasons why someone bereaved following a death in custody may suffer from complicated grief. A healthy grief process following a sudden or unexpected death involves a bereaved person having a narrative which explains why the death occurred. Delayed access to the truth can leave a grieving individual struggling to come to terms with a death. Also, when a grieving person creates a narrative to explain a death, which is then challenged at a later date (when the truth is established), it can result in a renewed sense of grief. This research shows that an inquest is vitally important in allowing families to understand the true account of a death, therefore assisting a healthy grief process. Effective participation at an early stage ensures families can incorporate facts about a death into their narrative. Unfortunately, delays in the inquest process can still prevent families being able to move on until all the hearings are finished.

Recommendation 2: The impact of an inquest on the grief process of a bereaved family should be understood, especially in relation to the delays in the system. The obligation to hold an inquest in a timely manner must take account of negative impacts on the grief process if a family has to wait years for closure. In addition to steps to minimise delays, ensuring families are provided with support and accurate information about the process and the death should be a priority.

This book has gone beyond the current understanding of participation as seen as a benefit to families themselves and shown that participation is also beneficial to the legitimacy of the inquest system itself. One function of the inquest system is

[27] *Letts v Lord Chancellor* (2015).

to fulfil Article 2 requirements to identify the circumstances leading to a death and to ensure culpability is established and future deaths are prevented. Family participation can have the instrumental benefit of improving the effectiveness of the system in relation to all three of these objectives to hold the State to account for any deaths that occur in custody. Family participation can help maximise the likelihood of a fair and accurate outcome, therefore ensuring any State failings are identified. Families can provide relevant information to the process and the families (with the support of their legal representative) can play a vital role in scrutinising the evidence presented at an inquest. In addition to influencing the outcome of an inquest, families also play an important role in disseminating verdicts following a critical inquest verdict, which can improve transparency and therefore public confidence in the process. Disseminating outcomes can also improve the opportunities for lessons to be learnt beyond specific institutions or individuals involved in any death. Families have also been involved in bringing legal challenges which have resulted in changes to the investigatory process as well as specific practices in relation to how State agents use their power to detain and restrain individuals.

Recommendation 3: The benefit of fair and effective participation of bereaved families in optimising a fair outcome for an inquest should be acknowledged in policy provisions. This may well necessitate additional scrutiny or follow-up of learning by an independent party where a bereaved family is unwilling or unable to participate in the inquest process. There are broader positive implications for appointment of an independent party to participate in the process (including representing the public), but with an understanding of resource restrictions, prioritisation should be for those cases where families are not willing or able to engage in the process by scrutinising the evidence.

Participation of bereaved families can go beyond having an instrumental effect on the inquest process. It can also have an intrinsic impact on the legitimacy of the process. Rule of law principles reflect the need for processes to be transparent and to treat all parties equally. This is particularly relevant in a democratic society when State parties are involved in a legal process, as it is important they are seen to be held to the same standards as individuals. Procedural justice theory also links perceptions of how fair, transparent and unbiased a process is with perceptions about the legitimacy of the system governing the process. Fair and effective participation of bereaved families can increase their sense of having been treated fairly and improve their perceptions of the fairness of the inquest system, therefore influencing how legitimate they believe the system to be and ultimately how much trust and confidence they have in the outcome of the inquest. In addition to procedural justice theory governing perceptions of legitimacy about the inquest system, issues of fairness and justice can also influence family perceptions of other agencies involved in an inquest. So family involvement increases their perception of the legitimacy of the inquest system, and family interaction with State parties can also influence their perception about those agencies. It has also been shown that wider public views about the legitimacy of the system can be positively impacted through positive family involvement and perceptions that the processes holding State agents to account are fair to all parties.

Recommendation 4: Any decision-maker who can influence and impact the participation of bereaved families in an inquest process (particularly coroners) should receive training and guidance to ensure they are aware of the positive impact that fair and effective participation of bereaved families in an inquest process has on the legitimacy of the process and the system itself.

Procedural justice theory also highlights the importance of parties being treated respectfully by decision-makers during a process. In relation to the inquest system, it is obvious that where families feel they are treated respectfully by the coroner and their staff, they will perceive the process to be more legitimate. However, this also relates to how families perceive their treatment by State parties involved in an inquest; where families perceive that State parties (either in the form of institutions or individual State officers) treated them fairly and with respect during the whole inquest process, they are more likely to perceive them as legitimate. Conversely, if State parties are perceived to be disrespectful by obfuscating, lying or not treating families with respect and dignity, confidence and trust in them and the legitimacy of how they utilised their powers to restrain or detain are damaged. So if a loved one dies in police custody, a family's interactions with both the police involved in the death and the Independent Office for Police Conduct (IOPC) influence the family's views of those separate institutions, respectively. If the police themselves are seen to be disrespectful to the family and hide facts from them, the family end up with negative views about the police. If (in the same case) the IOPC are seen to be helpful to the family, then this positive experience results in families trusting this investigatory body. It is therefore important for all those involved in an inquest to treat the bereaved family with respect.

Recommendation 5: Any decision-makers (especially investigatory bodies, FLOs and those who act as point of contact to the bereaved families) who can influence and impact the participation of bereaved families in an inquest process should receive appropriate training and guidance so they ensure the family is treated with respect and dignity throughout the process. Particular focus should be on providing all coroners with training about how procedural justice theory relates to the legitimacy of an inquest.

This book has shown varied benefits resulting from families participating in an inquest including the protection of their legitimate interests, improving the effectiveness of an inquest, particularly as a means of holding the state to account, and increasing the legitimacy of the investigatory system and wider State agencies. In order to achieve these benefits, what should participation look like? Some aspects relating to the legal right for a bereaved family to participate in an inquest following a death in custody are clearly set out, but in order to ensure this right is protected, participation must be effective not just in law but also in practice. Fair and effective participation relies on the right for a family to be heard at all stages of an inquest. It also demands that family participation is able to influence the outcome. This means families should have effective access to the different stages of the inquest process and be able to engage positively with opportunities to be heard and to influence the process. Families should be supported and informed about the inquest process, as well as how they will be able to participate. Families should also be able to influence the investigation that frames the inquest.

Ensuring access to specialised legal representation at an early stage and providing families with full and early access to all documents relating to the case are vital aspects in ensuring families are able to effectively participate. If families are able to participate in a fair, independent and transparent process, they will perceive it to be legitimate, which will in turn ensure they have trust and confidence in the outcome. The book shows that two important factors are particularly important: providing early access to all the evidence surrounding the death and funding specialised legal representation for families. Support and advice provided by specialised legal representation can ensure families are informed about the inquest process, get access to all the evidence and are able to participate in the process through being heard and influencing the outcome. Fair and effective participation maximises the potential for families to influence the outcome and secure an accurate verdict.

Recommendation 6: Families should be assured of fair and effective participation which requires the following:

(1) Bereaved family members who indicate they would like to participate must be given interested party status;
(2) Bereaved families are signposted to independent advice and support relevant to the inquest system;
(3) Bereaved families are informed of their legal rights in relation to participating in an inquest;
(4) Information should be provided to families on the unique aspects of complex or Article 2 inquests;
(5) Families should be able to input into and influence any investigation into the death;
(6) Relevant decision-makers (including LAA staff) should recognise complex inquests following a death in custody as adversarial and not inquisitorial processes;
(7) Bereaved families should have an established right to legal aid funding, to ensure they can access experienced legal representation from the start of an inquest process. Legal aid must be the presumed default to allow families to access specialised legal representation soon after any death, rather than having to negotiate the complex exceptional funding system;
(8) Bereaved families should be given access to all documents or evidence relating to a death as soon as practically possible. It must be agreed that where there are concerns about information being in the public domain, this should not prevent families being provided with said information. Measures can be taken during an inquest process to restrict public access to information, but families must have access to all relevant information in order to participate effectively and fairly.
(9) Reasonable steps should be taken to support families' attendance at the inquest: including giving families information about the location of the inquest, including nearest accessible parking, and providing a separate waiting room during the inquest.

This book has explained how participation of a bereaved family following a death in custody can protect their legitimate interests by ensuring they know the truth, receive an apology, can be confident lessons are learnt and anyone culpable for a death is punished. Participation can ensure the voice of the deceased is represented and also allow the inquest process to have a positive impact on the family's grief process. In addition to benefitting the families themselves, participation can benefit the process by maximising the likelihood of an accurate outcome and positively impacting on the legitimacy of the process and the system itself. Confidence and trust in the process only comes from families being able to fairly and effectively participate without having to fight for their rights. It is therefore important that all decision-makers actively protect and promote families' participation.

The inquest system is set up as an inquisitorial process and therefore it is inherent within the system that the decision-maker (in this case the coroner) has wide discretionary powers, allowing for adaptation of rules depending on context, with the aim of ensuring the process finds the truth. Although inquests are governed by legislation, at many points the rules empower coroners to use their discretion to decide how the process will be conducted. In addition, there are many opportunities for other decision-makers to influence the participation of families, from the LAA deciding on whether to provide legal aid funding for legal representation to State investigatory bodies controlling family involvement in an investigation prior to the inquest hearing. It is therefore very important that all decision-makers understand the benefits of family participation and how to ensure that the participation is fair and effective.

Conclusion

In England and Wales, an inquest is carried out into any death that occurs in custody or where the actions of a State agent might be found to be a causal factor in the death. Unless an enquiry is set up, an inquest is the mechanism for fulfilling the requirements of an Article 2 compliant investigation. An inquest differs from other domestic jurisdictions as it is inquisitorial instead of adversarial: a coroner presides over the process which aims to find the facts rather than adjudicate between two opposing parties. The law establishes a right for families to participate in the inquest system following a death in custody, in order to protect their 'legitimate interests'. The right of family participation has evolved in United Kingdom (UK) law via common law, domestic legislation and UK case law reflecting European Court of Human Rights (ECtHR) judgments.

The evidence compiled by Professor Scraton, INQUEST and others indicates that families experience huge challenges in accessing their right to participate in Article 2 inquests.[1,2] Families' stories about the inquest system have been represented by the organisation INQUEST as well as academics such as Professor Scraton, with some families telling their own stories publicly, including Audrey Edwards' book about the death of her son and Sean Riggs' family giving evidence to parliamentary committees.[3,4] The different stories have illustrated not just the grief of families or their frustration at the State failing to protect the lives of their loved ones but also their negative experiences of the inquest system itself. This book builds on the previous work, putting family experiences alongside those of people who either work or have participated in the system. It places those experiences within an academic context of both law and theory to explain why the lack of participation of bereaved families is such an important problem with

[1]Thomas and others *R v Neil Gordon Graham* [Northern Ireland Unreported Judgments] (Northern Ireland Crown Court).

[2]For all the negative experiences expressed by these families, it should be noted that the families who engage with the media are often supported by INQUEST as well as experienced legal representatives but the majority of families have to negotiate the system with no support at all and their voices are rarely heard.

[3]Edwards, No Truth, No Justice (Hampshire: Waterside Press 2002).

[4]Home Affairs Committee, Independent Police Complaints Commission: Eleventh Report of Session 2012-3. HC494 (2013); Ev16-9.

Death in Custody, 201–204
Copyright © 2020 Jo Easton
Published under exclusive licence
doi:10.1108/978-1-83909-025-720201018

negative consequences for State accountability. This book also sets out practical solutions through recommendations relating to law, policy and practice.

The previous work has illustrated problems with the law, policy implementation and differing practice around England and Wales; this book clarifies how these problems contribute to families' negative perceptions. Firstly, although the law ensures each family has the right to be legally represented, the lack of equity in funding for said representation is a gap in the law that leaves families struggling to find and pay for adequate legal support. Secondly, policy directives to relevant police and prison investigative agencies require them to provide families with access to all relevant evidence related to an investigation; but in practice there can be delays before families are given the documents, if they even receive them at all without the intervention of their legal representation forcing disclosure. Thirdly, although family access to the inquest process is legally protected, in practice lack of information about the process as well as a lack of support provided to families prevents them participating fully. Access depends on decisions taken by coroners, their officials as well as other State agencies; and although there are examples of good practice, many do not take a process value approach which would ensure positive engagement with families. Even where families are able to participate effectively with the support of INQUEST and legal representatives, where they feel they have had to fight for their rights, families are left with negative perceptions about the process and the State actors involved. Previous campaigns have highlighted these problems but positive change has been slow. This book takes a new approach by going back to the basics of why family participation is important, focusing not just on what the benefits are to families themselves but also the positive impact on the wider system.

The right for families to participate in an Article 2 inquest has been established to protect their legitimate interests, which are set out as learning the truth, being confident any State failings have been identified and future deaths prevented.[5] This book also illustrates how effective participation for families could directly impact on the grief process, with early involvement and support being very important in limiting negative and prolonged complicated grief. In addition, it is clear that family participation can improve the system's ability to hold the State to account for its actions. This occurs in two ways; firstly, effective participation for a bereaved family increases the likelihood of a fair outcome which assures failings are identified. Secondly, the bereaved family is often responsible for disseminating the outcomes of the inquests, which can be linked to both forcing change and ensuring the system is transparent and therefore that the public can be confident it is robust.

Richardson argues that the need for fair procedures can be justified in two ways: the instrumental affect which states fair processes optimise fair outcomes, and the process value affect which states fair processes protect values (including human dignity) irrespective of impact on the outcome.[6] The benefits of a fair

[5] *Letts v Lord Chancellor* (2015), para 70.
[6] Richardson (1993, pp. 26–30).

process were set out by Lord Reed in *Osborn v Parole Board*, where he stated there were three positive 'virtues of procedurally fair decision-making': to optimise the likelihood of better outcomes, to ensure parties affected by the outcome feel they have been justly and respectfully treated in being able to participate in the process and to ensure actions by decision-makers are correctly governed by the rule of law.[7] Ensuring effective participation for families as representatives of the deceased, victims in their own right and those most directly affected by the death is a key aspect of a procedurally fair inquest process. In considering the impact of treating individuals unfairly in relation to participation in a legal process, this research looked to procedural justice theory to understand the impact of families being left with negative perceptions about participating in an inquest process. Tyler has lead research on procedural justice theory which considers the impact of negative perceptions of participants in varied criminal justice procedures including police interactions, criminal prosecutions and prison adjudications.[8] The research shows negative experiences relating to how unfairly an individual feels they were treated during a process leads to negative perceptions about the legitimacy of the process, which are then linked to reduced confidence in and compliance with the outcome. The evidence gathered in this book shows the same impact occurs in relation to families' participation in an inquest process. Family participation can therefore be linked to the legitimacy of the system, both by ensuring the process follows rule of law principles and by improving perceptions of a fair process which positively correlate with perceptions about the legitimacy of the process.

It is important to understand the potential benefits to family participation not just to encourage change in law and policy but also to improve practice which impacts on enabling participation. This is particularly relevant to the inquest system as important aspects relating to family participation are left to the discretion of decision-makers. An individual coroner adjudicates over an inquest and, as it is an inquisitorial system, the coroner has considerable discretion to make decisions about aspects important to family participation. Another important factor affecting participation is access to legal representation, but unless families can fund this themselves, the decision of whether to provide funding is left to the discretion of the Legal Aid Agency. One of the purposes of this book is to encourage those exercising discretionary powers relating to family participation to make decisions in a way that maximises fair and effective family participation, leading to positive perceptions about the process itself.

Where discretion exists, decision-makers must be aware of what is required for effective participation and what optimises the opportunity for positive perceptions by families. Negative perceptions around State parties as well as sometimes coroners themselves do not just leave families angry and resentful, they also result in a lack of trust and confidence in the system and therefore the outcomes.

---

[7] *Osborn v The Parole Board* (2013) UKSC 61, para 67–71.

[8] Lind and Tyler (1998), Tyler (1990), Tyler and Huo (2002), Tyler (1998), Reisig and Mesko (2009), Jackson and others (2010).

The purposes of complex inquests are linked to ensuring compliance with Article 2 requirements and mean fundamental questions about the use of State powers have to be answered. The legitimacy of the system is therefore intrinsically important. As procedural justice theory illustrates correlations between trust, confidence and perceptions of legitimacy, decision-makers, in particular coroners, should be aware of the key aspects of procedural justice to ensure families effectively participate and have positive perceptions about the process.

Bibliography

European Case Law

Airey v Ireland (A/32) (1979-80) 2 EHRR 305 (European Court of Human Rights).
Aksoy v Turkey (1997) 23 EHRR 553 (European Court of Human Rights).
Andronicou v Cyprus (1998) 25 EHRR 491 (European Court of Human Rights).
Angelova and Iliev v Bulgaria (2008) 47 EHRR 7 (European Court of Human Rights).
Association X v United Kingdom (1978) DR 14 (European Commission (Plenary)).
Aydin v Turkey (2006) 42 EHRR 44 (European Court of Human Rights).
Banel v Lithuania (2013) ECHR 558 (European Court of Human Rights).
Botta v Italy (1998) 26 EHRR 241 (European Court of Human Rights).
Bubbins v United Kingdom (2005) 41 EHRR 24 (European Court of Human Rights).
Bures v The Czech Republic (2012) ECHR 1819 (European Court of Human Rights).
Byrzykowski v Poland (2008) 46 EHRR 32 (European Court of Human Rights).
Calvelli and Ciglio v Italy (2002) ECHR 3 (European Court Human Rights).
Da Silva v United Kingdom (2016) ECHR 314 (30 March 2016). (European Court of Human Rights).
Dodov v Bulgaria (2008) 47 EHRR 41 (European Court of Human Rights).
Edwards v United Kingdom (2002) 35 EHRR 19 (European Court of Human Rights).
Enukidze and Girgvliani v Georgia (2011) ECHR 735 (European Court of Human Rights).
Ergi v Turkey (2001) 32 EHRR 18 (European Court of Human Rights).
Gul v Turkey (2002) 34 EHRR 28 (European Court Human Rights).
Jordan v United Kingdom (2003) 37 EHRR 2 (European Court of Human Rights).
Keenan v United Kingdom (2001) 33 EHRR 38 (European Court of Human Rights).
Kelly and others v United Kingdom (2001) ECHR 328 (European Court of Human Rights).
Koladenko and Others v Russia (2013) 56 EHRR 2 (European Court of Human Rights).
LCB v United Kingdom (1999) 27 EHRR 212 (European Court of Human Rights).
Leray and Others v France (2001) ECHR 880 (European Court of Human Rights).
Mahmut Kaya v Turkey (2000) ECHR 129 (European Court of Human Rights).
Mastromatteo v Italy (2002) ECHR 694 (European Court of Human Rights).
McCann v United Kingdom (1996) 21 EHRR 97 (European Court of Human Rights).
McKerr v United Kingdom (2002) 34 EHRR 20 (European Court of Human Rights).
McShane v United Kingdom (2002) 35 EHRR 23 (European Court of Human Rights).
Nikolova v Bulgaria (2009) 48 EHRR 40 (European Court of Human Rights).

Oneryildiz v Turkey (No.2) (2005) 41 EHRR 20 (European Court of Human Rights (Grand Chamber)).
Osman v United Kingdom (2000) 29 EHRR 245 (European Court of Human Rights).
Pereira Henriques v Luxembourg (2009) ECHR 2244 (European Court of Human Rights).
Ramsahai v The Netherlands (2008) 46 EHRR 43 (European Court of Human Rights).
Rantsev v Cyprus (2010) 51 EHRR 1 (European Court of Human Rights).
Renolde v France (2009) 48 EHRR 42 (European Court of Human Rights).
Salman v Turkey (2002) 34 EHRR 17 (European Court of Human Rights).
Selmouni v France (2000) 29 EHRR 403 (European Court of Human Rights).
Shanaghan v United Kingdom (2001) ECHR 330 (European Court of Human Rights).
Slimani v France (2006) 43 EHRR 49 (European Court of Human Rights).
Stubbings and Others v United Kingdom (1996) 23 EHRR 213 (European Court of Human Rights).
Tarariyeva v Russia (2009) 48 EHRR 26 (European Court of Human Rights).
Timurtas v Turkey (2001) 33 EHRR 6 (European Court of Human Rights).
Trubnikov v Russia (2005) ECHR 462 (European Court of Human Rights).
Vo v France (2005) 40 EHRR 12 (European Court of Human Rights (Grand Chamber)).
Yasa v Turkey (1999) 28 EHRR 408 (European Court of Human Rights).

United Kingdom Case Law

Antoniou, R. (on the application of) v Central and North West London NHS Foundation Trust & Ors (2013) EWHC 3055 (Admin) (England and Wales High Court (Administrative Court)).
Associated Provincial Picture Houses Ltd v Wednesbury Corp (1948) 1 KB 223; (1947) 2 All ER 680 (Court of Appeal).
Beckford v R. 1987 3 ALL ER 425 (Privy Council).
Chambers v HM Coroner for Preston and West Lancashire & Ors (2015) EWHC 31 (Admin).
Goodson v HM Coroner for Bedfordshire and Luton (2004) EWHC 2931 (Admin) (Queen's Bench Division (Administrative Court)).
Hill v Chief Constable of West Yorkshire (1989) AC 53; (1988) 2 WLR 1049 (House of Lords).
Kirkham v Chief Constable of the Greater Manchester Police (1990) 2 QB 283 (Court of Appeal (Civil Division)).
Mack, R (on the application of) v Coroner for Birmingham and Solihull & Ors (2011) EWCA Civ 712.
Maksovich v Attorney General 4 NSWLR 318 (Court of Appeal of New South Wales).
McDonnell v HM Assistant Coroner for West London (2016) EWHC 3078 (Admin).
Menson v United Kingdom (Admissibility) (2003) Inquest LR 146 (European Court of Human Rights).
Orange v West Yorkshire Police (2001) EWCA Civ 611 (Court of Appeal (Civil Division)).
Osborn v The Parole Board (2013) UKSC 61.

R. (Hicks) v Inner North London Senior Coroner (2016) EWHC 1726 (Admin).
R. (Joanna Letts) v Lord Chancellor (2015) EWHC 402 (Admin) (England and Wales High Court (Administrative Court)).
R. (Tainton) v HM Senior Coroner for Preston and West Lancashire (2016) EWHC 1396 (Admin).
R. v HM Coroner for Exeter and East Devon ex parte Palmer (2000) Inquest LR 78 (Court of Appeal).
R. v Neil Gordon Graham (Northern Ireland unreported judgments) (Northern Ireland Crown Court).
R. v Sussex Justices; Ex parte McCarthy 1 KB 256.
R. v Williams (Gladstone) (1987) 3 ALL ER 411 (Court of Appeal).
R. (on the application of Ahmed) v HM Coroner South East and Cumbria (2009) EWHC 1653 (Admin) (Queen's Bench Division (Administrative Court)).
R. (on the application of Amin (Imtiaz)) v Secretary of State for the Home Department (2003) UKHL 51 (UK House of Lords).
R. (on the application of Anderson) v HM Coroner for Inner North Greater London (2004) EWHC 2729 (Admin) (Queen's Bench Division (Administrative Court)).
R. (on the application of Bennett) v HM Coroner for Inner South London (2007) EWCA Civ 617 (Court of Appeal (Civil Division)).
R. (on the application of Bentley) v HM Coroner for Avon (2001) EWHC Admin 170 (Queen's Bench Division (Administrative Court)).
R. (on the application of Bloggs 61) v Secretary of State for the Home Department (2003) EWCA Civ 686 (Court of Appeal (Civil Division)).
R. (on the application of Cash) v HM Coroner for Northamptonshire (2007) EWHC 1354 (Admin) (Queen's Bench Division (Administrative Court)).
R. (on the application of Coker) v HM Coroner for Inner South London (2006) EWHC 614 (Admin) (Queen's Bench Division (Administrative Court)).
R. (on the application of D) v Inner South London Assistant Deputy Coroner (2008) EWHC 3356 (Admin) (Queen's Bench Division (Administrative Court)).
R. (on the application of Da Silva) v DPP (2006) EWHC 3204 (Admin) (Divisional Court).
R. (on the application of DF) v Chief Constable of Norfolk (2002) EWHC 1738 (Admin) (Queen's Bench Division (Administrative Court)).
R. (on the application of Gentle) v Prime Minister (2008) UKHL 20 (House of Lords).
R. (on the application of Humberstone) v Legal Services Commission (2010) EWHC 760 (Admin) (Queen's Bench Division (Administrative Court)).
R. (on the application of Hurst) v HM Coroner for Northern District London (2007) UKHL 13 (House of Lords).
R. (on the application of JL) v Secretary of State for the Home Department (2008) UKHL 68 (House of Lords).
R. (on the application of Jones) v Legal Services Commission (2007) EWHC 2106 (Admin); (Queen's Bench Division (Administrative Court)).
R. (on the application of Joseph) v Director of Legal Aid Casework (2015) EWHC 2749 (Admin); (Queen's Bench Division (Administrative Court)).
R. (on the application of LePage) v HM Assistant Deputy Coroner for Inner South London (2012) EWHC 1485 (Admin) (Divisional Court).
R. (on the application of Lewis) v HM Coroner for the Mid and North Division of Shropshire (2009) EWCA Civ 1403 (Court of Appeal (Civil Division)).

R. (on the application of Main) v Minister for Legal Aid (2007) EWCA Civ 1147 (Court of Appeal (Civil Division)).

R. (on the application of McLeish) v HM Coroner for the Northern District of Greater London (2010) EWHC 3624 (Admin) (Queen's Bench Division (Administrative Court)).

R. (on the application of Middleton) v HM Coroner for Western Somerset (2004) UKHL 10 (House of Lords).

R. (on the application of Platts) v HM Coroner for South Yorkshire (East District) (2008) EWHC 2502 (Admin) (Queen's Bench Division (Administrative Court)).

R. (on the application of Sacker) v HM Coroner for West Yorkshire (2004) UKHL 11 (House of Lords).

R. (on the application of Sharman) v HM Coroner for Inner North London (2005) EWHC 857 (Admin) (Queen's Bench Division (Administrative Court)).

R. (on the application of Smith) v Oxfordshire Assistant Deputy Coroner (2008) EWHC 694 (Admin) (Queen's Bench Division (Administrative Court)).

R. (on the application of Smith) v Oxfordshire Assistant Deputy Coroner (2010) UKSC 29 (Supreme Court).

R. (on the application of Speck) v HM Coroner for District of York (2016) EWHC 6 (Admin) (Queen's Bench Division (Administrative Court)).

R. (on the application of Takoushis) v HM Coroner for Inner North London (2005) EWCA Civ 1440; (2006) 1 WLR 461 (Court of Appeal (Civil Division)).

R (on the application of The Public Law Project) (Appellant) v Lord Chancellor (Respondent) (2016) UKSC 39.

R. (on the application of Wiggins) v HM Assistant Coroner for Nottinghamshire (2015) EWHC 1658 (Admin) (Queen's Bench Division (Administrative Court)).

R. v DPP Ex p. Manning (2001) QB 330 (Queen's Bench Division (Administrative Court)).

R. v DPP Ex p. Treadaway Times, October 31, 1997 (Divisional Court).

R. v Galbraith (George Charles) (1981) 1 WLR 1039; (1981) 2 All ER 1060; (Court of Appeal (Criminal Division)).

R. v HM Coroner for Greater London Southern District Ex p. Driscoll (1995) 159 JP 45; (1994) COD 91 (Divisional Court).

R. v HM Coroner for Hammersmith Ex p. Peach (1980) QB 211 (Court of Appeal (Civil Division)).

R. v HM Coroner for Inner London South District Ex p. Douglas-Williams (1999) 1 All ER 344 (Court of Appeal (Civil Division)).

R. v HM Coroner for North Humberside and Scunthorpe Ex p. Jamieson (1995) QB 1; (1994) 3 WLR 82 (Court of Appeal (Civil Division)).

Rabone v Pennine Care NHS Trust (2010) EWCA Civ 698 (Court of Appeal (Civil Division)).

Reeves v Commissioner Of Police For Metropolis (2000) 1 AC 360 (House of Lords).

Savage v South Essex Partnership NHS Foundation Trust (2010) EWHC 865 (QB) (Queen's Bench Division).

Tyrell v Hm Senior Coroner County Durham and Darlington (2016) EWHC 1892 (Admin) Divisional Court.

Van Colle v Chief Constable of Hertfordshire (2008) UKHL 50 (House of Lords).

Worcester County Council and Worcestershire Safeguarding Children Board v HM Coroner for the County of Worcester (2013) EWHC 1711 (QB).

Law: Legislation, Rules and Regulations

Convention for the protection of human rights and fundamental freedoms (European Convention on Human Rights, as amended) (ECHR).

Coroners Act 1988.

Coroners Rules 1984. No 552.

Coroners and justice Act 2009.

Criminal law Act 1967.

Crown prosecution service, prosecution policy and guidance: Deaths in custody (2004).

Human Rights Act.

Legal Aid, sentencing and punishment of offenders Act 2012.

Lord Chancellor, Lord chancellor's exceptional funding guidance (Inquests) (2015).

Lord Chancellor's Exceptional Funding guidance (Inquests).

Ministry of Justice, United Kingdom government, guide to coroner services (2014).

Prisons and Probation Ombudsman, Disclosing policy (2009).

The coroners (inquests) Rules 2013; No. 1616.

The coroners (investigations) Regulations 2013; No. 1629.

United Kingdom Government, Prison Rules 1964 (1964).

United Nations, Universal declaration of human rights (UNG. A. Res 1948).

United Nations, Basic principles on the use of force and firearms by law enforcement officials (1990).

Reports

Association of Chief Police Officers. (2003). Manual of guidance on police use of firearms.

Brodrick Committee. (1971). Report of the committee on death, certification and coroners. HM Stationery Office, London.

Butler, G. (1999). Inquiry into Crown Prosecution Service decision-making in relation to deaths in custody and related matters. Butler Report.

Corston, B. (2007). The Corston report: A report of a review of women with particular vulnerabilities in the criminal justice system. Home Office.

Home Office. (1999). Deaths in police custody: Guidance to the police on pre-inquest disclosure.

Home Office. (2003a). Death certification and investigation in England, Wales and Northern Ireland (the Luce report).

Home Office. (2003b). Death certification and the investigation of deaths by coroners: The third report (the shipman inquiry).

Home Office. (2004). Reforming the coroner and death certification service: Position paper. Cm 6159.

Home Office. (2014). Legal aid for representation at inquests Standard Note: SN/HA/4358.

House of Commons Constitutional Affairs Committee. (2006). Reform of the coroners' system and death certification: Eighth Report of Session 2005–06.

House of Lords Committee Stage Policing and Crime Bill. (2016, December 7).

Independent Police Complaints Commission. (2007). Stockwell Two: An investigation into complaints about the Metropolitan Police Service's handling of public statements following the shooting of Jean Charles de Menezes on 22 July 2005.

Keith, B. (2006). *Report of the Zahid Mubarek inquiry* (Vols. 1 and 2).
Macpherson, S. W., & Britain, G. (1999). The Stephen Lawrence inquiry: Report of an inquiry. TSO.
Ministry of Justice UG. (2010). The government's response to coroners' recommendations following the inquests of Gareth Myatt and Adam Rickwood.
The Chief Coroners Office. (2013). The chief Coroner's guide to the coroners and justice Act 2009.
The Rt Hon The Lord Goldsmith. (2003). A review of the role and practices of the crown prosecution service in cases arising from a death in custody.

References

Adams, G. (1973). The small claims court and the adversary process: More problems of function and form. *The Canadian Bar Review*, *51*, 583.
Legal Aid Agency. (2013). Inquests – exceptional cases funding – provider pack. Retrieved from https://www.gov.uk/government/uploads/system/uploads/attachment_data/file/309095/legal-aid-ecf-inquest-provider-pack.pdf
Allan, T. (1998). Procedural fairness and the duty of respect. *Oxford Journal of Legal Studies*, *18*, 497.
Aranda, S. M. D. (2000). Guidelines for the assessment for complicated bereavement risk in family members of people receiving palliative care. Centre for Palliative Care Melbourne, Australia.
Armour, M. (2007). Violent death: Understanding the context of traumatic and stigmatized grief. *Journal of Human Behavior in the Social Environment*, *14*, 53.
Ashworth, P. (2003). Conceptual foundations of qualitatitive pyschology. In Smith J. (Ed.), *Qualitative psychology: A practical guide to research methods*. California: SAGE Publications.
Back, C., Gustafsson, P. A., & Berterö, C. (2013). Sexually abused children–prosecutors' experiences of their participation in the legal process in Sweden. *Psychiatry, Psychology and Law*, *20*, 273.
Beckett, C. (1999). Deaths in custody and the inquest system. *Critical Social Policy*, *19*, 271.
Beetham, D. (1991). *The legitimation of power*. London: Humanities Press Intl.
Biddle, L. (2003). Public hazards or private tragedies? An exploratory study of the effect of coroners' procedures on those bereaved by suicide. *Social Science & Medicine*, *56*, 1033.
Bierie, D. M. (2013). Procedural justice and prison violence: Examining complaints among federal inmates (2000–2007). *Psychology, Public Policy, and Law*, *19*, 15.
Bies, R. J., & Shapiro, D. L. (1988). Voice and justification: Their influence on procedural fairness judgments. *Academy of Management Journal*, *31*, 676.
Blader, S. L., & Tyler, T. R. (2003). A four-component model of procedural justice: Defining the meaning of a "fair" process. *Personality and Social Psychology Bulletin*, *29*, 747.
Bonilla, Y., & Rosa, J. (2015). # Ferguson: Digital protest, hashtag ethnography, and the racial politics of social media in the United States. *American Ethnologist*, *42*, 4.
Braithwait, J. (2002a). Setting standards for restorative justice *British Journal of Criminology*, *42*, 563.
Braithwaite, J. (2002b). *Restorative justice and responsive regulation*. Cambridge, MA: Oxford University Press.

Brems, E., & Lavrysen, L. (2013). Procedural justice in human rights adjudication: The European court of human rights *Human Rights Quarterly*, *35*, 176.

Brockner, J., & Wiesenfeld, B. M. (1996). An integrative framework for explaining reactions to decisions: Interactive effects of outcomes and procedures. *Psychological Bulletin*, *120*, 189.

Bryman, A. (2015). *Social research methods*. Oxford University Press.

Buckler, K., & others. (2011). Racial and Ethnic Perceptions of Injustice; Does prior personal and vicarious incarceration experience alter the racial/ethnic gap in perceptions of injustice? *Criminal Justice Review*, *35*, 269.

Burnham, P., & others. (2004). *Research methods in politics*. London: Palgrave Macmillan Basingstoke.

Campbell, F. R. (1997). Changing the legacy of suicide. *Suicide and Life-Threatening Behavior*, *27*, 329.

Campbell, R. (2002). *Emotionally involved: The impact of researching rape*. London: Psychology Press.

Cavadino, M., & Dignan, J. (1992). *The Penal system; an introduction*. California: SAGE Publications.

Cooper, J. Q. (2011). Ensuring that justice is understood. *Criminal Law and Justice Weekly*, 1.

Cropanzano, R., & Ambrose, M. L. (2001). Procedural and distributive justice are more similar than you think: A monistic perspective and a research agenda. *Advances in Organizational Justice*, *119*, 151.

Crosby, F. (1976). Model of egotistical relative deprivation. *Psychological Review*, *83*, 85.

Cross, C., & Garnham, N. (Eds.). (2016). *The inquest book: The Law of coroners and inquests*. Bloomsbury, London: Hart Publishing.

Damaška, M. (1975). Presentation of evidence and factfinding precision. *University of Pennsylvania Law Review*, *123*, 1083.

Demi, A. S., & Howell, C. (1991). Hiding and healing: Resolving the suicide of a parent or sibling. *Archives of Psychiatric Nursing*, *5*, 350.

Denzin, N. K., & Lincoln, Y. S. (2005). *The Sage handbook of qualitative research*. Thousand Oaks, CA: SAGE Publications.

Dobson, A. (2012). Shifting sands: Multiple counts in prosecutions for corporate manslaughter. *Criminal Law Review*, 200.

Dorpat, T. (1972). Psychological effects of parental suicide on surviving children. *Survivors of Suicide*, 121.

Dowdney, L. (2000). Annotation: Childhood bereavement following parental death. *Journal of Child Psychology and Psychiatry*, *41*, 819.

Drew, P. (2005). Conversation analysis. *Handbook of Language and Social Interaction*, *71*, 102.

Dunne-Maxim, K., Dunne, E. J., & Hauser, M. J. (1987). When children are suicide survivors. In E. J., Dunne, J. L., McIntosh, & K. Dunne-Maxim (Eds.), *Suicide and its aftermath* (p. 234). New York, NY: W. W. Norton.

Dworkin, R. (1963). Judicial discretion. *The Journal of Philosophy*, *60*, 624.

Dworkin, R. (1986). *Law's empire*. Cambridge, MA: Harvard University Press.

Dyregrov, K., Nordanger, D., & Dyregrov, A. (2003). Predictors of psychosocial distress after suicide, SIDS and accidents. *Death Studies*, *27*, 143.

Edwards, A. (2002). *No truth, no justice*. Hampshire: Waterside Press.

Elliott, D., & McGuinness, M. (2002). Public inquiry: Panacea or placebo? *Journal of Contingencies and Crisis Management, 10*, 14.

Falk, G. (2001). *Stigma: How we treat outsiders.* Buffalo, NY: Prometheus Books.

FitzGerald, M., & others. (2002). *Policing for London.* Devon: Willan.

Fuller, L. L. (1961, 1971). The adversary system. H. J. Berman (Ed.), *Talks on American law* (Rev. ed.). New York, NY: Vintage.

Fuller, L. L. (1969). *The morality of law* (Rev. ed., p. 33). New Haven and London.

Gau, J. M. (2014). Procedural justice, police legitimacy, and legal cynicism: A test for mediation effects. *Police Practice and Research*, 1.

Gaubatz, K. T. (1995). *Crime in the public mind.* Ann Arbor, MI: University of Michigan Press.

Gearty, C. A., & Kimbell, J. A. (1995). *Terrorism and the rule of law: A report on the laws relating to political violence in Great Britain and Northern Ireland.* London: King's College, London, Civil Liberties Research Unit.

Gekoski, A., Adler, J. R., & Gray, J. M. (2013). Interviewing women bereaved by homicide: Reports of secondary victimization by the criminal justice system *International Review of Victimology, 19*, 307.

Giddens, A. (1977). *Studies in social and political theory.* London: Basic Books.

Goffman, E. (1963). *Stigma: Notes on the management of spoiled identity.* New York, NY.

Greenberg, J., & Folger, R. (1983). *Procedural justice, participation, and the fair process effect in groups and organizations.* In P. B. Paulus. (Ed.), *Basic Group Processes.* (pp. 235–256). Springer: New York.

Greer, C., & McLaughlin, E. (2012). 'This is not justice' Ian Tomlinson, institutional failure and the press politics of outrage. *British Journal of Criminology, 52*, 274.

Group, W. I. (1985). The inquest as a theatre for police tragedy: The Davey Case. *Journal of Law and Society, 12*, 35.

Harding, D. J. (2003). Jean Valjean's dilemma: The management of ex-convict identity in the search for employment. *Deviant Behavior, 24*, 571.

Harris, D. (1994). The right to life under the European convention on human rights. *Maastricht Journal of European and Comparative Law, 1*, 122.

Harris, A. (2017). 'Natural' and 'unnatural' medical deaths and coronial law: A UK and international review of the medical literature on natural and unnatural death and how it applies to medical death certification and reporting deaths to coroners: Natural/unnatural death: A scientific review. *Medicine, Science & the Law, 57*, 105.

Her Majesty's Inspectorate of Constabulary. (2015). The welfare of vulnerable people in police custody. Retrieved from http://www.justiceinspectorates.gov.uk/hmic/wp-content/uploads/the-welfare-of-vulnerable-people-in-police-custody.pdf

Heuer, L., & others. (2002). The role of resource and relational concerns for procedural justice. *Personality and Social Psychology Bulletin, 28*, 1468.

Hirschfield, P. J., & Piquero, A. R. (2010). Normalization and legitimation: Modeling stigmatizing attitudes toward Ex-offenders. *Criminology, 48*, 27.

Hollway, W., & Jefferson, T. (2000). *Doing qualitative research differently: Free association, narrative and the interview method.* Thousand Oaks, CA: SAGE Publications.

Home Affairs Committee. (2013). Independent Police Complaints Commission: Eleventh Report of Session 2012-3. HC494, Ev16-9.

Hung, N. C., & Rabin, L. A. (2009). Comprehending childhood bereavement by parental suicide: A critical review of research on outcomes, grief processes, and interventions. *Death Studies*, *33*, 781.

Hyam, J. (2010). Where inquests raise A question of Human Rights. 1 Crown Office Row.

INQUEST. (2013). Updated briefing on Jimmy Mubenga. Retrieved from http://www.inquest.org.uk/pdf/briefings/INQUEST_briefing_Jimmy_Mubenga_updated_may_2013.pdf.

INQUEST. (2007). Gareth Myatt briefing. Retrieved from http://inquest.gn.apc.org/pdf/INQUEST_gareth_myatt_briefing_feb_2007.pdf.

INQUEST. (2011). The inquest handbook; A guide for the bereaved families, friends and their advisors. Retrieved from https://hub.supportaftersuicide.org.uk/wp-content/uploads/2019/04/INQUEST_handbook2016.pdf.

INQUEST. (2011a). Response to Consultation Paper CP 5/2011 "The draft Charter for the current coroner service". Retrieved from https://www.inquest.org.uk/Handlers/Download.ashx?IDMF=30b0b319-674c-4afd-b19a-e9625594babc.

INQUEST. (2012). Learning from death in custody inquests: A new framework for action and accountability. Retrieved from https://www.inquest.org.uk/Handlers/Download.ashx?IDMF=b826fe00-307c-40e3-8e35-9cd604207a04.

INQUEST. (2014). Briefing: 10 reasons to vote against the legal aid residence test. Retrieved from https://justice.org.uk/wp-content/uploads/2015/01/150715-NGO-Residence-Test-Briefing-Paper.pdf.

Jackson, J., & others. (2010). Legitimacy and procedural justice in prisons. *Prison Service Journal*, *191*, 4.

Jackson, J., & others. (2012). Why do people comply with the law? Legitimacy and the influence of legal institutions. *British Journal of Criminology*, *52*, 1051.

Jaconelli, J. (2002). *Open justice: A critique of the public trial*. London: Oxford University Press.

Jamieson, R., & McEvoy, K. (2007). *Conflict, suffering and the promise of human rights*. Devon: Willan Publishing.

Kaltman, S., & Bonanno, G. A. (2003). Trauma and bereavement: Examining the impact of sudden and violent deaths. *Journal of Anxiety Disorders*, *17*, 131.

Kant, I., & Gregor, M. J. (1996). *Kant: The metaphysics of morals*. Cambridge: Cambridge University Press.

Kennedy, N. (2014). An interpretative phenomenological analysis of prisoners' experience of riotous behaviour in an adult male prison. *Journal of Forensic Practice*, *16*, 203.

Kessler, A. D. (2004). Our inquisitorial tradition: Equity procedure, due process, and the search for an alternative to the adversarial. *Cornell Law Review*, *90*, 1181.

King, R. D. (1985). Control in prisons In M. Maguire & R. Morgan. (Eds.), *Accountability and prisons*. London: Tavistock.

Klass, D. E., Silverman, P. R., & Nickman, S. L. (1996). *Continuing bonds: New understandings of grief* (1st ed.). London: Taylor & Francis.

Kukavica, J., & Fikfak, V. (2015). Strasbourg's U-turn on independence as part of an effective investigation under article 2. *The Cambridge Law Journal*, *74*, 415.

Lane, R. E. (1988). Procedural goods in a democracy: How one is treated versus what one gets Social Justice Research, 2, 177.

Larkin, M. (2013). Interpretative phenomenological analysis - introduction. Retrieved from http://prezi.com/dnprvc2nohjt/interpretative-phenomenological-analysis-introduction/?auth_key=3d2c098e0db0a31ea05f2d9f60148ed5144e6d06.

LaTour, S. (1978). Determinations of participant and observer satisfaction with adversary and inquisitorial modes of adjudication. *Journal of Personality and Social Psychology*, *36*, 1531.

Lawrence, R. G. (2000). *The politics of force: Media and the construction of police brutality*. Oakland, CA: University of California Press.

LeBel, T. P. (2008). Perceptions of and responses to stigma. *Sociology Compass*, *2*, 409.

Lerner, M. J. (1982). The justice motive in human relations and the economic model of man: A radical analysis of facts and fictions. *Cooperation and helping behavior: Theories and research, 249*.

Leventhal, G. S. (1980). What should be done with equity theory? In K. J. Gergen MSG & R. H. Willis (Eds.), *Social exchange: Advances in theory and research*. New York: Springer.

Leverick, F. (2002). Is English self-defence law incompatible with Article 2 of the ECHR? *Criminal Law Review*, *347*.

Levine, M., & Pyke, J. (1999). *Levine on Coroners' court*. London: Sweet & Maxwell.

Liebling, A. (2001). Suicides in prison: Ten years on. *Prison Service Journal*, 35.

Lind, E. A., & Lissak, R. I. (1985). Apparent impropriety and procedural fairness judgments. *Journal of Experimental Social Psychology*, *21*, 19.

Lind, E. A., & others. (1980). Procedure and outcome effects on reactions to adjudicated resolution of conflicts of interest. *Journal of Personality and Social Psychology*, *39*, 643.

Lind, E. A., & Tyler, T. R. (1988). *The social psychology of procedural justice*. New York: Springer.

Lind, E. A., Kanfer, R., & Earley, P. C. (1990). Voice, control, and procedural justice: Instrumental and noninstrumental concerns in fairness judgments. *Journal of Personality and Social Psychology*, *59*, 952.

Long, J. J. (2003). Compliance in small claims court: Exploring the factors associated with defendants' level of compliance with mediated and adjudicated outcomes'. *Conflict Resolution Quarterly*, *21*, 139.

Love, A. W. (2007). Progress in understanding grief, complicated grief, and caring for the bereaved. *Contemporary Nurse*, *27*, 73.

Lynch, G. E. (1997). Our administrative system of criminal justice *Fordham Law Review*, *66*, 2117.

Marsh, D., & Stoker, G. (1995). *Theory and methods in political science*. London: Palgrave Macmillan.

McHugh, M., & Snow, L. (2002). Suicide prevention: Policy and practice. Suicide in Prisons 1.

McIvor, C. (2010). Getting defensive about police negligence: The Hill principle, the human rights Act 1998 and the house of lords. *The Cambridge Law Journal*, *69*, 133.

Mclean, M. (2017). Contradictory coroners? Decision-making in death investigations. *Journal of Clinical Pathology*, *70*.

Merrills, J. G. (1993). *The development of International Law by the European court of Human Rights*. Manchester: Manchester University Press.

Milanović, M. (2008). From compromise to principle: Clarifying the concept of state jurisdiction in human rights treaties. *Human Rights Law Review*, *8*, 411.

Millar, R. W. (1923). Formative principles of civil procedure. *Illinois Law Review*, *18*, 1.

Mitchell, A. M., & others. (2006). Effective communication with bereaved child survivors of suicide. *Journal of Child and Adolescent Psychiatric Nursing*, *19*, 130.

Moore, M. M., & Freeman, S. J. (1995). Counseling survivors of suicide: Implications for group postvention. *Journal for Specialists in Group Work*, *20*, 40.

Mowbray, A. (2004). *The development of positive obligations under the European convention on Human Rights by the European court of Human Rights*. Bloomsbury: Bloomsbury Publishing.

Mowbray, A. (2005). The creativity of the European court of human rights. *Human Rights Law Review*, *5*, 57.

Neimeyer, R. A., & others. (2010). Grief therapy and the reconstruction of meaning: From principles to practice. *Journal of Contemporary Psychotherapy*, *40*, 73.

Neimeyer, R. A. (2001). Reauthoring life narratives: Grief therapy as meaning reconstruction. *The Israel Journal of Psychiatry and Related Sciences*, *38*, 171.

Neria, Y., & Litz, B. T. (2004). Bereavement by traumatic means: The complex synergy of trauma and grief. *Journal of Loss & Trauma*, *9*, 73.

Newman, J. O. (1985). Rethinking fairness: Perspectives on the litigation process. *The Yale Law Journal*, *94*, 1643.

Nickman, S. L., Silverman, P. R., & Normand, C. (1998). Children's construction of a deceased parent: The surviving parent's contribution. *American Journal of Orthopsychiatry*, *68*, 126.

Nonami, H., & others. (2015). Effects of voice and similarity on procedural fairness and trust: A dual process model of public acceptance based on representatives' participation. *Asian Journal of Social Psychology*, *18*, 216.

Park, C. L., & Folkman, S. (1997). Meaning in the context of stress and coping. *Review of General Psychology*, *1*, 115.

Paternoster, R., & others. (1997). Do fair procedures matter? The effect of procedural justice on spouse assault. *Law & Society Review*, *31*, 163.

Price, K. H., & others. (2006). Judging the fairness of voice-based participation across multiple and interrelated stages of decision making *Organizational Behavior and Human Decision Processes*, *99*, 212.

Prigerson, H. G., & others. (1997). Traumatic grief as a risk factor for mental and physical morbidity. *American Journal of Psychiatry*, *154*, 616.

Principe, M. L. (1999). Albert Venn Dicey and the principles of the rule of law: Is justice blind-A comparative analysis of the United States and great Britain *Loyola of Los Angeles International & Comparative Law Review*, *22*, 357.

Provini, J. R. E., Cynthia, R., & Pfeffer, C. (2000). Adults mourning suicide: Self-reported concerns about bereavement, needs for assistance, and help-seeking behavior. *Death Studies*, *24*, 1.

Raphael, B., & Martinek, N. (1997). Assessing traumatic bereavement and posttraumatic stress disorder. In J. P. Wilson & T. M. Keane (Eds.), *Assessing psychological trauma and PTSD*. New York: Guilford.

Reisig, M. D., & Mesko, G. (2009). Procedural justice, legitimacy, and prisoner misconduct. Psychology, Crime and Law, 15, 41.

Richardson, G. (1993). *Law, process and custody: Prisoners and patients*. London: Weidenfeld and Nicolson.

Rolston, B., & Scraton, P. (2005). In the full glare of English politics Ireland, inquiries and the British state. *British Journal of Criminology*, *45*, 547.

Schütz, A. (1973). *The structures of the life-world* (Vol. 1). Evanston, IL: Northwestern University Press.

Schwartz, R. D., & Skolnick, J. H. (1962). Two studies of legal stigma. *Social Problems*, *10*, 133.

Scraton, P., & Chadwick, K. (1987). *In the arms of the law: Coroners' inquests and deaths in custody*. London: Pluto Press.

Scraton, P., Sim, J., & Skidmore, P. (1991). *Prisons under protest*. Bristol: Open University Press.

Seidman, I. (2012). *Interviewing as qualitative research: A guide for researchers in education and the social sciences*. New York: Teachers College Press.

Shear, K., & others. (2005). Treatment of complicated grief: A randomized controlled trial. *The Journal of the American Medical Association*, *293*, 2601.

Shepherd, D., & Barraclough, B. The aftermath of parental suicide for children. The British Journal of Psychiatry, 129, 267.

Silverman, P. R., & others (2003). The effects of negative legacies on the adjustment of parentally bereaved children and adolescents. *Journal of Death and Dying*, *46*, 335.

Simmel, G. (1950). *The Sociology of Georg Simmel* (Vol. 92892). New York: Simon & Schuster.

Smiley, C. J., & Fakunle, D. (2016). From "brute" to "thug:" the demonization and criminalization of unarmed Black male victims in America. *Journal of Human Behavior in the Social Environment*, *26*, 350.

Smith, J. A., & Osborn, M. (2003). Interpretative phenomenological analysis. In *Qualitative psychology: A practical guide to research methods*. Thousand Oaks, CA: SAGE Publications.

Smith, G. (2001). Police complaints and criminal prosecutions. *The Modern Law Review*, *64*, 372.

Smith, J. A. (2007). *Qualitative psychology: A practical guide to research methods*. Thousand Oaks, CA: SAGE Publications.

Snow, L., & McHugh, M. (2000). The aftermath of a death in prison custody. In G. J. Towl, L. Snow, & M. McHugh (Eds.), *Suicide in prisons*. Oxford: BPS Blackwell.

Society, T. L. (2017). ACCESS DENIED? LASPO four years on: A Law & Society Review.

Sparks, J. R., & Bottoms, A. (1995). Legitimacy and order in prisons. *British Journal of Sociology*, *46*.

Stroebe, M., Schut, H., & Stroebe, W. (1960). Health outcomes of bereavement. *The Lancet*, *370*.

Sunshine, J., & Tyler, T. R. (2003). The role of procedural justice and legitimacy in shaping public support for policing. *Law & Society Review*, *37*, 513.

Sykes, G. M. (1958). *The society of captives*. Princeton, NJ: Princeton University Press.

Thibaut, J., & others. (1973). Procedural justice as fairness. *Stanford Law Review*, *26*, 1271.

Thibaut, J. W., & Walker, L. (1975). *Procedural justice: A psychological analysis*. New Jersey: L. Erlbaum Associates.

Thibaut, J., & Walker, L. (1978). A theory of procedure. *California Law Review*, *66*, 541.

Thomas, L., & others. (2014). *Inquests; a practitioner's guide* (3rd ed.). London: Legal Action Group.

Tyler, T. R., & Blader, S. L. (2000). *Cooperation in groups: Procedural justice, social identity, and behavioral engagement.* Ontario: Hogrefe & Huber.

Tyler, T. R., & Huo, Y. J. (2002). *Trust in the law: Encouraging public cooperation with the police and courts.* New York: Russell Sage Foundation Publications.

Tyler, T., & others (1998). Conflict with outsiders: Disputing within and across cultural boundaries. *Personality and Social Psychology Bulletin, 24*, 137.

Tyler, T., Degoey, P., & Smith, H. (1996). Understanding why the justice of group procedures matters: A test of the psychological dynamics of the group-value model. *Journal of Personality and Social Psychology, 70*, 913.

Tyler, T. R. (1988). What is procedural justice?: Criteria used by citizens to assess the fairness of legal procedures. *Law & Society Review*, 103.

Tyler, T. R. (1990). *Why people obey the law: Procedural justice, legitimacy, and compliance.* New Haven, CT: Yale University Press.

Tyler, T. R. (2003). Procedural justice, legitimacy, and the effective rule of law. *Crime & Justice, 30*, 283.

Tyler, T. R. (2007). Procedural justice and the courts. *Court Review, 44*, 26.

Valentine, G. (1997). Tell me about...: Using interviews as a research methodology. *Methods in Human Geography, 2*, 27.

Van den Bos, K., Vermunt, R., & Wilke, H. A. (1997). Procedural and distributive justice: What is fair depends more on what comes first than on what comes next. *Journal of Personality and Social Psychology, 72*, 95.

Walsh, D. P. J., & Conway, V. (2011). Police governance and accountability: Overview of current issues. *Crime, Law and Social Change*, 1.

Ward, T., & Coles, D. (1997). *Investigating suspicious deaths in police custody.* Hampshire: Waterside Press.

Warren, M. (1972). Some psychological sequelae of parental suicide in surviving children. *Survivors of Suicide*, 112.

Wolcott, H. F. (1994). *Transforming qualitative data: Description, analysis, and interpretation.* Thousand Oaks, CA: SAGE Publications.

Wolfe, S. E., & Piquero, A. R. (2011). Organizational justice and police misconduct. *Criminal Justice and Behavior, 38*, 332.

Young, J. (1999). *The exclusive society: Social exclusion, crime and difference in late modernity.* Thousand Oaks, CA: SAGE Publications.

Annex I

Participant Information Sheet for the PhD Research of Jo Easton

September 2012

Please read the following information carefully before reading the consent form below. You may want to save this document or print it out to keep.

Project title: Impact of bereaved families participating in the inquest system following a death in custody.

Principal researcher: Jo Easton, PhD candidate at the Human Rights Centre of Essex University.

Supervisors: Professor Maurice Sunkin and Ms Lorna McGregor.

I would like to invite you to participate in my research project. It is important that you understand what the aim of the project is and what your participation may involve, so please read the following information carefully. Your participation in this project must be your own choice – there will be no negative consequences if you decide not to take part. If anything in this document is not clear or you have any questions regarding my research, please contact me at jeeast@essex.ac.uk.

What Is the Purpose of This Study?

This aim of this research is to gather information from varied stakeholders involved in the inquest system in relation to deaths in custody. I would like to investigate the perceptions of fairness within the process – both whether participants feel the current procedures allow for fair treatment of all those involved and how important participants feel fairness is within the process. An inquest is an inquisitorial process that stands apart from both civil and criminal justice procedures; however, in relation to deaths in custody, cases can raise issues of conflict between parties. I would like to consider how important procedural fairness as a principle may be to an inquest that is investigating a death in custody. The issues I am interested in include equity of parties, respectful treatment and any other aspects to the process that participants feel are important in ensuring effective participation and fairness for all interested parties.

Why Have I Been Invited?

You have been invited as a stakeholder in the inquest process. I will be speaking with a variety of people who have been involved in inquests following a death in custody – including interested parties, lawyers who have represented parties and coroners themselves. You may choose to remain anonymous, in which case no one other than myself and my two supervisors will know your name or that you have participated in the project: we will ensure your details remain confidential. In this case, some details may have to be edited to ensure you cannot be identified through the information you give me.

What Do I Do if I Decide to Take Part?

You can contact me at jeeast@essex.ac.uk to discuss your participation. I have a questionnaire prepared and preferably we will set up a time that is convenient to you so that I can interview you (either in person or over the phone). I can send you a summary of some of the issues I would like to discuss so you can prepare your thoughts. The interviews will be recorded to ensure the information is accurately recorded. I will be carrying out the transcription of these recordings myself, so no one else will have access to the information. If an interview is either inconvenient or otherwise not possible, I may agree to send you a copy of the questionnaire to complete in your own time. At any point, if you decide you no longer wish to take part, you may withdraw from the process without giving a reason.

What Are the Possible Benefits of Taking Part?

I hope that the opportunity to express your views on the inquest process may be a positive experience.

What Are the Possible Risks of Taking Part?

The questions may involve issues or memories that are painful or distressing; you are under no obligation to answer any questions that you are not comfortable with.

Confidentiality

All data will be collected and stored in accordance with the Data Protection Act 1998. This means that all of the personal information that you give for this survey will be treated as confidential. It will only be used for the purposes of my PhD and will not be available to anyone other than myself and my two supervisors. The data will also be stored on a secure computer and hardcopies will be held in a locked cabinet.

Giving Informed Consent

If you are still interested in participating in the research – please read the Informed Consent Form below and sign it if you agree with the statements.

If you have any queries in regard to your participation, please contact me at jeeast@essex.ac.uk or either of my supervisors Professor Maurice Sunkin at sunkm@essex.ac.uk or Lorna McGregor at lmcgreg@essex.ac.uk.

Informed Consent Form

Thank you for your interest in taking part in this research. Before you agree to take part, you must be clear about what the project involves. If you have any queries, please contact the researcher Jo Easton at jeeast@essex.ac.uk.

If you complete this form, you are giving your consent to take part in a survey on your perceptions of the inquest system.

- I have read the Participant Information Sheet and understand what my participation in the research would involve.
- I understand that if I ask for my name or contact details to remain anonymous, the information I give will only be available to the researcher and her supervisors and if referenced, this information will not be able to identify me.
- I may choose for my name to be published, in which case details of particular cases that I discuss may be referenced and I may be identified alongside the information I give.
- I agree to any interviews between myself and the researcher, Jo Easton, as part of the project to be recorded to ensure the information is accurate.
- I understand that the information I give will be treated as strictly confidential and handled in accordance with the provisions of the Data Protection Act 1998.
- I understand that I can choose whether to participate or not and that I can withdraw at any time prior to the interview being completed without having to give a reason and without any adverse consequences
- I understand that the information I have divulged will be used to produce a PhD research project and may be published.

Name: ....
Signature: ....
Date: ....

Please tick one.

- I would like to remain anonymous and for it to be assured that it will not be possible to identify me from any publications ☐

OR

- I give my permission for my name to be used in relation to the information given within this questionnaire in any publications resulting from this project ☐

Annex II

Useful Acronyms

ACCT	Assessment, Care in Custody and Teamwork
ACPO	Association of Chief Police Officers
CO	Coroner Participant
ECHR	European Convention of Human Rights
ECtHR	European Court of Human Rights
ESP	Ex-senior Police Officer Participant
FA	Family Member Participant
FLO	Family Liaison Officer
HRA	Human Rights Act
IPA	Interpretative Phenomenological Analysis
IOPC	Independent Office for Police Conduct
LA	Legal Representative Participant
LAA	Legal Aid Agency
PFD	Prevention of Future Deaths (Reports)
PPO	Prisons and Probation Ombudsman
SP	Senior Police Officer Participant

Annex III

Skeleton Questions for Interviews

(1) Experiences of complex inquest process:
- First contact of bereaved families with coronial staff;
- How does inquest process compare/differ from expectation/experiences of criminal court processes?

(2) What is family experience of participating?
- Identifying the next of kin;
- Families at the centre;
- How are families heard?
- How does the process respond to families?

(3) What is impact of families participating?
- What are possible benefits/problems with families participating?
- Impact on families themselves;
- Impact on outcome;
- Experiences of inquests with no family involvement.

(4) What affects family participation?
- Involvement early in process;
- Access to information;
- Legal support.

(5) What role do inquests have in holding the State to account?
- Rule R43's;
- Prevention of other deaths;
- Media interest.

Index

Printed and bound by CPI Group (UK) Ltd, Croydon, CR0 4YY
13/09/2026
14961027-0001